PETER JORDAN (ED.)

REGIONAL DEVELOPMENT AND REGIONALISATION IN THE ADRIATIC SPACE

PROCEEDINGS OF THE 3rd CONFERENCE OF THE ADRIATIC FORUM
VIENNA, SEPTEMBER 23-25, 2010

ISR-FORSCHUNGSBERICHTE

HERAUSGEGEBEN VOM
INSTITUT FÜR STADT- UND REGIONALFORSCHUNG

HEFT 38

REDAKTION: PETER JORDAN

ÖAW
Österreichische Akademie der Wissenschaften

VERLAG DER ÖSTERREICHISCHEN AKADEMIE DER WISSENSCHAFTEN
WIEN 2012

PETER JORDAN (ED.)

REGIONAL DEVELOPMENT AND REGIONALISATION IN THE ADRIATIC SPACE

Proceedings of the 3rd Conference of the Adriatic Forum, Vienna September 23-25, 2010

ÖAW
Österreichische Akademie der Wissenschaften

VERLAG DER ÖSTERREICHISCHEN AKADEMIE DER WISSENSCHAFTEN
WIEN 2012

Umschlagfoto: Rovinj/Rovigno (Foto: Peter Jordan, 2008)

Die Arbeit unterliegt ausschließlich der Verantwortung des ISR
und wurde der phil.-hist. Klasse nicht vorgelegt.

ISBN-978-3-7001-7266-6

Medieninhaber und Herausgeber: Österreichische Akademie der Wissenschaften

Institut für Stadt- und Regionalforschung, Postgasse 7, A-1010 Wien

Tel. (+43-1)-51581/3520-3532

Telefax (+43-1)-51581/3533

Redaktion: Peter Jordan

Druck: Novographic, A-1230 Wien

Preface

The 3rd Conference of the Adriatic Forum took place September 23-25, 2010, in Vienna, Austria. It was the follow-up of the *First Conference of Geographers of the Upper Adriatic – Joint Management of a Borderless Area*, held in Koper/Capodistria, 27-28 November 2008, organised under the direction of Prof. Milan Bufon by the Science and Research Centre of Koper/Capodistria and the Faculty of Humanities of the University of Primorska, as well of the 2nd Conference titled *Construction and Deconstruction of Nationalism and Regionalism: A Long Journey to Europe*, held in Trieste, 1-2 October 2009, organised under the direction of Prof. Maria Paola Pagnini by the University of Trieste.

Vienna was chosen as the third venue, although it is – much in contrast to the first two venues – certainly not an Adriatic city. Its choice may, however, be regarded as an acknowledgement of the fact that it was not only historically well-connected with the Adriatic, but cultivates many relations to the Adriatic space up to the present day and is the home of several geographers interested in it.

The event was organized by the Austrian Academy of Sciences' Institute of Urban and Regional Research (director: Heinz Fassmann) in cooperation with the Institute of Geography and Regional Research, University of Vienna (head: Helmut Wohlschlägl), the International Geographical Union (IGU) – Political Geography Commission (chair: Anton Gosar), the International Cartographic Association (ICA) – Commission on National and Regional Atlases (chair: Peter Jordan), and the Austrian Geographical Society (OEGG, chair: Christian Staudacher). It took place in the Theatersaal of the Austrian Academy, right in Vienna's historical downtown.

The conference was devoted to the general theme *Regional Development and Regionalisation* which corresponds to global and European challenges as well as to demands for research in the wider Adriatic region. Political geographers as well as regional, cultural and social geographers, spatial planners, geographers of tourism and transportation were addressed. But studies from other fields of geography and interdisciplinary approaches were by no means excluded.

The Adriatic space in the sense of the coastlands of the Adriatic Sea and their hinterlands was to be the focus of this conference in regional terms. But this spatial concept was not regarded as clearly defined, and comparison with situations elsewhere as well as methodological and theoretical approaches applicable on regional research were also accepted with pleasure.

These proceedings comprise just a smaller selection of papers presented at the conference, i.e. the papers closest to the conference theme in regional and thematic terms.

They start with transnational views followed by focuses on individual countries in the Adriatic space.

While Milan BUFON (Koper/Capodistria) and Damir JOSIPOVIČ (Ljubljana) present surveys over the development of trans-border relations and ethno-demographic situations, resp., in the wider region of the Upper Adriatic, Maria Paola PAGNINI (Rome) and André Louis SANGUIN (Paris) draw a comparison between the development of border regions in the Southern Alps and the Pyrenees. Peter JORDAN (Vienna) closes this transnational part by an analysis of administrative decentralisation processes in all Adriatic countries.

Contributions on individual countries start with Slovenia, of which Lučka LORBER (Maribor) discusses the development of spatial disparities in recent decades followed by Anton GOSAR (Koper/Capodistria), who presents the various attempts of regionalising Slovenia for purposes of tourism branding. Simon KERMA (Koper/Capodistria) then focuses on the Slovenian coastal region Primorska, when he describes efforts to promote wine tourism.

Jelena LONČAR and Zoran STIPERSKI (both Zagreb) deal with a Croatian topic, when they highlight the relative socio-economic role and development of Central Croatia within the country. Jan WENDT (Gdańsk) throws finally a glance on Polish tourism to Croatia and Slovenia.

The editor would like to thank all authors for their valuable contributions, his colleague Florian PARTL for his careful proof reading and skilful layout as well as the Institute of Urban and Regional Research of the Austrian Academy of Sciences and its director Heinz FASSMANN for the opportunity to include these proceedings into the Institute's renown series of research reports.

Peter JORDAN, editor

Contents

Preface 5

Transnational Views 9

The Changeable Political Map of the Upper Adriatic Region Between Conflict and Coexistence
Milan Bufon, Koper/Capodistria 11

Recent Ethnodemographic Developments in the Central Part of the Alps-Adriatic Region: Slovenia, Croatia, Friuli-Venezia Giulia and Carinthia
Damir Josipovič, Ljubljana 27

Borders and Transportation, Autonomy and Linguistic Minorities in the Julian Alps and Eastern Pyrenees. A Comparative Case Study in Political Geography
Maria Paola Pagnini, Rome, and André Louis Sanguin, Paris 43

Administrative Regionalisation in the Adriatic Space
Peter Jordan, Vienna 57

Focus on Countries 95

Development of Regional Disparities in Slovenia
Lučka Lorber, Maribor 97

Re-defining Slovenian Touristic Regions
Anton Gosar, Koper/Capodistria 109

Wine Tourism as a Development Factor of the Primorska Wine Region
Simon Kerma, Koper/Capodistria 127

Regional Economic Development of Central Croatia in the Transition Period
Jelena Lončar, Zoran Stiperski, Zagreb 141

Changes in Polish Tourist Flows to the Eastern Adriatic
Jan A. Wendt, Gdańsk 159

Transnational Views

The Changeable Political Map of the Upper Adriatic Region between Conflict and Coexistence

Milan Bufon, Koper/Capodistria*

with 4 tables in the text

Content

Summary ... 11
1 Introduction ... 12
2 The construction of political space in the Upper Adriatic ... 13
3 Changes in ethnic structure within the cultural contact areas of the Upper Adriatic as a consequence of the political partition ... 15
4 Building harmony in the Upper Adriatic borderlands ... 18
5 Conclusions ... 23
6 References ... 24

Summary

*The paper presents a geopolitical and political geographical overview of the Upper Adriatic region as an area of contact between different cultural, social, economic and political entities, producing potential of conflicts, particularly in the period of growing nationalism and emerging nation-state formulation in this region. The first part of the 20*th *century represented a classic example of geopolitical conflict through two world wars and their related peace conferences that produced several versions of political organization of the Upper Adriatic region and a huge number of border proposals. Conflicts arising from the mid-century solution of the so-called Trieste question transformed the Upper Adriatic region into an example in geopolitical handbooks and*

* Milan Bufon, Prof. PhD., Institute for Geographical Studies, Science and Research Centre (ZRS), University of Primorska, Titov trg 4, SI-6000 Koper/Capodistria, Slovenia; e-mail: milan.bufon@upr.si

a real laboratory of contemporary political geographic transformations. Changing geopolitical patterns have also produced considerable modifications in the political, social and ethnic construction of the Upper Adriatic region, driving neighbouring national policies to subordinate the ethno-linguistic structure to the existing state situation. The process of creating new international boundaries in the region actually ended in 1991 with the establishment of an independent Slovenia and Croatia.

In this long period of geopolitical transformations in the Upper Adriatic region an evolution of political-geographic attitudes can also be detected. Early on it followed RATZEL*'s geopolitical principles, according to which the flexibility of defining borders directly indicated the change in the power ratio between neighbouring countries, but later it has taken into account to a greater extent modern integrative ideas concerning an increasing interest in looking for harmony and the elimination of international conflicts. Greater attention has thus been given to the political geography of «everyday life», inter-ethnic relations and cross-border contacts.*

Research in the area has shown that the «new» borderlands of the Upper Adriatic region are more receptive to integration, because they are seeking to overcome conflicts caused by the division of traditionally homogeneous administrative, social, economic and cultural spaces.

The potential advantages deriving from sharing common spaces among different and hitherto rival ethnic groups on a local level are emerging following the decline or even elimination of political and ideological hindrances on the state level. Since the Upper Adriatic region is now divided among three countries – Italy, Slovenia and Croatia – it is becoming a new and special type of European borderland which will surely increasingly become an object of study for many scholars interested in its social and spatial problems. Moreover, it is now in the best interests of these countries that the region should continue to develop as an area of international and inter-ethnic integration and co-operation, providing thus a possible model of coexistence practices for other European contact areas. After all, the history of the Upper Adriatic region proves that it is much more difficult to divide the region than to bond it together.

1 Introduction

The paper will present a political-geographical overview of the Upper Adriatic region as an area of contact between different cultural, social, economic and political entities, producing potential of conflicts, particularly in the period of growing nationalism and emerging nation-state formation in this region. The first part of the 20th century represented a classic example of geopolitical conflict through two world wars and their related peace conferences that produced several versions of political organization of the Upper Adriatic region and a huge number of border proposals. Conflicts arising from the mid-century solution of the so-called Trieste question transformed the Upper

Adriatic region into an example in geopolitical handbooks and a real laboratory of contemporary political geographic transformations. Changing geopolitical patterns have also produced considerable modifications in the political, social and ethnic construction of the Upper Adriatic region, driving neighbouring national policies to subordinate the ethno-linguistic structure to the existing state situation. The process of creating new international boundaries in the region actually ended in 1991 with the establishment of an independent Slovenia and Croatia.

In this long period of geopolitical transformations in the Upper Adriatic region an evolution of the political-geographic attitude can also be detected. Early on it followed RATZEL's geopolitical principles, according to which the flexibility of defining borders directly indicated the change in the power ratio between neighbouring countries, but later it has taken into account to a greater extent modern integrative ideas showing an increasing interest in looking for harmony and the elimination of international conflicts. Greater attention has thus been given to the political geography of 'everyday life', inter-ethnic relations and cross-border contacts. Research in the area has shown that the 'new' borderlands of the Upper Adriatic region are more receptive to integration, because they are seeking to overcome conflicts caused by the division of traditionally homogeneous administrative, social, economic and cultural spaces. The potential advantages deriving from sharing common spaces among different and hitherto rival ethnic groups on a local level are emerging following the decline or even elimination of political and ideological hindrances on the state level. Since the Upper Adriatic region is now divided among three countries – Italy, Slovenia and Croatia – it is becoming a new and special type of European borderland which will surely increasingly be an object of study for many scholars interested in its social and spatial problems. Moreover, it is now in the best interests of these countries that the region should continue to develop as an area of international and inter-ethnic integration and co-operation, providing thus a possible model of coexistence practices for other European contact areas.

2 The construction of political space in the Upper Adriatic

The 'modern' borders in this region have their origin in the 16th century due to the Treaty of Worms between the Republic of Venice and the Habsburg Empire. Interestingly enough, this borders had undergone only minor adjustments until the First World War, and actually still represent the basis of the northern part of the current border between Italy and Slovenia. This border section is therefore one of the oldest and most stable boundaries in Europe.

Its southern part, however, is characterised by instability. After the Second World War this new section of the boundary between Italy and Yugoslavia was based on the totally new criterion of functionally adopted 'ethnic balance'. According to this criterion, the border was to coincide as much as possible with the ethnic divide between Italian and Slovene speakers, while at the same time having in both countries the same number of minority group members and the necessary conditions for internal communication. Nevertheless, this criterion created several problems in splitting up traditionally rather persistent integrated regions such as the Gorizia and Istria [Istra] historical regions as well as the Trieste functional region (Klemenčič & Bufon 1991).

In the case of Gorizia, the new political boundary coincided with the ethnic border between the Romance (Italian and Friulan) and Slovenian populations, in the sense that the ethnically mixed town of Gorizia and the transport connections the town needed with Trieste and Udine remained in Italy.

In the case of Istria and Trieste, the principle of 'ethnic balance' was used, since in this region there is no clear territorial ethnic border between the Romance and Slavic (Croatian and Slovenian) population (Moodie 1950). The difficulty of drawing up boundaries in this territory is clear if we consider the fact that for the most problematic segment, Trieste, a temporary solution was found by the creation of the so-called Free Territory of Trieste, itself divided into two zones. Zone A, including the city of Trieste, was ruled by the Anglo-American military forces, whereas Zone B, including Istria, came under Yugoslav rule. This situation was finally solved in 1954, when, with a slight modification of the border, the northern part of the Free Territory of Trieste (Zone A) was left to Italy, while the southern part (Zone B) was left to Yugoslavia. The validity of the entire border was than accepted and confirmed by Italy and Yugoslavia by the Treaty of Osimo in 1978, which introduced also small functional territorial modifications and important proposals for cross-border co-operation (Klemenčič & Bufon 1991).

A new problem arose with the independence of Slovenia and Croatia in 1991, when the republic boundary drawn along the ethnic border between Croatian and Slovenian population became an international border. At this point a more precise and more rational definition of the border on the ground was needed as it was on the sea, namely in the Gulf of Piran/Pirano – a problem not yet fully solved (Gosar & Klemenčič 1994, Gosar & Klemenčić 2000). It is interesting to note that these problems also emerged because the Slovenian-Croatian administrative border was based on the ethnic border with no functional modifications, as discussed above. Here, except for the ethnic Italian population in Istria, no national minorities are officially present.

Yet, it should be stressed how even the 'modern' political partitions of the Upper Adriatic in the 20th century have not modified the traditional multicultural nature of that region and how historical inter-ethnic and functional cross-border relations have 'survived' the prevailing 'cuius regio eius religio' homogenization policies.

3 Changes in ethnic structure within the cultural contact areas of the Upper Adriatic as a consequence of the political partition

After the First World War, the increasingly Fascist-like Italian policy of assimilation forced the traditionally ethnically mixed coastal towns to follow the new pattern of Italian 'ethnic purity', and hence they became 'città italianissime'. This in particular was the case with Trieste, where the 1910 census found 30% of the population in the commune to be Slovenian, whereas only ten years later this figure had decreased to only 8%. According to the analysis of ČERMELJ (1965), after the First World War about 100,000 Slovenians left their homes in the ethnically mixed towns of the occupied territories. The political migrants moved mainly to Yugoslavia, whereas the economic ones moved overseas, to both South and North America. The political emigration of Slovenian population from Trieste continued after World War II, especially after the Yugoslav administration departed, whereas the economic emigration increased after the end of the Free Territory of Trieste and the annexation of Trieste to Italy.

The first two decades after the Second World War were very dynamic and important for Trieste. Even though the number of its inhabitants remained virtually stable (about 250,000 inhabitants), the structure of the population changed radically (see Table 1). In this period, about 50,000 to 60,000 people immigrated from the areas that became part of Yugoslavia, whereas on the other hand about 30,000 to 40,000 people, including many Slovenians, emigrated abroad for economic reasons, mainly to Australia. Also among the immigrants the ethnic structure was different: mostly they were Italians from Istria and Rijeka (Fiume), but there were also from the same areas many Croats, and Slovenes from different part of Slovenia, whose ideas were pro-western and who disagreed with the Tito Communist regime.

Table 1: **Change in population structure of Trieste according to birthplace, in 1910 and 1991 (%)**

	1910	*1991*
Trieste	*49*	*62*
Istra	*8*	*14*
Western Slovenia	*12*	*1*
Italy	*11*	*17*
Rijeka and Dalmatia	*2*	*2*
Former Yugoslavia	*10*	*1*
Austria	*5*	*0*
Other countries	*3*	*4*

Source: Authors' analysis of statistical data

Generally speaking, the shift in political boundaries and the annexation of the city to Italy influenced also the immigration flow towards Trieste and hence also the territorial origins of its inhabitants. From the comparison of the situation in 1910 and 1991, an increase of people born in the town (from 49% to 62%) can be seen, this means a decline in immigration dynamics, and indirectly also in attractiveness of the town among hinterland inhabitants.

On the other hand, we can see also a different spatial orientation. Thus the percentage of people that immigrated to Trieste from Italy increased remarkably (from 11% to 17%) as did the number of immigrants from Istria (from 8% to 14%). On the contrary, the number of immigrants from western Slovenia decreased (from 12% to only 1%), as did the number of the immigrants from the rest of Yugoslavia (from 10% to less than 1%), and also from Austria (from 5% to 0%). The only figure that remained nearly unchanged is that of the immigrants from Rijeka and Dalmatia (2%) and from other countries (3% to 4%).

Also the census figures regarding the ethnic structure of Istria show the impact of political transformations on the ethnic and demographic situation of the area. According to the Austrian census of 1910 there were on the whole peninsula, excluding Trieste and Rijeka, about 250,000 inhabitants – 52% Italians, 39% Croats and 9% Slovenes; whereas according to the 1921 Italian census of a total of 265,000 inhabitants 66% were Italians, 24% Croats and 9% Slovenes. Thus it seems that in a mere decade the number of Italians increased by 50,000, whereas the number of Croats decreased by 30,000 (Bufon 2000).

It is clear that such a huge modification in ethnic structure cannot be explained solely by emigration of the native population and by immigration of Italian colonists and state employees. According to Schiffrer (1946), the figures of the real ethnic structure were rather distorted. His figures for 1939 are the following: about 150,000 Italians, 97,000 Croats, 44,000 Slovenes and at least 28,000 ethnically mixed inhabitants as well as nearly 10,000 inhabitants of other origin (Schiffrer 1946).

What is immediately clear from this analysis, besides the perhaps exaggerated number of Slovenes, is the difficulty of ethnic identification among the population. This can be seen by the big number of ethnically 'neutral' inhabitants, like in north-west Istria, speaking a mixed Croatian-Italian-Slovene dialect that cannot be said to be part of any of the involved ethnic 'parties'. Something similar was noticed by Rutar (1896) at the end of the 19th century.

All these difficulties of ethnic identification can be seen also in the post-war census of 1948 that somehow turned the statistics of 1921 upside down. Even though the emigration of Italians from Istria actually began in this period, this phenomenon was rather limited in the very first post-war years and therefore does not justify the finding that only 80,000 Italians remained in the region. Obviously many of them, who were included among the Italians 20 years before, changed their minds more or less 'voluntarily'. The real 'exodus' of the Italian population began after 1947 and lasted for a decade; by 1961 the number of Italians in Istria had decreased to 20,000, thus about 100,000 native Italians or one third of the whole population had joined the emigration flow. This gap has been only partly filled with new immigrants from the rest of Yugoslavia.

On the other side of the border the majority of the migrants from Istria was settled in the area around Trieste, which has been historically densely inhabited by Slovenes. Thus, a trend towards a 'normalisation' on both sides of the border is evident, which means that the political and ethnic border should better coincide: the north-west coast of Trieste mainly inhabited by Slovenes should have become 'Italian', whereas the western coast of Istria inhabited by Italians should have become 'Yugoslav'.

The influence of 'external' factors on ethnic identification and self-identification is also evident in the later movements of the Italian population in Istria. According to statistics their number had by 1981 decreased to only 13,000. On the contrary, in 1991, when there was a big political and economic crisis in Yugoslavia, the number of Italians increased again to 21,000 (Juri 1991, Repolusk 1990).

Usually the biggest changes in ethnic structure occurred in the traditionally ethnically mixed urban centres, to which Italians, Slovenes, Croats, and people of other origin had immigrated during the Austrian period. In this area a remarkable decrease of German population and of other more distant populations can be noticed, as can be seen a decrease in native population depending on nationality (see Table 2). Thus in Trieste

Table 2: **Changes in ethnic structure of selected towns in the Upper Adriatic between 1910 and 1991 (in %)**

		Italians	***Slovenes***	***Croats and other Yugosl. nations***	***Germans and other nations***
Gorizia	1910	*44.8*	*40.0*	*1.2*	*14.0*
	1991*	*77.0*	*14.0*	-	*9.0*
Trieste	1910	*64.7*	*24.8*	*1.0*	*9.5*
	1991*	*84.0*	*10.0*	*3.0*	*3.0*
Koper/ Capodistria	1910	*78.2*	*18.5*	*1.3*	*1.9*
	1991	*2.2*	*82.4*	*15.4*	-
Pula/Pola	1910	*52.0*	*4.9*	*23.2*	*19.9*
	1991	*8.1*	*1.9*	*88.0*	*2.0*
Rijeka	1910	*48.6*	*4.7*	*26.7*	*19.9*
	1991	*1.8*	*1.6*	*95.7*	*0.9*

* Estimation

Source: Bufon 1992, Perselli 1993

a decrease in Slovene population can be seen and at the same time Italian population, which has been traditionally the majority, has increased. In Koper/Capodistria, Pula/Pola and Rijeka the formerly dominant Italians have withdrawn and have been partly substituted by local Slovene or Croatian population as well as by immigrants from the less developed regions and republics of former Yugoslavia (Gosar 1993). For example, more than 30% of all immigrants that have moved to Koper/Capodistria were from these areas.

While the census figures show clear trends in ethnic identification and the influences of the political situation, they are not very useful in assessing the 'real' dimension of the ethnic structure, given that the ethnic minority groups often behave like 'submerged' linguistic communities and their 'visibility' depends primarily on the degree of social integration or on the protection measures taken. From more accurate surveys it is evident that in Slovenian Istria only 73% of the Italian speaking population identify themselves as Italians, and in Croatia this figure is even lower (Bogliun Debeljuh 1989, 1994, Milani Kruljac 1990). This difference between objective and subjective ethnic identification occurs to an even greater extent among Slovenes in Trieste, whose degree of formal protection is rather inferior. Here only 40% of the people, who can speak Slovenian or can understand it, identify themselves explicitly as Slovenes (Bufon 1992).

4 Building harmony in the Upper Adriatic borderlands

The contemporary image of the Upper Adriatic from a political-geographic point of view is thus completely different from the old image. Ethnic-political transformations in this area have erased to a great extent the formerly persistent ethnic borders. But, even though cultural spaces have lost many of their traditional traits, they still influence the shape of the specific territorial identity, which can be seen by the people who have moved into these places from somewhere else. Moreover, the emigration of native people has widened the space of original regional identity and has been influencing the forms of spatial bonds within a wider regional context (Klemenčič 1993).

In this way, especially the bonds between Trieste and Istria have become stronger, since in and around Trieste now lives the majority of the Istrian native Italians, who are still very bonded to their land of origin. Trieste consequently is becoming, in spite of the two borders that separate it from the rest of Istria, the new 'Caput Istriae', and it is likely that this function will become even stronger in the future, since Istria is devoid of a specific regional centre. Considering that contemporary processes of integration follow the principle of 'unity in diversity', it is likely that Trieste can assume again its regional function in this area, on the condition that at the same time its multicultural tradition is revived (MINGHI 1994).

It is a common rule for all 'new' borderlands that after the elimination of political and ideological hindrances, they are the most receptive to new forms of integration between neighbouring countries (BUFON 1994a, 2002). This search for a wider co-operation derives from the process of overcoming the conflicts caused by the division of traditionally homogeneous administrative, social, economic and cultural spaces, and it is becoming quite evident also in the case of the 'three-border' area of Trieste and Istria (SANGUIN 1996, ZUPANČIČ & REPOLUSK 1995). 'Old' borders – and the northern part of the current Italian-Slovene border is a good example of this – are based, in fact, on the 'old' concepts of defining borders, that coincide with the so-called natural, usually orographic boundaries, whereas 'new' borders often penetrate into urban and densely populated areas, where communication among inhabitants used to be intense (BUFON 1993, KLEMENČIČ & BUFON 1994).

This is particularly true for the Gorizia region. Here, the area of the Goriška Brda/Collio was cut in two and thus lively social and economic relations between the Goriška Brda/Collio and Friulian centres, representing the main outlet for the Brda agricultural products, were interrupted. Moreover, the new border hampered the access from the major part of the Goriška Brda/Collio to the villages of Solkan and Šempeter, where a new urban centre, an 'alternative' to the town of Gorizia, was developing, making thus the Goriška Brda/Collio a dead enclave within its own state territory. On the other hand, the very birth of the town of Nova Gorica (The New Gorizia) was unusual – not because it meant the construction of a 'twin' town along the border, a relatively frequent phenomenon, – but rather because it had to grow virtually overnight for a precise purpose: that of joining the two villages of Solkan and Šempeter into a larger and more attractive urban centre which would have to overshadow the 'old' Gorizia (BUFON 1996).

These examples show that the border, drawn between Italy and Yugoslavia in 1947, opened up two possible, but extremely different perspectives: on the one hand, the strenghtening of the dividing character of the border and the limitation of cross-border relations would provoke a gradual disintegration of the social and economic tissue of the border area, but on the other, the opening of the border and the promotion of traditional local ties would contribute to the integration and the development of the two border areas.

It is not clear to what extent this dilemma influenced the drawing up of that part of the Peace Treaty in which the two parties are required to jointly solve certain 'technical' problems regarding water and power supply. Nevertheless, the important fact is that already in 1949 the Italian and Yugoslavian governments agreed to make the boundary more permeable, initially only with regard to cross-border traffic of those farmers whose land remained on the other side of the border. But from 1955 onwards they agreed to include all local cross-border transit within a range of 10 km on either side of the border. During the same year local trade within the same area was greatly liberalized.

The effects of these agreements were extraordinary and undoubtedly contributed to the amicable settlement of other open questions and to the creation of a more favorable political climate both at a local and national level. Towards the end of the 1960s, after the abolition of entry visas for international traffic and the stabilization of political relations, the Italian-Yugoslavian border became known as one of the 'most open' boundaries between Western and Eastern Europe, which was undoubtedly true considering the substantially less permeable borders between other neighbour states with profoundly different political systems.

But the openess of the current Italian-Slovene border, particularly with regard to local relations, was even greater than that of many other 'stable' Western European cross-border regions (Bufon 1995). Intense local relations may not be so important from a macro-economic point of view, but they certainly contribute to the shaping and development of more integrated cross-border regions.

In this way, not only the 'berlinization' of both major urban centres along the border was avoided, but the adopted policy also deeply influenced cross-border social and economic transactions. Cross-border trade stemmed on the local level from the rather asymmetric political division: in the Gorizia region, Italy obtained only 8% of the territory of the former Province of Gorizia, but 74% percent of its population and 52% of commercial businesses. It was like an apple cut in two parts: one smaller, but containing the core, the other greater, but without the core. The local border agreements permitted this 'apple' to link up again, and therefore it is not surprising that after the liberalization of local cross-border traffic in 1955, the latter increased in only five years by nearly 900% (Bufon 2003).

The intensity of the local cross-border traffic has undoubtedly influenced the shaping of a particular and complementary type of economic border space around the towns of Gorizia and Trieste, where the Slovenian area still attracts the inhabitants of the Italian side with its cheaper petrol and food-stuff, restaurants and duty-free shops, as well as its casinos, but also with its better preserved environment, while the Italian border area has been traditionally more attractive for the Slovene neighbours because of its job and shopping opportunities.

A particular phenomenon, which by far exceeds the local cross-border relations, was represented by the Trieste and, on a minor scale, Tarvisio daily shopping fair (Minghi 1999). The former has known its 'golden age' in the 1970s and 1980s thanks to the Yugoslavian shoppers, the latter, instead, has always been an Austrian target.

On the other hand, several researchers (Sussi 1973, Delli Zotti 1982) have revealed the importance of social cross-border transactions. Investigations revealed that economic ties could develop only when local personal cross-border contacts had been established, based on cultural homogeneity, kindships and friendships. On the basis of these contacts several social contacts and other events, such as sports and cultural, could first develop. Only then, could political relations develop. Significantly, these were strenghtened and finally 'normalized' in the late 1970s.

It seems that particularly knowledge of both languages and national or ethnic intertwining of the border population provide for more sophisticated and intense forms of social and cultural cooperation and integration. Traditionally as much as two thirds of local cross-border 'official' contacts were maintained by the Slovene ethnic community in Italy, a minority which is present along the entire Italian-Slovene borderland (Bufon 1994b).

This situation has only partially changed after the independence of Slovenia, even though there are now increasing efforts to give a more structured frame to these extraordinarily intense local cross-border contacts and to create a new Euroregion in the Upper Adriatic, which will most probably be generated by different areas of interest such as the northern border sector, the Gorizia sector, and the Trieste sector, which could also act as the leading Euroregion for the Istrian three-border area.

But besides an increasing process of re-integration of the Upper Adriatic within the frame of the European Union and the established Schengen space, there is also a process of social and spatial dis-integration on the Slovenian-Croatian border, showing how influential remain wider political-geographical transformations on this interesting European contact area.

Recent investigations (Bufon 2008) have revealed that expectations for future developments in cross-border cooperation are quite different among Slovene respondents at the border with Italy and Croatia: positive expectations prevail on the former, whilst negative expectations persist on the latter, as shown in Table 3. Nevertheless, both border areas are sharing the same level of potential social cross-border connection, as 81% to 83% of respondents at the border with Italy and Croatia indicated that they have friends living on the other side of the border.

Significantly different is, instead, the structure of functional cross-border traffic, both in terms of intensity and motivations (see Table 4). On the Slovenian-Italian border, as much as 19% of the population is used to cross the border daily or at least weekly, whilst those types of visits involve only 5% of the population on the Slovenian-Croatian border. Moreover, in this border area not less than 18% of the population never cross the border in comparison with only 7% at the border with Italy. For what the motivations for cross-border movements are concerned, shopping prevails at the border with Italy (48%), whilst the same percentage goes on the border with Croatia for recreation.

Table 3: **Recent convergence and divergence processes in the Upper Adriatic – different expectations for the development of cross-border cooperation among Slovene respondents at the border with Italy and Croatia (in % of respondents)**

a) How have croos-border relations changed after Slovenia joined the EU?

	SLO/I	*SLO/CRO*
To the better	*36.0*	*6.0*
Remained the same	*55.0*	*29.0*
To the worse	*6.0*	*62.0*

b) How will cross-border relations change after the Slovenian entrance into the Schengen space?

	SLO/I	*SLO/CRO*
To the better	*49.0*	*14.0*
Remain the same	*42.0*	*29.0*
To the worse	*4.0*	*52.0*

Source: Bufon 2008

Table 4: **Recent convergence and divergence processes in the Upper Adriatic – different structure of cross-border visits among Slovene respondents at the border with Italy and Croatia (in % of respondents)**

a) Intensity of cross-border visits

	SLO/I	*SLO/CRO*
Every day	*7.2*	*1.6*
At least once a week	*12.0*	*3.6*
At least once a month	*33.5*	*20.2*
At least once a year	*40.2*	*56.7*
Never	*7.1*	*17.9*

b) Motivations for cross-border visits

	SLO/I	*SLO/CRO*
Work	*5.6*	*3.6*
Supply	*48.2*	*8.7*
Visits to relatives/friends	*17.5*	*15.5*
Visits of cultural events	*4.0*	*2.4*
Recreation/Excursion	*14.3*	*48.4*

Source: Bufon 2008

5 Conclusions

The Upper Adriatic is a region of intense cross-border intertwining on a cultural, social, economic and political level. The diffused practice of bilingualism has been in recent times reinforced by developments in local cross-border relations and cross-border information exchange produced by the neighbouring mass media, in which border minorities have taken an important role in creating contact opportunities.

This area provides an interesting illustration of an apparently paradoxical process within borderlands: the greater the conflicts in political partitioning of a previous homogeneous administrative, cultural and economic region, the greater have been opportunities for such a divided area to develop into an integrated cross-border region, once the appropriate conditions are given.

Reflecting on the border landscape concept on the basis of this case study, it becomes clear that the political or economic 'macro' approach in studying cross-border regions is not sufficient. The real qualities of these regions, however, may be found when local cultural and social elements of cross-border relations are taken into account. This great variety of micro-transactions, supported by the border population, is the result of its spatial mobility in satisfying daily needs regarding basic social functions such as shopping, work, leisure time, housing or even education. But they are also the result of the activity of the border population in maintaining traditional cultural links within historical regions.

Hence, the study of border regions undoubtedly brings additional aspects to bear on the standard theory of centre-periphery relations, while opening up a range of new problems and possibilities. Many of these are becoming increasingly more topical in today's world, as we try to enhance our mutual understanding in the culturally rich and diverse European space. The geography of border landscapes in its social and cultural dimension is thus definitely assuming an important role in the process of 'humanisation' of the traditional geographical approach to borders and border conflict resolution (Rumley & Minghi 1991).

The Upper Adriatic remains therefore a very interesting area subject to continuous geopolitical transformations. Since this area is now divided into three states it is fastly becoming a new and special kind of European borderland or 'Euro-region' where both convergence and divergence processes could be studied, providing thus continuous stimula for boundary researchers. Moreover, the states involved in this region should see that their vested interests are best served by allowing it to remain an area of international and both functional and multicultural integration and co-operation into the future. The history of the Upper Adriatic region proves, after all, that it is much more difficult to divide than to bond it together.

6 References

Bogliun Debeljuh L. (1989), Analisi dell'autoidentificazione etnica tra i figli dei matrimoni nazionalmente misti. In: Atti del Convegno Lingue e culture in contatto, pp. 138–149. Fiume, Università degli Studi.

Bogliun Debeljuh L. (1994), L'identità etnica – gli Italiani dell'area istro-quarnerina. Rovigno, Centro di Ricerche Storiche.

Bufon M. (1992), Prostorska opredeljenost in narodna pripadnost: obmejna in etnično mešana območja v evropskih razvojnih silnicah – primer Slovencev v Furlaniji-Julijski krajini. Trst, ZTT.

Bufon M. (1993), Cultural and social dimensions of borderlands: the case of the Italo-Slovene transborder area. In: GeoJournal, 3, pp. 235–240.

Bufon M. (1994a), Local aspects of transborder cooperation: a case study on the Italo-Slovene border landscape. In: Gallusser W. (ed.), Political Boundaries and Coexistence, pp. 19–29. Bern, Peter Lang.

Bufon M. (1994b), Nacionalne manjšine in njihova funkcija v mednarodnih integracijskih procesih: iluzija ali realnost? In: Štrukelj I., Sussi E. (eds.), Narodne manjšine danes in jutri, pp. 87–95. Trst, SLORI.

Bufon M. (1995), Prostor, meje, ljudje – razvoj prekomejnih odnosov, struktura obmejnega območja in vrednotenje obmejnosti na Goriškem. Trst, SLORI.

Bufon M. (1996), Social integration in the Italo-Slovene border landscape: the Gorizia transborder region. In: TESG, 3, pp. 247–258.

Bufon M. (2000), Transformations ethniques et geopolitiques en Adriatique septentrionale: entre conflits et perspectives d'integration. In: Sanguin A.L. (ed.), Mare nostrum: dynamiques et mutations géopolitiques de la Méditerranée, pp. 63–72. Paris, L'Harmattan.

Bufon M. (2002), Confini, identità ed integrazione – nuove prospettive per l'Alto Adriatico. Trieste, SLORI.

Bufon M. (2003), Cross-border cooperation in the Upper Adriatic. In: Anderson J., O'Dowd L., Wilson T.M. (eds.), New Borders for a New Europe, pp. 177–196. London, Frank Cass.

Bufon M. (2008), Na obrobju ali v osredju? Slovenska obmejna območja pred izzivi evropskega povezovanja. Koper, Annales.

Bufon M., Minghi J. (2000), The Upper Adriatic borderland – from conflict to harmony. In: GeoJournal, 52, pp. 119–127.

Čermelj L. (1965), Slovenci in Hrvatje pod Italijo med obema vojnama. Ljubljana, Slovenska Matica.

Delli Zotti G. (1982), Transnational relations in a border region: the case of Friuli-Venetia Julia. In: Strassoldo R., Delli Zotti G. (eds.), Cooperation and Conflicts in Border Areas, pp. 25–60. Milano, Angeli.

Gosar A. (1993), Nationalities of Slovenia – changing ethnic structures in Central Europe. In: GeoJournal, 3, pp. 215–223.

Gosar A., Klemenčič V. (1994), Current problems of border regions along the Slovene-Croatian border. In: Gallusser W.A. (ed.), Political Boundaries and Coexistence, pp. 30–42. Bern, Peter Lang.

Gosar A., Klemenčić M. (2000), Les problemes de la delimitation de la frontiere Italie-Slovenie-Croatie en Adriatique septentrionale. In: Sanguin A.L. (ed.), Mare Nostrum – Dynamiques et mutations geopolitiques de la Mediterranee, pp. 123–134. Paris, L'Harmattan.

Juri F. (1991), Manjšinsko vprašanje v etnično mešanih okoljih: primer Istre. In: Geografija v šoli, 1, pp. 23–25.

Klemenčič V. (1993), National minorities as an element of the demographic and spatial structure of the Alpine-Adriatic-Pannonian region. In: GeoJournal, 3, pp. 207–214.

Klemenčič V., Bufon M. (1991), Geographic problems of frontier regions: the case of the Italo-Yugoslav border landscape. In: Rumley D., Minghi J.V. (eds.), The Geography of Border Landscapes, pp. 86–104. London, Routledge.

Klemenčič V., Bufon M. (1994), Cultural elements of integration and transformation of border regions: the case of Slovenia. In: Political Geography, 1, pp. 73–83.

Milani Kruljac N. (1990), La comunità italiana in Istria e a Fiume fra diglossia e bilinguismo (= Etnia, 1). Rovigno, publisher.

Minghi J.V. (1994), The impact of Slovenian independence on the Italo-Slovene borderland: an assessment of the first three years. In: Gallusser W.A. (ed.), Political Boundaries and Coexistence, pp. 88–94. Bern, Peter Lang.

Minghi J.V. (1999), Borderland "day tourists" from the East: Trieste's transitory shopping fair. In: Visions in Leisure and Business, 17, pp. 32–49.

Moodie A.E. (1950), Some new boundary problems in the Julian March. In: Transactions and Papers, Institute of British Geographers, pp. 81–93.

Perselli G. (1993), I censimenti della popolazione dell'Istria, con Fiume e Trieste, e di alcune città della Dalmazia tra il 1850 e il 1936 (= Etnia, IV). Rovigno, Centro di Ricerche Storiche.

Repolusk P. (1990), Spreminjanje narodnostne strukture prebivalstva kot element demo-geografskega razvoja v Koprskem primorju. Primorje. In: Zbornik, 15, pp. 107–112.

Rumley D., Minghi J.V. (1991), The Geography of Border Landscapes, pp. 86–104. London, Routledge.

Rutar S. (1896), Trst in mejna grofija Istra. Ljubljana, Matica Slovenska.

SANGUIN A.L. (1996), La 'communaute submergee': les Italiens de l'Istrie croate et slovene. In: Bulletin de l'Association de Geographes Francais, 73, pp. 55–64.

SCHIFFRER C. (1946), La Venezia Giulia: saggio di una carta dei limiti nazionali italo-jugoslavi. Roma.

SUSSI E. (1973), L'emergenza della regione transfrontaliera Alpe-Adria: transazioni 'pubbliche' tra Carinzia, Friuli-Venezia Giulia e Slovenia. In: STRASSOLDO R. (ed.), Confini e regioni, pp. 135–146. Trieste, Lint.

ZUPANČIČ J., REPOLUSK P. (1995), Regionalism in Istria. In: KOTER M. (ed.), Region and Regionalism – Social and Political Aspects, pp. 109–116. Opole – Łódź, University of Lodz, Silesian Institute in Opole.

Recent Ethnodemographic Developments in the Central Part of the Alps-Adriatic Region: Slovenia, Croatia, Friuli-Venezia Giulia and Carinthia[1]

Damir Josipović, Ljubljana*

with 2 figures and 7 tables in the text

Content

Summary 27
1 Introduction 28
2 Recent ethnodemographic developments in the four regions 30
3 Conclusion 41
4 Bibliography 41

Summary

The Northern Adriatic space is a contact zone between several differing macro-regions. As much as it is a transit area, state borders have changed several times. Its population shows a wide linguistic variety, but interethnic relations are close. The 20th century left delimitations, which played and still play an important role for the ethnodemographic development of the region. Changes can systematically be traced back to the first modern census of 1857. In about one and a half century this area has gradually been transformed from a kaleidoscope of ethnic groups across the borders to a multitude of fluctuating and small ethnic identities.

[1] This chapter is a result of the basic research project "Constitution of new national and ethnic identities in the Alps-Adria region with special regard to border areas and the city of Trieste, and to the "community-making" aspects of contemporary media (code: J6-0825)" lead by Dr Marija Jurič Pahor from the Institute for Ethnic Studies. (duration: 1.2.2008 - 30.1.2011) funded by the Slovenian Research Agency

* Damir Josipović, PhD., Scientific Associate, Institute for Ethnic Studies, Ljubljana, Erjavčeva c. 26, SI-1000 Ljubljana, Slovenia; e-mail: damir.josipovic@guest.arnes.si

Accordingly, available demographic data tend to concentrate on objectively measurable phenomena. Due to the gradual omitting of some traditionally observed population features like language or religion, national statistics leave little space for diachronic comparisons. But the data basis is good enough to confirm that the last few decades have witnessed completely new characteristics of demographic development.

This paper will firstly present a diachronic ethnodemographic analysis of the region from the times, when it was part of two monarchies until now, when it is split into four nation states. Secondly, the paper focuses on recent changes in ethnodemographic structure and on the new phenomenon of accelerated migration based on national statistics. In this respects it highlights the cases of Slovenia (especially its western region Littoral [Primorska/Littorale], Croatia (especially the regions of Istria [Istra/ Istria] and Kvarner/Quarnero), Italy (especially its northeasternmost region Friuli-Venezia Giulia), and Austria (especially its southernmost province Carinthia [Kärnten/ Koroška]).

1 Introduction

Perhaps one of the scientifically most intriguing places in the entire Alpine-Adriatic-Danubian region, the Northern Adriatic space is a unique contact zone between several differing macro-regions. The Northern Adriatic space in this context is understood as a geographically heterogeneous area, composed of land and sea and stretching from the Kvarner/Quarnero[2] and the Istrian peninsula in the South to the alpine province of Carinthia [Kärnten/Koroška] in the North. This concept does not claim any kind of exclusivity for this space, but functions just as a frame for investigating into some typical aspects of contact and transition by placing them into a broader context.

It may be argued that such a view on the Northern Adriatic overlooks wide areas of the Adriatic space truly north-bound, especially those in the West of this imagined region. But it includes four macro-regions getting into contact here: the Adriatic basin, the Dinaric karst, the Alps and alpine piedmonts as well as the Po valley. The plethora of physical-geographic features with a linguistic and ethnic kaleidoscope made this region always being in motion (cf. Massey et al. 1998). Thus, we deal with a prominent investigative geographical laboratory.

As much as it is a transit area, state borders have changed several times and are shaped in an extraordinary way. They divide cultural landscapes – neglecting both the sense of place and the fates of populations – and do often not correspond to the "real

[2] In this contribution all endonyms are presented, whether they are standardized and official or not, and separated by a slash. When an English exonym is used, the corresponding endonym(s) appear(s) in rectangular brackets with the first mentioning of the name. An endonym is by the United Nations in their most recent version of the Glossary defined as "name of a geographical feature in an official or well-established language occurring in that area where the feature is situated." (Kadmon 2007, p. 2)

world". However, the boundaries drawn half a century ago became gradually producers of space-related identities themselves (cf. PAASI 1986). While superimposed at the beginning with the main goal of establishing an equilibrium between war-faring parties (cf. JONES 1959) and disregarding central place systems and catchments, they were later accepted as the new "reality" and started shaping new central place systems.

Despite a wide linguistic variety in the region, close relations among populations exist. Before the advent of the national idea, in the times of supranational empires, people developed feelings of belonging to a ruler and his territory, and the cohesive power of a region was based on the strength of its leadership. After 1848, when nationalist movements emerged, the Northern Adriatic space became a contested terrain of antagonistic national ideas.

Being rather peripheries in the political and economic sense, the regions of the Northern Adriatic never developed centripetal forces based on a concept of their own. On the contrary, they welcomed the ruthless political plays of the 20th century producing always new delimitations, which played, and still play an important role in the ethnodemographic development of the region.

Ethnodemographic changes may well be traced back to the first modern census of 1857. During about one and a half century this region has gradually turned from a mosaic of ethnic identities crossing borders into a multitude of individualized perceptions of identities. This was supported by national homogenization and the internally invasive nation state. The end of WWI brought a break-up of the Austro-Hungarian Empire and the creation of several new states. The Northern Adriatic, thus, became a contact area between Italy, Austria and the Kingdom of Serbs, Croats, and Slovenes, which later became the Kingdom of Yugoslavia. The whole area between the Adriatic Sea and the Alps represented a contested terrain for decades to come. It looks as if it will take about one hundred years from World War I to a reunification of the four neighbours (Austria, Croatia, Italy and Slovenia) by European integration.

It seems also that a globalizing economy and pertaining issues somehow veiled the local "ethnic" concerns. In the course of the past century the neighbouring states have slowly omitted statistical indicators which "measure" ethnic, linguistic and other cultural features of the population, although we still witness the importance ascribed to "ethnic" issues by the local population (e.g. treating the rights of national minorities). This ambivalence leads us to a confirmation of the "glocal" character of "things". Moreover, it implies that we have moved further in a sequence of time-space compression (cf. HARVEY 1989 p. 240, MASSEY 1993).

The question here is why certain countries omit or restrain the aforementioned indicators. We may, accordingly, argue that the available demographic data nowadays tend to concentrate around more objectively measurable phenomena. Furthermore, by gradually omitting the traditionally observed cultural population features like language, religion etc. national statistics raise methodological questions as well. They leave little space for diachronic comparisons.

Besides, the last few decades have witnessed completely new aspects of demographic development. They may well be addressed as the "third demographic transition" (Coleman 2006). Former dualistic relationships are superimposed by high numbers of immigrants and migrant communities. Spatial relations tend to be more complicated and blurred. And the national statistical agencies are incapable of capturing the heavily accelerated population dynamics.

This paper will firstly present a diachronic ethnodemographic analysis of the region from the times, when it was part of two monarchies until now, when it is split into four nation states. Secondly, the paper focuses on recent changes in ethnodemographic structure and on the new phenomenon of accelerated migration based on national statistics. In this respects it highlights the cases of Slovenia (especially its western region Littoral [Primorska/Littorale], Croatia (especially the regions of Istria [Istra/Istria] and Kvarner/Quarnero), Italy (especially its northeasternmost region Friuli-Venezia Giulia), and Austria (especially its southernmost province Carinthia [Kärnten/Koroška]).

2 Recent ethnodemographic developments in the four regions

To get a better imagination of ethnodemographic developments we have to refer in the first line to statistical data which are usually collected and published by national statistical agencies according to contemporary administrative divisions. Since the study focuses on recent developments, the censuses around 1991 and 2001 are most important. In 2011 only Croatia conducted a traditional census with questions for ethnic and religious affiliation, while Austria and Slovenia practiced a so-called "register census" lacking possibilities to ask for such characteristics. Italy had anyway also with traditional censuses not asked for such criteria.

In addition we used material from other sources, such as migration statistics, which are collected annually, and other demographic data on residents, migrant population, etc.

2.1 Carinthia (Austria)

Carinthia is situated in the South of modern Austria. Its geographical location contributes to its transit function. Although it is rather mountainous, it has in its centre a wide basin. The main communication corridors cross the province in NW-SE and NE-SW direction. The Karawanken/Karavanke mountain range forms a physical-geographical border towards Slovenia. After World War I the south-easternmost part of Carinthia around Gutenstein/Ravne was ceded to the Kingdom of Serbs, Croats, and Slovenes. Additionally, the municipality of Seeland/Jezersko was exchanged for the municipality of Weißenfels/Fusine/Bela Peč in the north-westernmost part of Carniola [Kranjska]. Curiously enough, the latter was not attached to the first Austrian republic, but to Italy.

Nowadays, Carinthia occupies an area of 9,536 km^2 with about 560,000 inhabitants (see Table 1), which ranks it among less densely populated regions (58.5 inhabitants per km^2).

Table 1: **Carinthia's resident population in absolute figures and indices 1981-2011**

Year	*Carinthia (Land)*	*Chain indices*
1981	536,179	...
1991	547,798	102.2
2001	559,404	102.1
2009	560,605	100.2
2011*	558,085	99.6

* First quarter of 2011

Source: STATISTIK AUSTRIA 2011

Carinthia's traditional ethnodemographic characteristic is the dualism of two linguistic groups, German- and Slovene-speakers. Political debates frequently circle around this feature and the question of legal protection of the Slovene minority.[3] Official numbers on the size of the Slovene group in the ethnic sense are not available. Only colloquial language data were officially collected and published up to and including the 2001 census. As regards ethnic affiliation we can only refer to estimates.[4]

The tradition of asking for the colloquial language with population censuses can – with the exception of the interwar period – be traced back to the censuses of the Habsburg Empire. But since then the function of Slovene as a colloquial language has changed dramatically. While in the former compact rural society Slovene was in predominantly Slovene villages indeed the language predominantly spoken also in the public sphere, this is not anymore so in the modern network society. Declaring to speak Slovene as the colloquial language has today rather the meaning of a political or ethnic confession (cf. DAMJANIĆ 2002, ŠUMI & JOSIPOVIČ 2008). Moreover, it is used to demonstrate the diminuation of Slovenes under German-speaking rule (e.g. KLEMENČIČ 1990, ZUPANČIČ 1999).

3 There is a harsh debate on Slovene place names in Carinthia. For a very instructive contribution on exo- and endonyms see JORDAN 2007

4 STEINICKE (2001) estimates the number of Carinthians with Slovene mother tongue at around 50,000.

The turn from a spatially compact rural cultural group into a network spread over most parts of Carinthia, also over typically non-Slovene speaking areas, can well be observed in Table 2.

Table 2: **Colloquial language by Carinthian Political Districts and resident population 2001**

	absolute number		***percentage (%)***			
Political District	***Slovene***	***»Windisch«***	***German***	***Slovene***	***»Windisch«***	***Other***
Carinthia	14,010	556	*92.39*	*2.50*	*0.10*	*5.01*
Klagenfurt (city)	1,722	8	*89.43*	*1.91*	*0.01*	*8.65*
Villach (city)	382	6	*90.62*	*0.66*	*0.01*	*8.70*
Feldkirchen	48	0	*96.37*	*0.16*	*0.00*	*3.47*
Hermagor	147	38	*96.62*	*0.74*	*0.19*	*2.44*
Klagenfurt (surroundings)	3,290	104	*90.24*	*5.83*	*0.18*	*3.74*
Sankt Veit an der Glan	147	1	*96.06*	*0.25*	*0.00*	*3.69*
Spittal an der Drau	289	0	*95.29*	*0.35*	*0.00*	*4,36*
Villach (surroundings)	1,928	70	*92.84*	*2.98*	*0.11*	*4.07*
Völkermarkt	5,920	329	*82.48*	*13.59*	*0.76*	*3.18*
Wolfsberg	137	0	*96.52*	*0.24*	*0.00*	*3.23*

Source: Statistik Austria, Census 2001

As we will see also in the other regions under investigation, the former linguistic and ethnic dualism is gradually replaced by a variety of ethnic groups. In the case of Carinthia, the Slovene-German antagonism is de facto outdated after the fall of the Iron Curtain and the Yugoslavian wars. This becomes obvious when we look at data by citizenship. Even if only Austrian citizens are regarded, the former divide into German-speakers and Slovene- (and "Windisch-")[5] speakers is contested by an in many places higher share of other languages (see Table 3).

[5] »Windisch« is in fact not a linguistic, but an ethnic category, although it is regarded by Austrian censuses as a linguistic classification. Those among Carinthian Slovenes regarding themselves as a part of the German, later Austrian nation used to classify themselves in this way. The word »windisch« as such is the former general German designation for all variants of Slavonic people – as opposed to »walisch« (in Carinthia) or »welsch« in other parts of the German-speaking lands for Romance people.

Table 3: **Colloquial language by Carinthian Political Districts and resident Austrian citizens 2001**

	absolute number		***percentage (%)***			
Political District	***Slovene***	***»Windisch«***	***German***	***Slovene***	***»Windisch«***	***Other***
Carinthia	12,554	555	*96.44*	*2.38*	*0.11*	*1.08*
Klagenfurt (city)	1,308	8	*96.15*	*1.58*	*0.01*	*2.26*
Villach (city)	198	6	*98.00*	*0.38*	*0.01*	*1.61*
Feldkirchen	28	0	*99.10*	*0.10*	*0.00*	*0.80*
Hermagor	122	37	*98.81*	*0.65*	*0.20*	*0.35*
Klagenfurt (surroundings)	3,115	104	*92.98*	*5.80*	*0.19*	*1.03*
Sankt Veit an der Glan	66	1	*99.14*	*0.12*	*0.00*	*0.74*
Spittal an der Drau	144	0	*99.04*	*0.19*	*0.00*	*0.77*
Villach (surroundings)	1,758	70	*96.13*	*2.87*	*0.11*	*0.89*
Völkermarkt	5,742	329	*84,80*	*13.71*	*0.79*	*0.70*
Wolfsberg	73	0	*99,36*	*0.13*	*0.00*	*0.50*

Source: Statistik Austria, Census 2001

While Slovene-speakers are much less then before concentrated on their former homelands, the Political Districts of Völkermarkt, Klagenfurt (surroundings) and Villach (surroundings), but dispersed all over Carinthia (and major Austrian cities outside Carinthia), they meet in many places a higher number of people with a third ethnic background, although foreign citizens are residing in Carinthia still well below the Austrian average (see Table 4).

Migrants in Austria make up for one ninth of the whole population. If the 3.3% share of naturalized population is added, Austria's population is at least at a share of 14% born outside the country. Carinthia has always been lagging behind the national average, except in the 1940s and 1950s, when it hosted a "repatriated" German-speaking population from former Yugoslavia and other eastern European countries. This situation has been accentuated after 1990, when especially Vienna [Wien] and other economically prosperous parts of Austria received a lot of migrants. Today, Carinthia hosts about 8.5% foreign-born population (see Table 4). Its overwhelming majority (60% or about 20,000 persons) descends from former Yugoslavia (Figure 1).

Table 4: **Foreign citizens in Carinthia and Austria 2011**

		Austria	*Carinthia*
Resident foreign citizens	1951	322,598	23,640
	%	*4.7*	*5.0*
	1961	102,159	7,752
	%	*1.4*	*1.6*
	1971	211,896	9,173
	%	*2.8*	*1.7*
	1981	291,448	8,156
	%	*3.9*	*1.5*
	1991	517,690	17,072
	%	*6.6*	*3.1*
	2001	710,926	32,071
	%	*8.9*	*5.7*
	2009	868,947	37,561
	%	*10.4*	*6.7*
	2010	895,144	38,407
	%	*10.7*	*6.9*
Naturalizations	2000/2010	277,414	8,644
	%	*3.3*	*1.5*

Source: STATISTIK AUSTRIA, 2011

Figure 1: **Citizenship of foreign residents in Carinthia 2001**

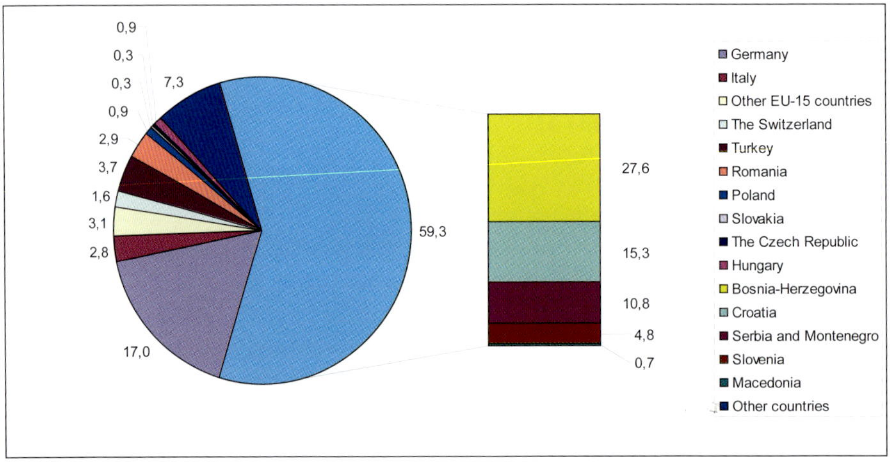

Source: STATISTIK AUSTRIA, Census 2001

2.2 Friuli-Venezia Giulia (Italy)

Friuli-Venezia Giulia is one of Italy's five autonomous regions. It is located in the Northeast of the country and shares territorial borders with Slovenia and Austria. It occupies an area of 7,856 km^2 with about 1,235,000 inhabitants (Statistical Office of Italy 2011). With a population density of 156.7 inhabitants per km^2, Friuli-Venezia Giulia is the most densely populated region in the central part of the Alps-Adriatic area. Administratively, it consists of the four provinces Udine/Udin, Pordenone/Pordenon, Trieste/Trst and Gorizia/Gurize/Gorica. Italy was the first of the four neighbours to avoid "ethnic" statistics. The last census collecting these data was conducted in 1921, i.e. on the eve of fascism. Later, only some estimates were made.

Traditional Slovene-speaking areas in Friuli-Venezia Giulia are Valcanale/Kanaltal around Tarvisio/Trbiž/Tarvis (formerly part of Carinthia), Slavia Veneta around Cividale del Friuli/Cividât/Čedad, the area of Gorizia/Gurize/Gorica and the province of Trieste/Trst. In Slavia Veneta (Beneška Slovenija) according to the last official census of 1921 36,000 out of 52,000 residents in 15 municipalities were Slovenes. The vast majority of the rest were Friulians (a.o. Roglić 1946). Roglić (1946) estimates the Slovene-speaking population of Valcanale/Kanaltal at about 3,000 persons before WWII. Together with the provinces of Gorizia/Gurize/Gorica (28,000) and Trieste/Trst (62,000) the Slovenes roughly amounted to between 130,000 and 150,000 before WWII (Roglić 1946, Stranj 1999). But the last Austrian census of 1910 and its revision in 1911 rather suggests that the number of Slovenes in the Trieste/Trst province was underestimated. The corrected number reached 80,000 (Roglić 1946) and was later supported by the results of the 1911 elections, according to which the number of Slovenes was 83,000 (Stranj 1999, p. 299).

After the exodus (about 40,000) of Slovenes under fascism (Stranj 1999), the post-war number of Slovenes was estimated at between 85,000 and 110,000 persons (Stranj 1983). The lower estimation was, accordingly, confirmed by Bufon (1992).

Apart from that, some official inquiries were carried out, mostly in connection with censuses. In spite of their official character, their only aim was to assess the ratio between Italian - and Slovene - speakers. They sheerly neglected the presence of other languages, first of all Friulian.

In 2001 Act No. 38 on the protection of the Slovene-speaking minority in Friuli-Venezia Giulia was passed, but did not define the area of application concretely. So it took another couple of years to see its at least partial implementation. Only the Presidential Decree of 2007 defined 32 municipalities, on which the Act had to be applied. They included indeed almost all of the traditional Slovene-speaking area except four municipalities to which the Act was only partially applied.

This local and regional struggle for minority rights did, however, not pay attention to radical changes in population dynamics. Firstly, peripheral border areas were almost depopulated. The population of Drenchia/Dreka in the Udine/Udin province, e.g., decreased by 86%, from 1,392 inhabitants in 1951 to 197 in 2001. Secondly, a significant increase of international migration after the fall of the Iron Curtain led to larger shares of migrant population and to major changes in the demographic structure of the region.

Table 5: **Migrant population in Friuli-Venezia Giulia by provinces 2003-2009**

	Friuli-Venezia Giulia	*Udine*	*Gorizia*	*Trieste*	*Pordenone*
2003	43,498	15,564	4,283	10,655	12,996
%	*3.7*	*3.0*	*3.1*	*4.4*	*4.5*
2004	51,889	18,654	5,165	11,432	16,638
%	*4.3*	*3.6*	*3.7*	*4.8*	*5.7*
2005	58,915	21,689	5,953	11,541	19,732
%	*4.9*	*4.1*	*4.2*	*4.8*	*6.6*
2006	65,185	24,166	6,600	12,406	22,013
%	*5.4*	*4.6*	*4.7*	*5.2*	*7.3*
2007	72,462	26,680	7,451	13,436	24,895
%	*6.0*	*5.0*	*5.3*	*5.7*	*8.2*
2008	83,306	31,313	8,360	14,852	28,781
%	*6.8*	*5.8*	*5.9*	*6.3*	*9.4*
2009	94,976	35,588	9,688	16,528	33,172
%	*7.7*	*6.6*	*6.8*	*7.0*	*10,6*

Source: Italian Statistical Office 2011

Table 5 shows that the period 2003-2009 was marked by an extensive increase of migrants. In total they doubled, while the most significant increase was registered in the Pordenone/Pordenon province, where their number eventually tripled. This province is the only one with a migrant population exceeding the 10% margin. This ranks it to the top of all four regions compared. Friuli-Venezia Giulia surpasses Carinthia's share of foreign residents (7.7% vs. 6.9%), but its growth occurred mainly in the last decade, while it was more continuous in Carinthia.

The migrant population in Friuli-Venezia Giulia is far from homogeneous. By citizenship it is much more complex than Carinthia's. While the share of migrants from former Yugoslavia amounts to only 26%, Romanians and Albanians are the largest groups contributing in total more than 30%. The remaining 44% are heavily dispersed: 7% come from the former Communist countries Poland, Ukraine and Moldova, 5% from Maghreb countries (Morocco and Tunisia), another 5% from Ghana, 3% each from India and the People's Republic of China (see Figure 2).

It is significant that the notorious issue of Chinese immigration especially to the city of Trieste/Trst is far from being overwhelming. It comprises less than 3% of the whole migrant population of Friuli-Venezia Giulia, although Chinese citizens show a certain concentration on the Trieste/Trst province (35% of the region's Chinese citizens).

Recent statistical and demographic data demonstrate that Friuli-Venezia Giulia is undergoing significant population shifts. On the one hand there are signs of social emancipation of Slovenes and Friulians, on the other migrants settle down in downtowns and suburbs replacing there the former population.

Figure 2: **Citizenship of migrant population in Friuli-Venezia Giulia 2011**

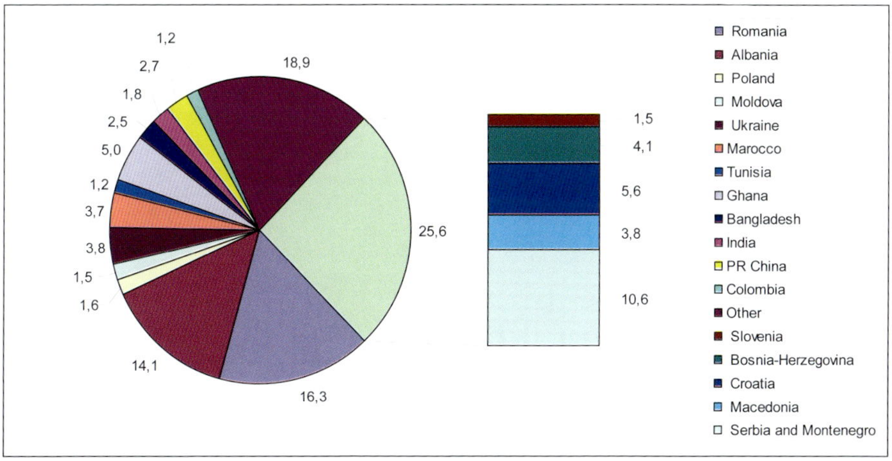

Source: Italian Statistical Office 2011

2.3 *Primorska/Littorale (Slovenia)*

Slovenia lacks administrative regions at the NUTS-3 level and is thus a rather centralized country (Josipovič 2009). It was also the only Yugoslavian republic that bordered as much as three other countries and only one other republic. Its geographical position between Italy, Austria, Hungary, Croatia and with an access to the Adriatic Sea ranks Slovenia among the physically and geopolitically most diverse countries compared to its size.

Nevertheless, even a relatively small country may have its periphery. Such a periphery is Primorska/Littorale. It is located in the far West of Slovenia bordering

Table 6: **Ethnic structure of Slovenia and Primorska/Littorale in 2002**

	Slovenia	*Notranjsko-kraška Region*	*Goriška Region*	*Obalno-kraška Region*	*percentage (%)*			
Total	**1,964,036**	**50,243**	**118,511**	**102,070**	***100.00***	***100.00***	***100.00***	***100.00***
Ethnically declared - Total	1,766,982	45,438	107,756	87,143	*89.97*	*90.44*	*90.92*	*85.38*
Slovenes	1,631,363	41,876	103,133	73,357	*83.06*	*83.35*	*87.02*	*71.87*
Italians	2,258	19	100	1,866	*0.11*	*0.04*	*0.08*	*1.83*
Hungarians	6,243	23	35	77	*0.32*	*0.05*	*0.03*	*0.08*
Roma	3,246	4	14	6	*0.17*	*0.01*	*0.01*	*0.01*
Albanians	6,186	225	476	538	*0.31*	*0.45*	*0.40*	*0.53*
Austrians	181	1	1	8	*0.01*	*0.00*	*0.00*	*0.01*
Bosniaks	21,542	554	667	2,174	*1.10*	*1.10*	*0.56*	*2.13*
Montenegrins	2,667	26	80	169	*0.14*	*0.05*	*0.07*	*0.17*
Croats	35,642	923	702	4,279	*1.81*	*1.84*	*0.59*	*4.19*
Macedonians	3,972	80	295	397	*0.20*	*0.16*	*0.25*	*0.39*
Muslims	10,467	237	365	676	*0.53*	*0.47*	*0.31*	*0.66*
Germans	499	8	3	31	*0.03*	*0.02*	*0.00*	*0.03*
Serbs	38,964	1,411	1,733	3,160	*1.98*	*2.81*	*1.46*	*3.10*
Other	3,752	51	152	405	*0.19*	*0.10*	*0.13*	*0.40*
Ethnically undeclared - Total	22,141	748	923	3,309	*1.13*	*1.49*	*0.78*	*3.24*
Undeclared - Yugoslavs	527	10	24	64	*0.03*	*0.02*	*0.02*	*0.06*
Undeclared - Bosnians	8,062	380	428	481	*0.41*	*0.76*	*0.36*	*0.47*
Undeclared - regional affiliation	1,467	8	16	1,245	*0.07*	*0.02*	*0.01*	*1.22*
Undeclared - other	12,085	350	455	1,519	*0.62*	*0.70*	*0.38*	*1.49*
Did not want to reply to the question on ethnicity	48,588	1,127	2,244	3,140	*2.47*	*2.24*	*1.89*	*3.08*
Unknown ethnicity	126,325	2,930	7,588	8,478	*6.43*	*5.83*	*6.40*	*8.31*

Source: Statistical Office of Republic of Slovenia, Census 2002

Italy and Croatia and having access to the Adriatic Sea. Once it had also a common border with Carinthia.[6] These features characterize it as a transitional region.

It is difficult to agglomerate data for the whole historical region of Primorska/ Littorale. So, for the purpose of a comparable analysis, we referred to the three westernmost statistical regions of Slovenia as constituting Primorska/Littorale, and data for these three regions are compared with the national average.

Since Slovenia (as well as Austria) did not conduct the 2011 census in a traditional manner by door-to-door inquiries, but as a register census, we have not anymore data on ethnic affiliation available to compare them with earlier situations. Some relatively recent data (from the 2002 census) on ethnic structure are nevertheless at our disposal (see Table 6).

The main differences between the 2002 census and the censuses 1981 and 1991 are due to methodological changes. While the 2002 census did not consider the so-called "gastarbeiter" population, both previous censuses did. Another issue is the new possibility not to answer the question for ethnicity. This resulted in a high share of the "did not want to reply" category. Together with the extremely high share of "unknown ethnic affiliation", this resulted in a reduced number of Slovenes. If, however, the non-response category is not included into the overall breakdown, the result is an even higher share of Slovenes (Josipovič 2007).

The 2002 census shows also reduced shares of other ethnic groups, especially of those from former Yugoslavia, which may hint at accelerated assimilation (Josipovič 2007). But the new migration trends in Slovenia show the opposite: The share of residents with foreign citizenship is increasing, but still well below 10%.

As far as the Primorska/Littorale is concerned, the region undergoes the same processes, combining significantly higher shares of former Yugoslavian nations and the continued presence of a relatively small Italian constitutionally recognized minority (around 3,000 persons).

2.4 Istria and Kvarner/Quarnero (Croatia)

For Croatia as well as for its Northern Adriatic regions Istria and Kvarner/Quarnero much of the same is true as it was said about Slovenia. The two regions are located next to or not far from the Slovenian and Italian border.

Croatia, as Slovenia, has not a high share of ethnic groups other than the dominant nation. Among non-Croats ethnic groups from the former Yugoslavia prevail (see Table 7). The period after independence saw a radical decrease of Serbs due to the exodus from the former para-military Krajina. Still, Serbs remained above the national average in Kvarner/Quarnero. Italians and Slovenes remain concentrated on Istria and Kvarner/ Quarnero, where Italians (Venetians) were dominant in many places before World

[6] When Valcanale/Kanaltal was a part of Carinthia until 1918.

Table 7: **Ethnic structure of Croatia, Istria and Kvarner/Quarnero in 2001**

	Croatia	*Primorsko-goranska County*	*Istarska County*	*percentage (%)*		
Total	**4,437,460**	**305,505**	**206,344**	***100.00***	***100.00***	***100.00***
Croats	3,977,171	258,438	148,328	*89.63*	*84.59*	*71.88*
Albanians	15,082	2,063	2,032	*0.34*	*0.68*	*0.98*
Austrians	247	36	26	*0.01*	*0.01*	*0.01*
Bosniaks	20,755	3,021	3,077	*0.47*	*0.99*	*1.49*
Bulgarians	331	33	33	*0.01*	*0.01*	*0.02*
Montenegrins	4,926	643	732	*0.11*	*0.21*	*0.35*
Czechs	10,510	145	103	*0.24*	*0.05*	*0.05*
Hungarians	16,595	516	536	*0.37*	*0.17*	*0.26*
Macedonians	4,270	489	454	*0.10*	*0.16*	*0.22*
Germans	2,902	213	180	*0.07*	*0.07*	*0.09*
Poles	567	68	35	*0.01*	*0.02*	*0.02*
Roma	9,463	589	600	*0.21*	*0.19*	*0.29*
Romanians	475	27	48	*0.01*	*0.01*	*0.02*
Russians	906	88	45	*0.02*	*0.03*	*0.02*
Ruthenians	2,337	61	31	*0.05*	*0.02*	*0.02*
Slovaks	4,712	125	144	*0.11*	*0.04*	*0.07*
Slovenes	13,173	2,883	2,020	*0.30*	*0.94*	*0.98*
Serbs	201,631	15,005	6,613	*4.54*	*4.91*	*3.20*
Italians	19,636	3,539	14,284	*0.44*	*1.16*	*6.92*
Turks	300	67	57	*0.01*	*0.02*	*0.03*
Ukrainians	1,977	87	78	*0.04*	*0.03*	*0.04*
Vlachs	12	3	1	*0.00*	*0.00*	*0.00*
Jews	576	27	17	*0.01*	*0.01*	*0.01*
Muslims	19,677	3,402	3,831	*0.44*	*1.11*	*1.86*
Yugoslavs	176	25	28	*0.00*	*0.01*	*0.01*
Other	1,948	224	138	*0.04*	*0.07*	*0.07*
Ethnically undeclared	89,130	11,914	21,978	*2.01*	*3.90*	*10.65*
Regional affiliation (of that)	9,302	150	8,865	*0.21*	*0.05*	*4.30*
Unknown	17,975	1,774	895	*0.41*	*0.58*	*0.43*

Source: Statistical Office of Croatia, Census 2001

War II. Very significant is also the high share (above 10%) of ethnically non-declared population in Istria. The greater portion of it can be attributed to the so-called Istrians, who are not recognized as an ethnic group of their own (JOSIPOVIČ & KRŽIŠNIK-BUKIĆ 2010, pp. 89f).

3 Conclusion

Although methodological constraints and a lack of comparable data prevented us from a full comparison, the collected material has the potential to support basic hypotheses. Thus, it was possible to show that in all four regions the former linguistic and ethnic duality was gradually replaced by a multitude of ethnic affiliations. In Carinthia, e.g., the former Slovene-German antagonism is de facto outdated. In Slovenia and Croatia traditional, stable ethnic affiliations have partly been replaced by multiple identities in a specific hierarchical order or varying in order according to circumstances. Very significant is also the fact that three of the four countries in question (The exception is Croatia.) do not ask for ethnic or linguistic affiliation in their censuses anymore, just for citizenship. This corresponds to the concept of the third demographic transition presuming a profound questioning of ethnic/national affiliation and the European nation state. This is also in line with a growing number of ethnically undeclared. The Slovenian Statistical Office consequently introduced various new ethnic affiliations (formerly referred to as regional).

4 Bibliography

BUFON M. (1992), Prostorska opredeljenost in narodna pripadnost: obmejna in etnično mešana območja v evropskih razvojnih silnicah: primer Slovencev v Furlaniji-Julijski krajini. Trieste, Založništvo tržaškega tiska.

COLEMAN D. (2006), Immigration and ethnic change in low fertility countries. A third demographic transition. In: Population and Development Review, 32, 3, pp. 401–446.

DAMJANIĆ D. (2002), Politizacija vprašanja o veroizpovedi pri popisu prebivalstva. Degree, Faculty of Social Sciences, Ljubljana.

HARVEY D. (1989), The Condition of Postmodernity. Oxford, Blackwell Publishing.

MASSEY D. B. (1993), Power-geometry and a progressive sense of place. In: BIRD J. et al. (eds.), Mapping the Futures: Local Cultures, Global Change, pp. 59–69. London, Routledge.

MASSEY D.S. et al. (1998), Worlds in Motion – Understanding International Migration at the End of the Millennium. Oxford, Clarendon Press.

ITALIAN STATISTICAL OFFICE (www.istat.it)

JONES S.B. (1959), Boundary concepts in the setting of place and time. In: Annals of the Association of American Geographers, 49, 3, pp. 241–255.

JORDAN P. (2007), Considerations on the definitions of "endonym" and "exonym". In: JORDAN P., OROŽEN ADAMIČ M., WOODMAN P. (eds.), Exonyms and the International Standardization of Geographical Names – Aproaches Towards the Resolution of an Apparent Contradiction, pp. 95–105. Wien – Berlin, LIT Verlag.

JOSIPOVIČ D. (2007), Spremembe etnične strukture prebivalstva v Sloveniji po letu 1991. In: Treatises and Documents, 53-54, pp. 98–115.

JOSIPOVIČ D. (2009), Razprava o odnosu center – periferija: peripanonski slovensko-hrvaški stik v sistemu širitve EU. In: GOSAR A. (ed.), Development opportunities of Slovenian border regions, pp. 197–211. Annales, Koper.

JOSIPOVIČ D., KRŽIŠNIK-BUKIĆ V. (2010), Slovensko-hrvaški obmejni prostor: etnične vzporednice med popisi prebivalstva po letu 1991. Ljubljana, Institute for Ethnic Studies.

KADMON N. (ed.) (2007), Glossary of Terms for the Standardization of Geographical Names. ST/ESA/STAT/SER.M/85/Add.1. New York, United Nations Secretariat.

KLEMENČIČ V. (1990), Metodologija uradnih popisov prebivalstva pripadnikov slovenske manjšine v Italiji, Avstriji in na Madžarskem. In: Narodne manjšine, Ljubljana, pp. 31–45.

PAASI A. (1986), Institutionalization of Regions. In: Fenia, pp. 1–46.

ROGLIĆ J. (1946), Le Recensement de 1910: ses méthodes et son application dans la Marche Julienne. Sušak.

STEINICKE E. (2001), Potential for conflicts in areas of ethno-linguistic minorities of the Eastern Alps. In: Annales, Ser. hist. sociol., 11, 2 (26), pp. 259–266.

STRANJ P. (1983), Demografsko gibanje v Furlaniji-Julijski krajini. In: Jadranski koledar, pp. 131–135.

STRANJ P. (1999), Slovensko prebivalstvo Furlanije-Julijske krajine v družbeni in zgodovinski perspektivi. Triest, SLORI.

STATE OFFICE FOR STATISTICS OF THE REPUBLIC OF CROATIA (www.dzs.hr)

STATISTICAL OFFICE OF THE REPUBLIC OF SLOVENIA (www.stat.si)

STATISTICS AUSTRIA (www.statistik.at)

ŠUMI I., JOSIPOVIČ D. (2008), Avtohtonost in Romi: k ponovnemu premisleku načel manjšinske politike v Sloveniji. In: Two Homelands, 28, pp. 93–110.

ZUPANČIČ J. (1999), Slovenci v Avstriji (= Geographica Slovenica, 32). Ljubljana.

Borders and Transportation, Autonomy and Linguistic Minorities in the Julian Alps and Eastern Pyrenees. A Comparative Case Study in Political Geography

Maria Paola **Pagnini**, ***Rome, and André Louis*** **Sanguin**, ***Paris***[*]

Content

Summary 43
1 The territorial context and its constraints 44
2 Border communities: A story of wrangling and tossing 45
3 Politics of transport and circulation 47
4 The economy of small border territories 49
5 Cross-border cooperation in the heart of mountain ranges 50
6 Linguistic and cultural autonomy of small mountain territories 52
7 Conclusion: A game of similarities and differences 54
8 Bibliography 55

Summary

Although separated by 1,100 km, the three small Alps-Adriatic territories (Valcanale, Slavia Friulana, Goriziano) and the three small Eastern Pyrenees' territories (Val d'Aran, Andorra, Cerdanya) have many features in common. For all, mountain environmental constraints, partitioning by valleys, linguistic isolation and transport difficulties have generated micro-societies with pronounced individuality. In order to overcome these handicaps, these voluntaristic communities implemented trunk roads to facilitate economic development and create better connections with the state to which

[*] Maria Paola **Pagnini**, Prof. PhD., Dean, Faculty of Political Science and International Relations, Niccolo Cusano University, Via Casalmonferrato 2/B, I-00182 Roma, Italy; e-mail: mp.pagnini@virgilio.it; André Louis **Sanguin**, Prof. PhD., Faculty of Geography, University of Paris IV-Sorbonne, 191 rue Saint-Jacques, F-75005 Paris, France; e-mail: al.sanguin@orange.fr

they belong. The physical barrier formed by high mountains has been overcome due to a bold politics of road and rail tunnels. In both cases, cross-border cooperation is supposed to be strengthened by special European Union programs. The six territories in question are inhabited by linguistic minorities (Catalan, Friulian, German, Occitan, Slovene). Their autonomy is more or less strong depending on whether they belong to the quasi-federal Spain, the regionalized Italy or the centralized France. The same physical-political environments generate similar territorial solutions up to a certain point.

1 The territorial context and its constraints

From the triple border point Austria-Italy-Slovenia to the contact between the Julian Alps [Alpi Giulie/Julijske Alpe] and the Karst, the Valcanale or Tarvisiano, the Slavia Friulana and the Goriziano are literally sticked on the western side of the Julian Alps (Steinicke 2001). This branch of the Alpine arc reaching altitudes up to 3,000 m is a range with just a few easy passes and with just three natural corridors: the Slizza Valley (*Gailitz* in German) converging with the Gail Valley in Austria, the Natisone valleys and the Vipacco (*Vipava* in Slovene) Valley. Actually, the lower Vipacco basin constitutes the limit between Julian Alps and Karst. These three valleys prompted indeed the development of roads and urban centres functioning as crossroads and markets (Cattaruzza 2007).

Valcanale (*val Cjanal* in Friulian, *Kanalska dolina* in Slovene, *Kanaltal* in German) is a valley of the Eastern Alps extending from Pontebba to Coccau. It is actually composed of the valleys of Fella, a tributary of Tagliamento, and the valley of the Slizza torrent connected by a valley pass. The Valcanale separates the Carnic Alps [Alpi Carniche/Karnische Alpen] in the North from the Julian Alps in the South. The urban centre of the valley is Tarvisio (*Trbiž* in Slovene, *Tarvis* in German).

Slavia Friulana (*Scalavanie* in Friulian, *Benecija* or *Beneska Slovenija* in Slovene) is an area of hills and mountains located in the Julian prealps of eastern Friuli and extending from Cividale del Friuli to the Natisone Valley and the mountains near Kobarid (*Caporetto* in Italian) in Slovenia.

The Goriziano is located around the middle course of the Isonzo (*Soča* in Slovene), the "most beautiful blue river" of Europe, and includes Gorizia (*Gorica* in Slovene, *Görz* in German). This area is characterized by hills with vineyards and karstic soils.

Valcanale, Slavia Friulana and Goriziano are sharing a common feature: In all of them hills or mountains meet a plain. This explains why, since historical times, these mountain communities are a hub of different cultures and languages as well as places of complicated historical connections: Romance people (Friulians and Italians), e.g., co-exist with Slovenes and German-speakers (Bufon 2002).

In the heart of the Pyrenean cordillera [French *Pyrénées,* Spanish *Pirineos,* Catalan *Pirineus*, Occitan *Pirenèus*, Aragonese *Perinés*, Basque *Pirinioak*], the Val d'Aran, Andorra and Cerdanya are located in an upper mountain milieu which was not really sculptured by quaternary glaciers. Consequently, unlike the Alps, the Pyrenees do not feature traffic corridors, suffer from a "lack of aeration" and have only narrow valleys penetrating hardly to the divide.

The Val d'Aran (*Valle de Aran* in Spanish, *Vall d'Aran* in Catalan, *Val d'Aran* in French) constitutes the upper valley system of the Garonne and is an exception within Spain, because it is the only Spanish territory in the Pyrenees located on the Atlantic slope. Up to 1948, Val d'Aran was not connected with Spain by road.

Andorra comprises the upper valleys of Valira (a sub-system of the Ebro hydrographic basin) with two long and narrow valleys. Up to 1933, the country was not connected with France by road.

Cerdanya [*Cerdana* in Spanish, *Cerdagne* in French] is a graben of high altitude (1,600 m) located between two mountain ranges. Its access from France is not easy.

The three Eastern Pyrenees' territories share a common physiographic feature: The valleys perpendicular to the general axis of the cordillera dispose only of a few easy communications with neighbouring valleys. This explains why these mountain communities were more or less isolated during history and formed a kind of small Pyrenean republics, where the local language was able to survive.

2 Border communities: A story of wrangling and tossing

The modern border between Italy and Slovenia coincides more or less with the border between the Republic of Venice and the Habsburg Empire between 1521 and 1797. The section between Predil [Passo del Predil/Predel] and Natisone coincided with this former border also between 1866 and World War I. It makes use of the orography of the Julian Alps and represents one of the most stable boundaries in Europe.

But things were different north and south of this section. During the Napoleonic period, the border between the Kingdom of Italy and the Napoleonic Illyrian Provinces followed the Isonzo Valley from its source to its mouth into the Adriatic. Only after World War I, near the present Italian-Austrian-Slovenian triple point, the valley pass of Rateče became for the first time the international border. Despite its hydrographic aspect, the new border caused much unpleasantnesses for the local population living on both banks of the Isonzo.

If the expression of a wrangled and tossed border is used, this is because it underwent at least three major changes between 1866 and 1947. In 1866, when Austria abandoned the Lombardo-Venetian Kingdom in favour of the newly unified Italy, the new Austrian-Italian border was fixed in such a way that the central sector Predil-Natisone was awarded to Italy, while Valcanale and the lower Isonzo Valley (from Cormons and Gorizia to Grado) remained with Austria. All the way from Monte Croce Carnico/Plöckenpass to the laguna of Marano, this resulted in disruptions. Thus, the rail link Udine – Tarvisio lost its importance. On the other hand, Gorizia – well located in a wider hinterland and now far from the 1866 boundary – developed its role of a regional center (Prost 1973).

By the Treaty of Rapallo (12 November 1920) signed between Italy and the young Yugoslavian state, the border shifted towards the East along a line running from the present Austrian-Italian-Slovenian triple point to Sušak, an eastern suburb of Fiume [Rijeka]. The new Italian province of Gorizia preserved the town's role of a regional center, because its limits coincided with those of the former Austrian province of Görz.

The Treaty of Paris (10 February 1947) settled the issue of the Italian-Yugoslavian border (Moodie 1945). During the peace negotiations, the principle of ethnic balance, promoted by France, had been accepted: A political boundary must coincide as much as possible with ethnic boundaries, but, if this is not possible, leave in both countries an approximately identical number of members of ethnic minorities. Valcanale and Slavia Friulana were assigned to Italy, while the town of Gorizia was cut by the new boundary. As a result, thousands of Slovenes became Italian citizens without any consent. The same was true for Italians, even more numerous, in Tito's new Yugoslavia.

Gorizia and the Goriziano had hardly been affected by the 1866 and 1920 border changes. But by the 1947 border Gorizia was not only partitioned, but lost also most of its hinterland and became a mutilated town. Tito's Yugoslavia constructed the new town of Nova Gorica by structuring eastern quarters of the ante-partition Gorizia and new Socialist-type quarters. The new 1947 border meant a severe cut for this urban area. On an area of 309 km^2 Nova Gorica hosts currently 35,332 inhabitants, while Gorizia (41 km^2) suffered from the demographic consequences of the partition: while it had still 40,625 inhabitants in 1948, it were only 35,946 in 2009. Under the conditions of the Single Market, the Euro Zone and the Schengen Space, the critical question is how to convert two twin cities with almost the same population amounting to a total of 70,000 into a well-performing bi-national and cross-border Greater Gorizia (Cocco 2002).

In the Pyrenees, border location played another role than in the Julian Alps. The difficult orography led to the fact that many mountain communities lived in isolation and in the shape of small Pyrenean republics which changed their political affiliation according to historical circumstances. The Val d'Aran formed part of the Kingdom of Aragon, then of the County of Bearn, the County of Cominges, the County of Bigorre, the Kingdom of Catalonia and finally the Kingdom of Spain. All these political authorities respected and guaranteed the privileges and autonomy of Val d'Aran until their annulment by the Spanish monarchy in 1833 (Sanguin 1994).

The border location of Andorra and the competition for controlling it on the cordillera's both sides brought the competitors to an original political solution: condominium by self-government. So the famous Parity Act of 1278 was signed by the Bishop or Urgell and the Count of Foix. The Bishop and the Count became co-princes of Andorra and they grant self-government to the Andorran valleys. Consequently, from that date, Andorra had its own parliament and government. This subtle solution let Andorra escape all turmoils occuring during the following centuries. The principality remained safe of WW I, Spanish Civil War and WW II.

Cerdanya walked along another historical-political route. This altiplano belonged for a long time to the Crown of Catalonia (till the 15th century), then to the Kingdom of Spain. By the clauses of the Treaty of the Pyrenees (1659), Spain transfered the western half of historical Cerdanya to France, except the exclave of Llivia. In fact, from 1659 onward the Cerdan society slowly diverged in everyday life towards two different political and cultural spheres, France and Spain (Mancebo 1999).

3 Politics of transport and circulation

Located along the international rail track Venice [Venezia] – Vienna [Wien] and along the highway A23 Venice – Klagenfurt am Wörthersee, Tarvisio (4,800 inhabitants), the urban centre of the Valcanale, is virtually located at European crossroads. The small town is enjoying a new development of tourism due to skiing without borders between Italy, Austria and Slovenia as a direct consequence of the Single Market, the Euro Zone and the Schengen Space. The fall of the Berlin Wall and the European Unions' (EU's) enlargement to the East generated an increasing tourism from eastern Europe and an interesting urban development of Tarvisio.

Slavia Friulana as a network of three valleys (Natisone, Alberone, Cosizza) converging towards Cividale del Friuli (11,600 inhabitants) would have profitted, if this town had developed in a centre of tourism. But this did not happen, although the town has one of the most precious cultural heritages in Friuli-Venezia Giulia.

Gorizia, having lost the Isonzo and Natisone valleys as its natural hinterland, was duplicated beyond the Italian-Yugoslavian border by Nova Gorica, a new town with similar commercial functions. But even after the new highway H4 connected Gorizia with Ljubljana, the town, which had become famous by Hemingway's novel *The Farewell to Arms*, does not receive too much tourism. This is also due to the fact that it never had significant touristic ambitions (Gasparini & Del Bianco 2003).

In the Valcanale/Tarvisiano, trade and traffic experienced a significant increase. Actually, Tarvisio is acting as a kind of relay between Northern Italy and Austria, the Czech Republic and Slovakia.

Cividale and its valleys, however, had no increase of this kind. A small road connects the upper Natisone Valley with Kobarid in Slovenia. In the winter season, its continuation, the upper Isonzo [Soča] road, is closed just behind Bovec.

A few years ago the opening of the highway H4 Gorizia – Ljubljana via Postojna made circulation with Slovenia easier. The extension of the Schengen Space across the Italian-Slovenian border on 21 December 2007 considerably changed the transport context in the Goriziano. The autoporto (truck station) nearby Gorizia shares with the Trieste autoporto a considerable amount of traffic. Corridor 5, one of the multimodal European corridors, is under discussion regarding its practical implications. So far there is no definite solution for the project, which is supposed to connect the nodes along the axis Venice – Gorizia – Trieste – Ljubljana – Budapest – Bratislava – Užgorod – L'vìv. It is justified to say that along the Julian Alps one is attending the death of a border and the birth of a hinge (Zago 2000, Gasparini 2001).

With mass tourism appearing during the 1970s on the Iberian Peninsula, flows and circulation through the Pyrenees experienced an exponential increase. Like in other parts of the European Union, the acceleration of this phenomenon is due to the Single Market, the Euro Zone and, above all, the Schengen Space. Consequently, the role of the France-Spain-Andorra international border has considerably changed within three decades turning slowly into a kind of EU's inner border (Sanguin & Guiraud 1995).

Facing this radical change of transpyrenean relationships, France, Spain and the European Commission implemented politics and programs for erasing the physical barrier represented by the Pyrenean Cordillera. This politics began to take shape with the opening of transpyrenean road tunnels in the three territories. Val d'Aran, Catalonia's dead angle, had for a long time totally been isolated from Spain because of the mountain range. In 1948, a road tunnel was opened and a new high performing tunnel (the Juan Carlos Tunnel) has replaced it in 2007. Located on the Toulouse-Zaragoza axis, the Val d'Aran tunnel is a key link regarding the territorial recombining at work in the Pyrenees.

In Andorra, the Envalira Tunnel located below the Envalira Pass (2,407 m), the highest road pass in the Pyrenees, acts as a subsidiary for the Puymorens Tunnel. The Envalira Tunnel allows Andorra to catch tourist flows which would otherwise run through the double tunnel system, namely the Puymorens Tunnel and the Cadi Tunnel, both judiciously located on the European axis Toulouse – Barcelona.

Cerdanya benefits from the positive repercussions of this tunnel axis while Latour de Carol, a Cerdan village, is acting as railway crossroads from Barcelona, Toulouse and Perpignan.

4 The economy of small border territories

Tarvisio, the main centre of Valcanale, is decreasing in population since 1961. Its tourism is concentrated on winter thanks to the Three Borders Ski Resort (Austria, Italy, Slovenia). Tarvisio has the famous ski pist "Di Prampero" at the Monte Santo di Lussari. Frequently, Tarvisio accomodates the events of the Alpine Ski World Cup. Summer tourism enjoys the beautiful lakes of Fusine and Predil as well as the summits of the crestline which were the theatre of terrible trench warfare during World War I (Mangart, Monte Canin/Kanin, Monte Rombon...). Another source of economic activity is the *Mercato*, a kind of open-air cheaper store which attracts daily buyers coming from all eastern Europe. In the Natisone Valley, Cividale has a stable population since the 1921 Italian census and was most capable to develop an efficient hinterland as well as to make profit of its remarkable architectural and historical heritage (MINGHI 1994).

In less than 30 years, the Val d'Aran (10,000 inhabitants) shifted from a traditional peasant mountain economy to a well-performing service sector economy based mainly on high-category skiing. The famous Baqueira-Beret ski resort, established in the 1980s, is frequented every winter by King Juan Carlos, Queen Sofia, the Royal Court and the Madrid jet-society. Camping is more or less absent in the Val. Summer tourism is supported by an efficient network of 4- and 5-star hotels and by two *paradores* (state-operated luxury hotels). This economic context explains why the Val d'Aran enjoys the highest income per capita in Spain (SANGUIN 1994).

The Principality of Andorra (84,000 inhabitants), independent from Spain and France since 1278, became a sovereign State in 1993. Andorra is not a member of EU but de facto part of the Schengen Space. Its economic success is based upon the duty-free regime which is historically consubstantial with the Pyrenean micro-state (absence of customs duties and VAT). This regime came into force at the beginning of the 1960s due to the emergence of mass tourism. Since the 1970s, Andorra turned into the "biggest duty-free shop in Europe". Such a particular economic system justifies in itself the presence of 12 million visitors and daytrippers every year by means of four million vehicles. Consequently, the volume of imported goods is totally unconnected with the resident population. Actually, it corresponds to a market of more than 12 million consumers.

Pas de la Casa (3,000 inhabitants) represents the quintessence of a borderscape. This artificial village located at 2,050 m altitude has been built above the upper limit of the traditional ecumene. Where a ski resort and a duty-free small town are extending since 1960, only some shepherd cabins could be met in 1945! The place is frequented daily by chartered buses coming from Toulouse used by seniors only for duty-free border shopping without any other tourist activity. The duty-free regime generates a second kind of tourist attendance. Skiing and housing-catering are cheaper than in both neighbouring countries (France and Spain). Moreover, skiing is underlawn by an efficient network of ski resorts able to combine sunniness, snow cover and a long ski season – three ingredients so much looked for by skiers. All in all, Andorra appears as an oversized economy due to the duty-free regime (Sanguin 2006).

Cerdanya (27,000 inhabitants) is the only territory in question which is cut into two parts by the international boundary in absence of any physical obstacle. This bi-national entity has the privilege of including national and regional parks. In the most eastward section of the Pyrenean Cordillera, Cerdanya offers a network of 10 ski resorts either in Spain or in France (Mancebo 1999). To a large extent, Cerdanya plays the role of a winter playground for Spanish Catalonia and, above all, for Barcelona. For the French customers, Font Romeu, the biggest town in French Cerdanya, develops its function of a health resort (high-altitude treatments or *climatisme*).

5 Cross-border cooperation in the heart of mountain ranges

From 1949 onwards, and especially after 1955 with the signing of the Trieste and Gorizia Memoranda, the launching of local trade area agreements marked the beginning of a long-term process of opening the border. After the Osimo Treaty (1975) which allowed new peaceful relationships between Italy and Yugoslavia, the opening of the border paved the way to cross-border cooperation in the Julian Alps and in the Trieste area. Three years later, the Alps-Adriatic Working Community was implemented with the membership of 11 different political units: Baranya and Vas for Hungary; Upper Austria [Oberösterreich], Burgenland, Styria [Steiermark], Carinthia for Austria; Lombardy [Lombardia], Veneto, Friuli-Venezia Giulia for Italy; Slovenia, Croatia for Yugoslavia. With 190,000 km^2 and 26 million people today, Alps-Adriatic is viewed as a hot spot of European integration. Its aim is to bridge the linguistic, political and social differences making a positive move towards understanding, friendship and peace in this neuralgic part of the continent. Certainly, Alps-Adriatic was the first and most fruitful international association between former Western and Eastern Europe. The fall of the Berlin Wall and the independence of Slovenia and Croatia decreased the political relevance of the Alps-Adriatic project which, today, is somewhat differently carried by the Central European Initiative.

However, in these early cross-border cooperation actions, the Euroregion Euradria project has moved a few tentative steps. This macro-euroregion finds its main goals in the internationalization of the euroregional market, focusing on its bridging role on the West-East economic and transport axis. As a macro-euroregion, Euradria focuses mostly on the need for integrated logistic structures, thus favouring the economic sphere compared to the social and cultural ones. Such an approach is still struggling to develop into a concrete planning platform, the application of which is shared among all partners. The main aim of the partnership is to promote the mobility of workers in the cross-border region in the interest of matching labour demand and supply. At present, this cross-border region includes the entire territory of Friuli-Venezia Giulia and the statistical regions of Goriška, Obalno-Kraška and Notransko-Kraška in Slovenia. The framework agreement for cooperation was signed in Trieste in December 2007. In March 2008, this partnership was recognized by the European Commission. With approximately 1.5 million inhabitants, Euradria measures 12,681 km^2 (7,856 in Italy and 4,825 in Slovenia). The Euradria headquarter is located in Trieste (Gasparini 2001).

Therefore, it might be complementary and useful to put forward smaller-scale euroregional initiatives stimulating not only economic collaboration, but also the daily social and cultural cross-border life. Hence, the EureGo project linking the Italian Gorizia province with the Slovene Goriška Statistical Region appears as an appropriate effort to re-evoke the Upper Adriatic regional unity (Gasparini & Del Bianco 2005). On the border area between Italy and Slovenia, EureGo counts up to 72 municipalities, with a population of 355,127 inhabitants living in an area of 3,804 km^2. The EureGo territory hosts 26,775 productive units in different sectors. Commerce, construction and manufacturing are the most developed sectors in this euroregion, mainly in Italy. The EureGo project has at the beginning (2005) been supported by Interreg IIIA Italy-Slovenia. Now scheduled within the Interreg program 2007-2013, EureGo has turned into an EGTC (European Group of Territorial Cooperation).

In the Pyrenees, cross-border cooperation began in the early 1980s, when Spain was not yet a EU member, implemented by the Council of Europe. Established in 1983, the Working Community of the Pyrenees hosts eight political entities (Basque Country [País Vasco/Euzkadi], Aquitaine, Midi-Pyrénées, Navarra, Aragon, Andorra, Languedoc-Roussillon, Catalonia [Catalunya]) including three countries (France, Andorra, Spain). Even if the Council of Europe is not the EU, the Working Community of the Pyrenees is in charge of the program Interreg IV (2007-2013) for all the Pyrenees.

The Euroregion Pyrenees-Mediterranean has been created in 2008 in the shape of an EGTC (European Group of Territorial Cooperation). Five political entities are members of this euroregion: Aragon, Midi-Pyrénées, Catalonia, Languedoc-Roussillon and the Balearic Islands [Illes Balears]. Surprisingly enough, Andorra, a true Pyrenean state, is not member of the Euroregion, while the Balearic Islands, which have nothing to do with the Pyrenees, are a member.

Like in the case of the Julian Alps area, a third scale of cross-border cooperation is to be found by the Eurodistrict of the Catalan Cross-Border Space. Established in 2009 in the shape of an EGTC, this Eurodistrict is actually a regrouping of urban cooperations. Its members are the Department of Pyrénées-Orientales in France and the Comarca de Girona (Catalonia) in Spain. The most interesting result is the cross-border hospital of Cerdanya established in 2010 and located in Puigcerda, the capital of historical Cerdanya. This first EU cross-border hospital was financed by the program

Interreg IIIA with a 60% contribution from the EFRD (European Fund for Regional Development). The Puigcerda cross-border hospital is planned for 30,000 local patients and 100,000 in summer, due to the tourist activities in the area.

The EU has from the very beginning initiated and favoured the model of cross-border cooperation as a protoype of European integration. And there is indeed no doubt that putting together parts of different states, relying on their reciprocal trust, taking advantage of their reciprocal knowledge and making them cooperate in many fields starting from the most concrete is the stroke of genius on the concept of Europe. While such geniality must remain rather implicit, economic advantages are obvious affecting those who "dared" making projects and joint actions of reciprocal usefulness.

6 Linguistic and cultural autonomy of small mountain territories

It is not surprising that the combination of physical constraints and a turbulent history has generated a solid base for linguistic and cultural originality in the six small territories. Valcanale/Tarvisiano with its tri-border location is an area with a strong mixing of languages: Friulian, German, Slovene, Italian. According to the Hitler-Mussolini agreement (1939) about 5,600 German-speaking and 100 Slovene-speaking people *(optanti)* left the Tarvisiano towards the Third Reich. Only 20% of them came back after World War II; the others remained in Austria. In the 2000s, around 20% of the Tarvisiano population are German- or Slovene-speaking. The Valcanale/Tarvisiano represents the single case of a linguistic peninsula in Europe, because four linguistic communities peacefully coexist in an Alpine micro-region. Today, the German, Slovene and Friulian minorities living in the ten municipalities are protected by Italian State Law 482/99. Probably, Tarvisio is the single quadrilingual commune in the EU. Its multilingual school has good success and it conducts a policy of dialogue with and protection of local linguistic minorities.

In Slavia Friulana, the Natisone valleys are an important linguistic island since the 10th century, when Aquileia's patriarchs gave them many privileges. The long-lasting autonomy has resulted in a specific culture. For the protection of minorities, some Slovene-speaking schools were established. Unfortunately, the Natisone valleys' population is tragically decreasing since the implementation of the Italian-Yugoslavian border in 1947 which actually acted as a kind of a soft Iron Curtain. In 1951, Slavia Friulana's population amounted to 16,195 people within the seven historical communes. The present population is just 5,995 inhabitants. After 1866 and its attachment to Italy, the local elite gradually abandoned the Slovene language. Italianization accelerated after 1933, when Fascism prohibited the use of Slovene in churches. After 1947 and in the time of Cold War, even if the Slovene-speaking people of the Natisone valleys were loyal citizens of Italy, they were considered as suspects and accused of Communist propaganda and philo-Yugoslavism. For this reason the situation of the Slovenes in the Udine province is much worse than in the provinces of Gorizia and Trieste, notably in terms of school rights and cultural rights (VALUSSI 2000).

Gorizia as a town has a majority of Friulian and Italian speakers and a Slovene minority. The Austrian census of 1910 identified 11% German-speakers at a time when Gorizia was considered the *Nice of the Habsburg Empire*. Today, the German language has practically disappeared. During the last decades of Habsburg rule, tensions between Slovenes and Italians were recurrent in Gorizia. The Fascist regime implemented an Italianization process after 1922, but many Slovene schools and institutions remained. Understanding the issue of the Slovenes in Friuli-Venezia Giulia means regarding the centuries-old process of Romanization of Slavonic people. Up to the "national awakening" around 1850 social advancement was for them synonymous with a change to Italian language.

The Aranese idiom spoken in Val d'Aran, a true Occitan in Spain, is the legitimate child of the Catalonian autonomy in the frame of the new constitutional Spain (1978). Val d'Aran is in this way an autonomy within the autonomy. By a double legislative tool, the Law on the Special Regime of Val d'Aran (1990) and the new autonomy statute of Catalonia (2006), Occitan has been declared co-official with Catalan in Val d'Aran. Consequently, schools, the media and culture are managed both in Occitan and Catalan. According to the last census in Spain (2001), Spanish is the mother tongue of 39% of the Aranese, Occitan the mother tongue of 34% and Catalan the mother tongue of 19%.

Before and after its transformation into a fully sovereign State (1993), Andorra was always a bastion of the Catalan language in the Pyrenees. The local population is Catalan-speaking (native Andorrans) including the majority of Spanish immigrants, because they are Catalans from Catalonia!

The historical Cerdanya is suffering from its former partition, which was the direct consequence of the Treaty of the Pyrenees (1659). From a linguistic and cultural point of view, Cerdanya is an object of dichotomy between Spanish Cerdanya (Puigcerda) and French Cerdanya (Font Romeu). Roughly speaking, the local population is Catalan-speaking in Spanish Cerdanya. This territorial section of Cerdanya is enjoying the benefits of the Catalonian autonomy as regards schools and cultural life. French Cerdanya, in contrast, is a part of a country which is the archetype of the centralized unitarian state. Consequently, even if the place names are Catalan, the local population is essentially French-speaking despite its clear Catalan roots. The school network is French. Only at the entrance of villages bilingual signposts can be observed.

7 Conclusion: A game of similarities and differences

Among the six territories compared, an important contrast prevails between the territories in the Julian Alps and those of the Eastern Pyrenees: Val d'Aran and Andorra are subjected to natural barriers which do not exist in Tarvisiano, Slavia Friulana and Goriziano. Consequently, Val d'Aran and Andorra and, to a lesser extent, Cerdanya had to construct many road tunnels. This was especially vital for Val d'Aran: Without the Juan Carlos Tunnel linking it with Spain, this Occitan micro-region would have remained a pene-exclave, namely a Spanish territory which would be connected with the rest of Spain only through France. Due to its location at a dead angle and grey zone, Slavia Friulana was not able to overcome its relative isolation. In terms of transport and circulation, the Tarvisiano has two European major highways and railways at its disposal, while such key elements are absent in Val d'Aran, Andorra, Cerdanya and Slavia Friulana.

While Andorra with its duty-free regime and oversized economy appears to be an exception, the other territories share a more classical economic profile. Except the Goriziano and Slavia Friulana, the mountain communities have strongly developed skiing tourism and subsidiary activities. For all of them the economic future lies in the uitlisation of the Schengen Space and cross-border cooperation. Frequently, euroregions and similar cross-border projects are much more empty projects or flashing media annoucements than concrete realizations in the field. On this background the cross-border hospital of Puigcerda or Greater Gorizia are certainly exceptions.

A political aberration, namely the redundance and double use generated by the competition between the Council of Europe and the European Union, has to be mentioned here: Alps-Adriatic versus Euradria, Working Community of the Pyrenees versus Euroregion Pyrenees-Mediterranean. Such redundance results in political-administrative stacking, which is ineffective and sterile: in the Perpignan-Girona area working community, euroregion and cross-border district; in the Goriziano area Alps-Adriatic, Euradria, EureGo. Here and there, ironically, they are addressed as *cross-border lasagna or millefeuille*!

The existence of the "Yugoslavian" Iron Curtain (1947-1976), the Italian-Yugoslavian border implemented in 1947 and the late accesses of Austria (1995) and Slovenia (2004) to the EU are the main factors explaining the backwardness of the Julian Alps area compared to the Eastern Pyrenees regarding cross-border cooperation. The Catalonian way to autonomy starting in 1978 (in the new constitutional Spain) has secured significant autonomy also to the small Occitan-speaking Val d'Aran; and Catalonia's autonomy status allows Spanish Cerdanya to blossom in its language and culture, which is absolutely not so with French Cerdanya.

8 Bibliography

BUFON M. (2002), Confini, identità ed integrazione. Nuove prospective per l'Alto Adriatico. Trieste, SLORI.

CATTARUZZA M. (2007), L'Italia e il confine orientale. Bologna, Il Mulino.

COCCO E. (2002), Metamorfosi dell'Adriatico Orientale. Faenza, Homeless Book.

GASPARINI A. (ed.) (2001), Progetto di sviluppo e conoscenza reciproca Italo-Slovena. San Pietro al Natisone, Comunità Montana Valli del Natisone.

GASPARINI A., DEL BIANCO D. (2003), Modello flessible di sviluppo per l'Isonzo. Gorizia, ISIG.

GASPARINI A., DEL BIANCO D. (2005), EureGo. Progetto di una euroregione transfrontaliera. Gorizia, ISIG.

MANCEBO F. (1999), La Cerdagne et ses frontières, conflits et identités transfrontalières. Perpignan, Editions El Trabucaire.

MINGHI J. (1994), The Impact of Slovenian Independence on the Italo-Slovene Borderland: An Assessment of the First Three Years. In: GALLUSSER W. (ed.), Political Boundaries and Coexistence, pp. 88–94. Bern, Peter Lang Verlag.

MOODIE A.E. (1945), The Italo-Yugoslav Boundary: A Study in Political Geography. London, G. Philip.

PROST B. (1973), Le Frioul, région d'affrontements. Gap, Editions Ophrys.

SANGUIN A.L. (1994), Le Val d'Aran (Catalunya) ou la réémergence politico-culturelle du fait occitan dans les Pyrénées. In: Géographie et Cultures, 12, pp. 3–14.

SANGUIN A.L. (2006), Andorra, the European Micro-State's Archetype. The Borderscape's Original Features of a Duty-Free Exclave, www.unitn.it/events/borderscapes/abstracts.htm

SANGUIN A.L., GUIRAUD, F. (1995), The Pyrenees: Death of a Border, Birth of a Hinge? In: European Spatial Research and Policy, 2, 2, pp. 43–53.

STEINICKE E. (2001), The Val Canale. Ethno-Geographical Problems of a Quadrilingual Italian Border Region. In: KOTER M., HEFFNER K. (eds.), Changing Role of Border Areas and Regional Policies, pp. 222–227. Łodź, University of Lodz Press.

VALUSSI G. (2000), Il confine nord'orientale d'Italia. Gorizia, ISIG.

ZAGO M. (2000), La cooperazione transfrontaliera nel Friuli Venezia Giulia. Trieste, Regione Autonoma Friuli Venezia Giulia.

Administrative Regionalisation in the Adriatic Space

Peter Jordan, Vienna*

with 12 figures and 2 tables in the text

Content

Summary 57
1 Introduction 58
2 Italy 60
3 Slovenia 62
4 Croatia 66
5 Bosnia and Herzegovina 73
6 Montenegro 82
7 Albania 85
8 Conclusions 89
9 References 91

Summary

The paper highlights the current administrative structure as well as administrative developments and decentralisation processes of the countries of the Adriatic space (Italy, Slovenia, Croatia, Bosnia-Herzegovina, Montenegro, Albania) on the background of cultural and administrative traditions. Focal research questions are: How far is administrative decentralisation, especially at the regional level, advanced? Does regionalisation correspond to functional units and cultural-historical regional identities? What are the reasons for shortcomings?

* Peter Jordan, Hon. and Assoc. Prof., PhD., Austrian Academy of Sciences, Institute of Urban and Regional Research, Postgasse 7/4/2, A-1010 Wien, Austria; e-mail: peter.jordan@oeaw.ac.at

1 Introduction

In the period since the fall of Communism and the dissolution of Yugoslavia the administrative structure in the Adriatic space has changed significantly: four new states have emerged, and most of the transformation countries have adopted a new subnational administrative structure.

The following contribution concentrates on (1) identifying the developments that have taken place since the political turn-around in 1989/90, (2) presenting the current organisational structure of the administration together with its institutions, competencies and financing methods and (3) illustrating the successes as well as the difficulties of the decentralisation process. Furthermore, it appears of importance to (4) briefly highlight the cultural and administrative traditions, in order to promote a better understanding of the current situation.

It will focus on the transformation countries of the Adriatic space, i.e. Slovenia, Croatia, Bosnia-Herzegovina, Montenegro and Albania, while the situation in Italy, which had decentralized its administrative structures already earlier, will only briefly be outlined.

For a better understanding, the following definitions of terms shall provide a preface.

The term **territorial-administrative unit** describes a juridical person of the public administration with a territorially defined sphere of operation. This definition does not include planning regions, development regions or statistical regions, which – as a rule – do not have their own legal personality and are merely regional or local institutions that are combined for a particular purpose. They are dependent either on the constitutive territorial-administrative units, or on the central offices at state level. Territorial-administrative units are always endowed with executive authority, and in some cases they also have legislative (law-making) authority.

Executive authority is understood to mean the mandate to implement laws within their own territorial sphere of operation as well as the freedom to act within the framework of the operational sphere designated by law and within the available budget.

Legislative authority is understood as the mandate to pass laws. Where subordinated territorial-administrative units are endowed with this mandate, it is usually attached to the condition that laws passed by this territorial-administrative unit shall not contravene the legislation of superordinate territorial-administrative units.

The principle of **subsidiarity** is understood to be a political guideline that allows those duties, which can be carried out by a subordinate territorial-administrative unit, to actually be performed by these, by bestowing the required powers.

This requires a process of (administrative) **decentralisation** in the sense of a transfer of administrative competencies from superordinate to subordinate territorial-administrative units. As a rule, the competencies are shifted from the state level to territorial-administrative units located at the regional and local level. So that the term „decentralisation" can be properly applied, these territorial-administrative units must be self-governing and are therefore politically accountable for wielding this authority.

Self-government exists when the citizens of an administrative unit govern themselves through the institutions they directly elected. In other words, as a precondition, the policy-makers within the territorial-administrative units must be eligible for direct election, upon which they accept the political responsibility towards the local electorate. Depending on the size of the territorial-administrative unit concerned, it is referred to as regional or local self-government.

In the relatively rare instances of **delegated self-government** the functionaries of a superordinate administrative institution are not elected directly, but are instead provided by directly elected institutions of a subordinate territorial-administrative unit.

Self-government must be distinguished from deconcentrated and delegated state administration. Neither corresponds to the principles of subsidiarity and decentralisation.

Deconcentrated state administration signifies that territorial-administrative units assume state competencies on a regional or local level, doing so on behalf of the state and with accountability towards state institutions. In this case, territorial-administrative units act as outposts of central state administration. On the one hand, they provide state administration services that are spatially deconcentrated and therefore more accessible to citizens. On the other hand, on behalf of the state, they can also have the function of controlling and monitoring those territorial-administrative units acting as subsidiaries.

In the case of **delegated state administration**, self-governing territorial-administrative units assume public competencies on behalf of the state and with accountability towards state institutions. Frequently only one institution belonging to a territorial-administrative unit that otherwise acts as a subsidiary, will take on these competencies.

Regionalisation in the administrative sense is understood to mean the subdivision of a state into larger territorial-administrative units that are not attributable to the local level. It always applies across the entire national territory. The functional mode of the territorial-administrative unit plays no part here (self-government, deconcentrated state administration, delegated state administration).

This is to be distinguished from **regionalism** in the sense of efforts that use the means of political organisation and exertion of influence in order to obtain special privileges for a specific administrative region vis-à-vis the central authority of the state. The objective here is to achieve a privileged status compared with the rest of the state.

Regionalism is usually justified by citing historical, cultural, linguistic, religious or national/ethnic characteristics.

2 Italy [Italia][1]

Italy is at the first administrative level below the state divided into 20 **regions** [regione], of which 15 have an ordinary statute and 5 are autonomous regions with a special statute (see Figure 1). They correspond to the NUTS-2 level and were

Figure 1: **Northern section of Italy's Adriatic façade. Regions and provinces**

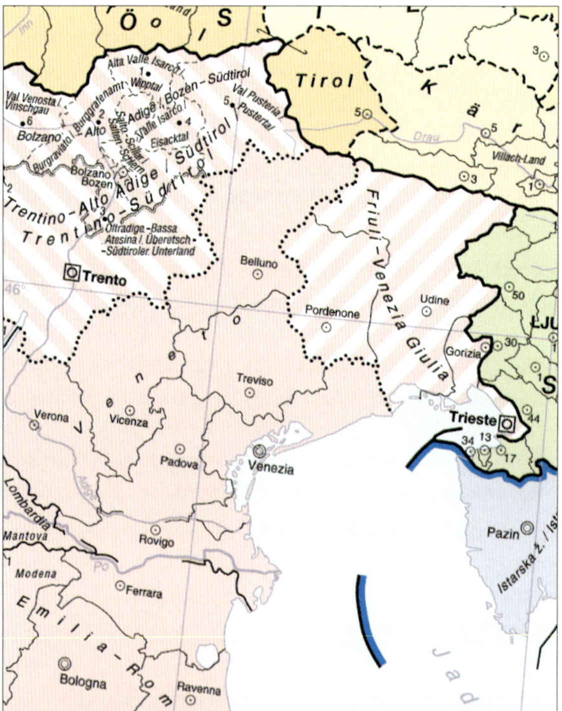

Source: Jordan 2010

[1] In rectangular brackets with the first mentioning of a name its official endonymic version in the first case singular is given.

established in 1970. Since the constitutional reform of 2001 they have not only executive, but also legislative powers. Their financial autonomy, however, is rather restricted and confined to levying taxes for the maintenance of the health system. Regions correspond – as a rule – to the historical components of Italy having enjoyed sovereign statehood or some kind of autonomy in various periods before Italy's unification between 1860 and 1870 or – in the case of Trentino-Alto Adige/Südtirol//Trentino-Südtirol, to some extent also Friuli-Venezia Giulia/Friûl-Vignesie Julie – to later acquisitions after World War I. They also coincide roughly with the catchment areas of macro-regional centres.

Autonomous regions with a special statute (Friuli-Venezia Giulia/Friûl-Vignesie Julie, Sardinia [Sardegna/Sardigna], Sicily [Sicilia], Trentino-Alto Adige/Südtirol// Trentino-Südtirol, Aosta Valley [Valle d'Aosta/Val d'Aost]) have a much higher financial autonomy and are entitled to keep between 60% (Friuli-Venezia Giulia) and 100% (Sicily) of all levied taxes. In return they have to finance the health-care system, the school system and most public infrastructures. Autonomous regions are based on linguistic and other cultural specifics, e.g. Friuli-Venezia Giulia on the large Friulian and several smaller ethnic and linguistic minorities, Trentino-Alto Adige on the German minority dominant in South Tyrol [Alto Adige/Südtirol] and the smaller minority of the Ladinians. Trentino-Alto Adige constitutes a special case among autonomous regions, since administrative powers rest mainly with the two autonomous provinces of the region, i.e. Trentino and South Tyrol, while the region plays more or less just a coordinating role.

Each region has an elected parliament called *regional council* [consiglio regionale] or *regional assembly* [assemblea regionale] and a government [giunta regionale], headed by the regional president [presidente]. The latter is directly elected by the citizens of each region, with the exceptions of the Aosta Valley and Trentino-Alto Adige, where he/she is chosen by the regional council. The president chairs the government, nominates and dismisses its members [assessori].

In Trentino-Alto Adige, the regional council is composed of the joint session of the two provincial councils of Trentino and South Tyrol, and the regional president is one of the two provincial presidents.

The 110 **provinces** [provincia] of Italy (see Figure 1) correspond to the NUTS-3 level as well as – in general – to the catchment area of meso-regional centres and have three main functions: local planning and zoning, provision of local police and fire services, transportation regulation (car registration, maintenance of local roads, etc.). Each province is headed by an elected president [presidente], assisted by the elected provincial council [consiglio provinciale] and an executive body, the provincial executive [giunta provinciale]. The executive is chaired by the president, who appoints its other members [assessori]. These representatives of regional self-government are balanced by a prefect [prefetto], who is appointed by the central government and heads the prefecture [prefettura] as an outpost of the central government. Thus, unlike the exclusively self-governing level of regions, at the level of provinces self-government and deconcentrated state administration are combined.

Trentino and South Tyrol are **autonomous provinces** with the legislative powers of regions. They are not subordinated to their region, but constituent parts of it.

The roughly 8,100 Italian **communes** [comune] correspond to the NUTS-5 level and are headed by a mayor [sindaco] assisted by a legislative body, the communal council [consiglio comunale], and an executive body, the *giunta comunale*. Mayor and the members of the communal council are elected by public vote. The *giunta comunale* is chaired by the mayor, who appoints others members [assessori]. Thus, communes enjoy exclusive self-government.

A commune usually consists of a principal town or village and other areas called **fractions** [frazione]. Only recently, fractions have been administratively upgraded by the implementation of fraction councils [consiglio di frazione], a local government representing the inhabitants of a fraction at the communal level.

So it may be justified to say that Italy has from the 1970s developed from a unitarian centralised state into a decentralised country with self-government at all three (including fractions even four) subnational administrative levels, of which only the provincial level has deconcentrated state administration in addition. Both regional administrative levels coincide very well with historical-cultural as well as gravitational units.

3 Slovenia [Slovenija]

3.1 Cultural and administrative traditions

Slovenia first emerged as a political entity in 1945, when it became a constituent republic of the federal Communist state of Yugoslavia. Prior to this, Slovenes only existed as an ethnic and linguistic category, which was dispersed across several countries and administrative units and which was dominated by majority populations or elites that belonged to other ethnic and cultural groups (with the limited exception of Yugoslavia during the inter-war years). The dominance by a variety of other cultures moulded Slovenian culture in different ways and left its traces in the cultural landscape, in regional identities and in the regional consciousness.

The most pronounced and diverse impressions were left by the Republic of Venice [Serenissima Repubblica di San Marco] in the Adriatic façade of modern Slovenia, and the Habsburg Empire in the remaining areas of the country. While the influence of Venice found its expression in the Mediterranean architecture and the Mediterranean lifestyle in parts of Slovenia, the Habsburg Empire left its mark in terms of Central European (Alpine, Pannonian) traditions. Looking beyond this cultural-historical bisection, the individual crownlands of the Habsburg Empire also left traces behind, producing a lively regional consciousness that exists to this day: the Slovenian Littoral [Primorska] that was Venetian until 1797, then became Austrian; the medieval Habsburg crownlands of Carniola [Kranjska], Styria [Štajerska] and Carinthia [Koroška], as well as Prekmurje [Prekmurje], which was ceded by Hungary after World War I.

None of the administrative-territorial structures implemented after 1918 reflected these historical and cultural identities. Instead, the area of present-day Slovenia was always subdivided in numerous smaller entities, varying in number between 20 and 62, and fluctuating in name between district [okraj, srez] and commune [občina]. Only for the time between 1922 and 1929, in the Kingdom of Serbs, Croats and Slovenes [Kraljevina Srba, Hrvata i Slovenaca, SHS] did the subdivision of the Slovene territory belonging to this state (the western areas belonged to Italy) into the regions [oblast] Ljubljana and Maribor correspond to the historical division between Carniola and Styria.

Between 1945 and 1991, Slovenia was one of the six constituent republics of Yugoslavia. This status, and particularly the degree of autonomy that was further deepened through the Yugoslav Constitution of 1974, can retrospectively be regarded as a necessary preliminary stage for the independence, which was gained in 1991. During this time, Slovenia was divided into greater communes [občina], numbering 62 in the end, which were self-governing. No further administrative level existed between these communes and the constituent republic.

3.2 Developments after 1991 and the current administrative-territorial system

The first administrative reform to take place in independent Slovenia on 3.10.1994 replaced the 62 communes with an average area of 336 sq.km and an average population of 28,000 with 147 communes [občina] with an average of 138 sq.km and 13,000 inhabitants. Consequently, they no longer corresponded to the NUTS-4 level (as the former greater communes had done), but to the NUTS-5 level instead. They too, were self-governing. By 1.1.2007 their number had been augmented in several stages (8.8.1998: 192, 15.6.2002: 193, 14.3.2006: 205, 14.6.2006: 210) to reach 210, gradually reducing the average area to 96 sq.km and the average population to 9,400. 11 of these are urban communes [mestna občina], these being Celje, Koper/Capodistria, Kranj, Ljubljana, Maribor, Murska Sobota, Nova Gorica, Novo Mesto, Ptuj, Slovenj Gradec and Velenje. Urban and other kinds of communes are each endowed with the same competencies.

The **communes** are defined as the basic local self-governing units according to the Constitution of 1991 and in the Local Government Act (72/1993). Following the

Constitution their number can only be increased up to a total of 300. The institutions of the communes (see Figure 2) are the communal council [občinski svet] elected for a four-year term and the mayor [župan], who is elected by the communal council and also serves for a term of four years. There can be up to three deputy mayors [podžupan]. The communal council also elects the communal government [občinska uprava].

Figure 2: **Slovenia's current administrative system**

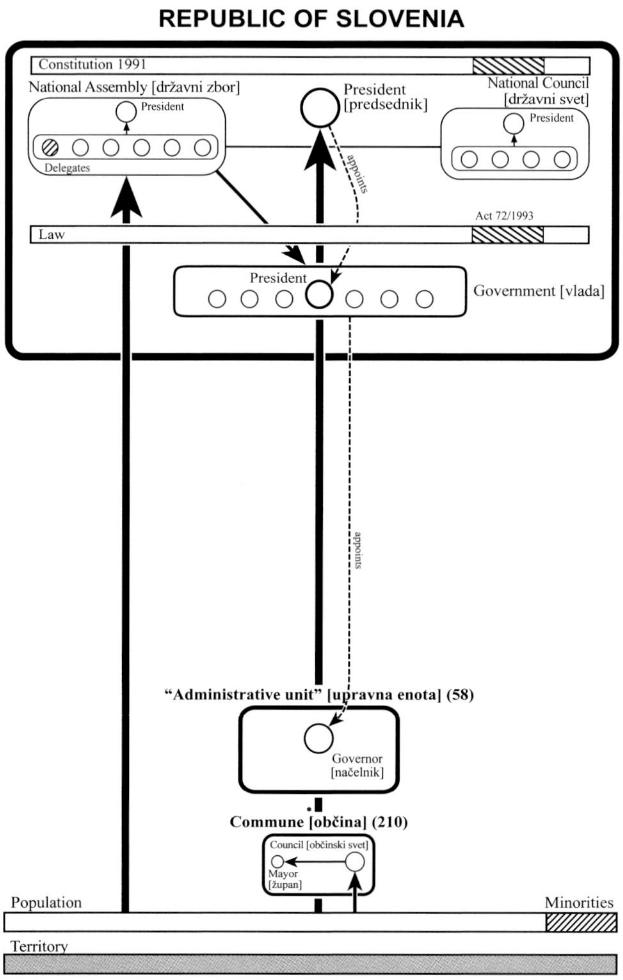

Source: JORDAN 2010

Communal revenues are sourced primarily from taxes and rates. Communes in peripheral areas, which are not able to finance themselves exclusively with self-generated revenues, receive state transfer payments in the way of disparity equalisation.

Simultaneously more or less with the new communes (4.10.1994), 50 so-called **„administrative units“** [upravna enota] were also established (see Figure 2 and 3). To a large extent they correspond to the territories of the former larger communes, and thus also to the NUTS-4 level, and they represent deconcentrated state administration by offering spatially dispersed governmental administrative services. They are led by a governor [načelnik], who is a civil servant.

Figure 3: **Slovenia's subdivision into „administrative units“ [upravna enota]**

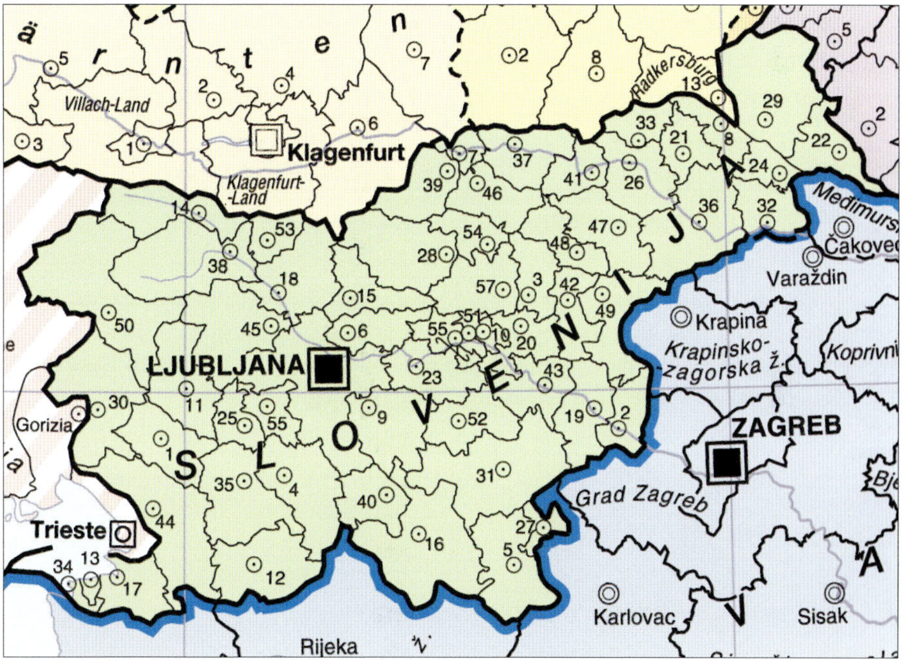

Source: Jordan 2010

To date, self-government has not been established at the regional level, even though the Constitution allows for this option and related discussions began as early as 1991. One possibility, which is repeatedly mentioned, would be the elevation of the 12 existing statistical regions [statistična regija] (see Table 1) to administrative regions [pokrajina]. They correspond to the NUTS-3 level, are largely well matched to the previously mentioned cultural landscapes and their respective subdivisions (e.g. the division of Carniola into Upper Carniola [Gorensko], Inner Carniola [Notransko] and Lower Carniola [Dolensko]) and also align with the functional territorial units (VRIŠER 1998). However, the political parties have been unable to agree upon a solution so far. There is also support for the widely held opinion that a small country such as Slovenia does not require an additional and costly administrative level. A further argument, mentioned less openly, suggests that self-governing regions could release centrifugal forces, if one considers that pronounced regional identities supported by self-government gain gravitas and could pose a threat to the statehood and national unity, which are still young and vulnerable.

Table 1: **Statistical regions [statistična regija] of Slovenia**

1	Pomurska regija	7	Jugovzhodna Slovenija
2	Podravska regija	8	Osrednjeslovenska regija
3	Koroška regija	9	Gorenjska regija
4	Savinjska regija	10	Notranjsko-kraška regija
5	Zasavska regija	11	Goriška regija
6	Spodnjeposavska regija	12	Obalno-kraška regija

Source: STATISTICAL OFFICE OF THE REPUBLIC OF SLOVENIA 2010

It was not until January 1, 2008, that Slovenia was divided into two statistical and funding regions at the NUTS-2 level, i.e. Eastern Slovenia [Vzhodna Slovenija] and Western Slovenia [Zahodna Slovenija] (see the contribution of LORBER to this book). They can, however, not be regarded as administrative regions.

4 Croatia [Hrvatska]

4.1 *Cultural and administrative traditions*

Similar to Slovenia, Croatia was first established as an administrative unit in the current shape in 1945. Very much in contrast to Slovenia, however, Croatian statehood can be traced back very far into history, in fact to the 9th century (852). However, this statehood was subject to several interruptions (the last one from 1919 to 1939), referred to shifting territories with shifting heartlands and varied in sovereignty from fully sovereign to a kind of autonomy. What is Croatia today was dominated for long periods by Venice along the Adriatic façade and by Hungary in the interior of the country, and later by Austria (1797-1805, 1813/15-1867) and Austria-Hungary (1867-1918) in both regions. Long-term territorial fragmentation and divergent rulers, each bringing with them their elites and cultural traditions, as well as late unification resulted, again very similar to Slovenia, in very distinct patterns of historical and cultural regional identities, even though the main dividing line runs between the former countries of the Hungarian Crown and the former "Austrian lands", the latter being successors of the Venetian possessions, which lasted until 1797.

The formerly Hungarian lands were composed of Slavonia [Slavonija] and Croatia Proper, both with a high level of autonomy until 1918, as well as Baranya, Međimurje and Fiume [Rijeka] (a *corpus separatum* of the Hungarian Crown), all of which were integrated parts of the Kingdom of Hungary until 1918. Croatia Proper is in turn composed of several smaller cultural regions like Hrvatsko zagorje, Banja, Kordun, Lika and the Croatian Coastland [Hrvatsko primorje]. With the exception of Hrvatsko zagorje and the Croatian Coastland, the cultural and socio-economic milieu of these subregions is mainly the result of the Austrian Military Frontier [Vojna krajina] against the Ottoman Empire. For several centuries this functioned as a military glacis, was directly subordinated to the Court Council of War in Vienna and in this way was excluded from Croatian-Slavonian self-government.

The former Austrian lands also enjoyed considerable self-governance. With regard to the territory of modern Croatia, they were composed of the Croatian share in the former Austrian Littoral, i.e. Istria [Istra] and the Kvarner, as well as of Dalmatia [Dalmacija].

While the former Hungarian lands, except Rijeka and the Croatian Coastland, have a rather Pannonian or Central European character, the former Austrian provinces skirting the Adriatic Sea (as well as Rijeka and the Croatian Coastland) feature the results of a pronounced Mediterranean and Venetian influence.

In recent times, apart from Serbian separatism, which lead to a *de facto* secession of areas with a Serbian majority coinciding to a large extent with the former Military Frontier between 1992 and 1995, Istria has displayed the strongest signs of a regional consciousness. This culminated in some endeavours towards autonomy in the early 1990s. In the population census of 1991, for example, 45% of the Istrian population declared ethnic affiliations other than Croatian, while 16% declared a "regional" rather than a national affiliation (see also Heilborn 1995). Istria had indeed never been part of any Croatian state before 1945.

With the exception of the years 1939-1941, when a Croatian Banate [Hrvatska banovina] was established, neither inter-war Yugoslavia, nor Tito-Yugoslavia after World War II reflected these historical regions in their administrative-territorial structures. From 1967 onward the communes [općina] were enlarged to the size of districts and endowed with considerable powers of self-government, functioning as the only administrative units below the republican level. Ultimately, their number had reached 102. With an average population of 40,000, however, they were too small to function as regions. Mainly for purposes of regional planning, communes joined associations [zajednica općina]. The entire territory of Croatia was covered by a total of 11 of these communal associations. They were very well aligned with the central place system, though they were not administrative-territorial units in their own right, but merely associations of independent communes for certain purposes.

4.2 Developments after 1991 and the current administrative-territorial system

Croatia had declared independence from Yugoslavia together with Slovenia on 25.6.1991, but continued to be troubled by violent conflicts until August 1995 and was burdened with significant refugee, political and economic problems for longer still.

In somewhat of a hurry and presumably also to prevent discussions, in 1993 Croatia completely reorganised its administrative-territorial system based on a Law dated 29.12.1992. It now consisted of 20 **counties** [županija] at the regional NUTS-3 level, plus the City of Zagreb [Grad Zagreb], which was equated to a county. This was achieved mainly by agglomerating existing communes. At that time, roughly a third of the country was not yet under the control of the Croatian state, but was occupied by the "Republic of Serbian Krajina" ["Republika Srpska Krajina"], neighbouring Bosnia-Herzegovina was still in a situation of war and Croatia as such was certainly still in danger of being involved into this war. This may go some way to explain why such a swift and centralistic approach was chosen.

In two counties (the Sisak-Moslavina County [Sisačko-moslavačka županija] and the Zadar-Knin County [Zadarsko-kninska županija]), subordinate self-governing districts [kotar] were established. These were territories with a majority Serbian population. These districts were conceived as an offer to give Serbs in Croatia self-organisation and representation vis-à-vis county and state on the one hand, and on the other hand, because they were subordinated to counties with a Croatian majority population, they were presumably intended as a mechanism for controlling the Serbs.

After war and violent conflict had come to an end in Croatia (August 1995), the county system was modified in shape in 1996 and on 7.2.1997. These boundary alterations applied particularly to the territory of the former „Serbian Republic“ and the areas around Zagreb. The total number of counties remained the same. Only the two districts conceived for Serbian self-government were abandoned, as the majority of Serbs had been expelled from these areas in 1995, and returned later in much smaller numbers. There have been no further changes to the system of counties. Figure 4 shows the county system in its current form.

The counties are self-governing territorial administrative units. Their institutions (see Figure 5) are the elected county assembly [županijska skupština], the county government [županijsko poglavarstvo] with the count [župan] at its head, who is elected

Figure 4: **Croatia's subdivision into counties [županija]**

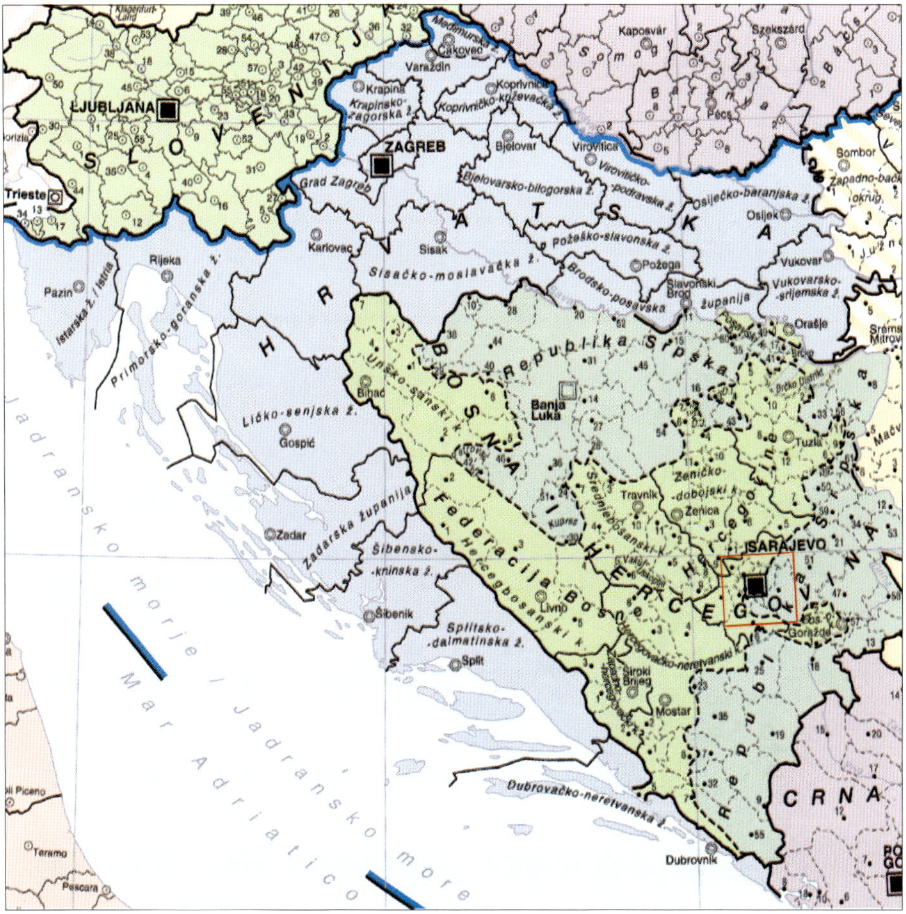

Source: Jordan 2010

by the assembly. The competencies of the counties comprise all regional matters that are not explicitly assigned to state authorities, in other words

- education,
- health care,
- communal planning,
- economic development,
- transportation and infrastructure,
- social and cultural facilities,
- construction permits,
- land management plans outside of larger cities.

Figure 5: **Croatia's current administrative system**

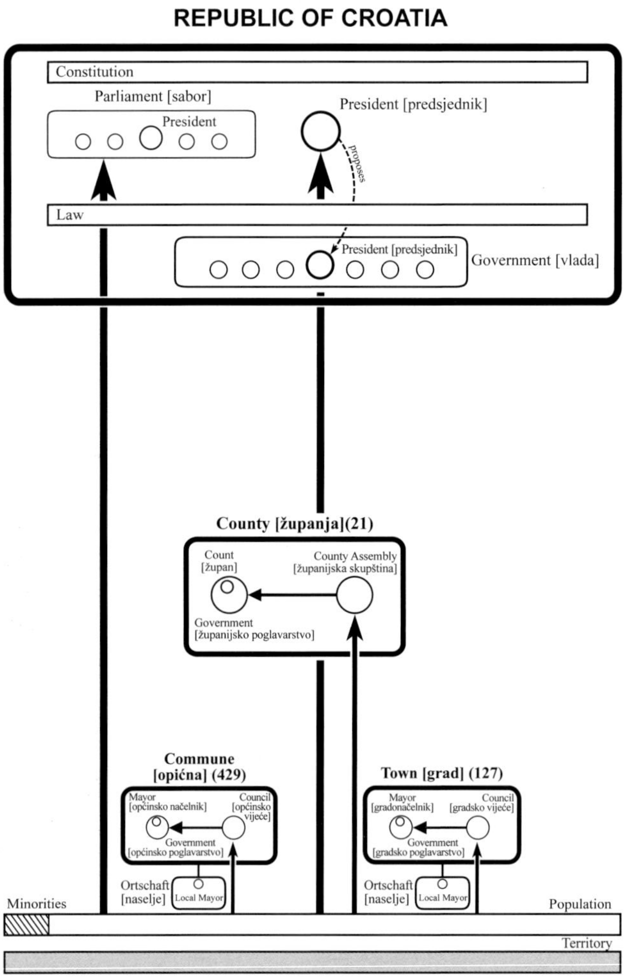

Source: Jordan 2010

In addition, some state functions are also transferred to the counties.

The counties procure their financing by levying taxes or (in the case of delegated state competencies) in the form of transfer payments from the state. Transfer payments from the state are also made available for the purpose of socio-economic disparity equalisation, should peripheral and economically weak counties not be able to finance their statutory functions through self-generated revenues.

Self-government at the county as well as at the local level was substantially reinforced in 2001, when centralistic attitudes prevailing in the Tuđman era (the 1990s) began to make way for other stances.

Although the county system split up the larger historical and cultural regions mentioned above, and only corresponds to smaller historical and cultural identities in three cases (the Istria County [Istarska županija] corresponds to Istria in the sense of the cultural region, not as a peninsula; the Dubrovnik-Neretva County [Dubrovačko-neretvanska županija] corresponds to the territory of the former city republic Ragusa [Dubrovnik]; Međimurje County [Međimurska županija] corresponds to the Međimurje region acquired from Hungary in 1919), it has established a kind of regional identity pattern itself in the meantime. It is, in general, well aligned with the central place system at the meso-level (meso-regions).

For these reasons it has so far been able to withstand wider public discussions, which evolved in a more liberal political climate after the end of the Tuđman era (2000) and circled around the replacement of the county system by "real" regions along the lines of historical and cultural units and in the dimensional range of NUTS-2. The most popular proposal brought forward encompassed five regions, i.e. Slavonia and Baranya [Slavonija i Baranja], Dalmatia [Dalmacija], Central Croatia [Središnja Hrvatska], Littoral and Lika [Primorsko-lička regija] and the City of Zagreb [Grad Zagreb] (Slobodna Dalmacija 23/8/2000, p. 7).

At the local level, the 102 large "Yugoslavian-type" communes [općina] were replaced by 70 **towns** [grad] and 419 **communes** [općina] in 1992 (see Figure 5). By the time of the population census in 2001, numbers had grown to 122 towns and 423 communes. As of 1.1.2007, the local administrative level comprised 127 towns and 429 communes, with an average of 100 sq.km and 8,000 inhabitants (NUTS-5). They are further subdivided into 6,751 settlements [naselje] at NUTS-6 level.

The significant reduction in size was motivated, amongst other things, by the experiences gained previously, i.e. that the former large communes had mainly favoured their centres, while other towns and larger settlements had lost economic activities and inhabitants. Another motive for the reduction in size was, to bring the administration closer to the local population and local interests.

Any settlement with more than 10,000 inhabitants qualifies as a town in the legal sense. Smaller settlements can also be declared towns for specific historical and economic reasons. A town has an elected council [gradsko vijeće] and a government [gradsko poglavarstvo] headed by the president of the council or the mayor [gradonačelnik], respectively. A commune also has an elected council [općinsko vijeće] and a government [općinsko poglavarstvo] headed by the president of the council or the mayor [općinski načelnik], respectively. In settlements, the population is usually represented by a local mayor.

Communes and towns do not differ with regard to competencies. Both are responsible for

- construction,
- regional planning,
- public services,
- childcare,
- social services,
- local health care,
- primary and secondary schools,
- culture,
- sport,
- consumer protection,
- protection of the environment,
- fire protection,
- civil defence.

In order to fulfil these functions they can levy their own taxes. National transfer payments support communes and towns that are financially weaker.

In 2007, three statistical regions were defined at the NUTS-2 level: Northwest Croatia [Sjeverozapadna Hrvatska], Central and East (Pannonian) Croatia [Središnja i istočna (Panonska) Hrvatska] and Adriatic Croatia [Jadranska Hrvatska]. They each combine several counties and replaced an earlier proposal for 4 statistical units, which, however, was rejected by the EU, because the regions did not have sufficient inhabitants. These statistical regions do not have the status of territorial-administrative units within the administrative system.

Despite a wealth of predictions to the contrary, the regional level of counties, which was hastily implemented under difficult external conditions and previously had no tradition in this form, has proved to be surprisingly stable in Croatia. Even though their competencies of self-government have been steadily expanded, they continue to correspond to the centralist concept, which formed the foundation for their implementation. This is because they are too small to effectively oppose central government, and they are unable to tap into the regional consciousness, which is oriented along the lines of the large cultural and historical units.

But it is precisely this regional consciousness combined with the highly varied cultural traditions that drive this state that is still young in years and has a very fragile national identity to push regionalisation forward at this level, rather than at the level of the large cultural-historical units. In this context, the small remaining group of Serbs (2001: 4.5%) that is widely scattered, no longer plays a part.

5 Bosnia and Herzegovina [Bosna i Hercegovina]

5.1 Cultural and administrative traditions

Bosnia and Herzegovina first achieved statehood in the High Middle Ages. However, they usually had to acknowledge the supremacy of greater powers, first those of Byzantium, then mainly those of Hungary and finally those of the Ottoman Empire. In 1463 the last territorial remnants of Bosnia and Herzegovina fell under direct Ottoman rule. Even under the rule of the Ottoman central state, Bosnia and Herzegovina remained an administrative unit, first as eyalet then, from 1845 as vilayet, in other words: one of the provinces and top-tier administrative units of the Empire. Unlike the territory inhabited by Albanians, it was not split between several units and can therefore be seen as a political entity with a strong historical identity among the successor states of Yugoslavia.

After long-lasting violent conflicts, which the weakening Ottoman Empire had been unable to settle, the Austro-Hungarian Monarchy occupied Bosnia and Herzegovina in 1878 with the consent of the Congress of Berlin. The Monarchy turned Bosnia and Herzegovina into a condominium of the Austrian and of the Hungarian half of the Monarchy and placed it under the control of the joint Ministry of Finance. In 1908, Bosnia and Herzegovina was formally annexed and received the status of an autonomous country with legislative and executive administrative competencies. It was divided into eight districts [Kreis/megye/kotar] (two urban, six rural), which followed the Austro-Hungarian model and were institutions of deconcentrated state administration. They were also closely aligned to the historical subregions such as Herzegovina [Hercegovina]. At the local level there were communes.

In this form, after World War I, Bosnia and Herzegovina became part of the first Yugoslavian state (Kingdom of the Serbs, Croats and Slovenes [Kraljevina Srba, Hrvata i Slovenaca], called Yugoslavia from 1929 onwards [Jugoslavija]). However, this country was organised along centralist lines and the borders of Bosnia and Herzegovina were not reflected in any administrative unit.

Not until the second, Communist, Yugoslavia with a federalist structure did Bosnia and Herzegovina arise again as constituent republic more or less in the borders of 1918. Compared to 1918, the only small alteration to the border was carried out in the Bay of Kotor [Boka Kotorska] near Herceg Novi, where the country had to hand over a narrow access corridor to Montenegro. Like the other constituent republics, during the period of the second Yugoslavian state, Bosnia and Herzegovina was merely divided into communes [opština/općina]. Ultimately, there were 104 of these, and they enjoyed far reaching rights of self-government.

5.2 Developments after 1991 and the current administrative-territorial system

When the multinational (Muslim, Serbian, Croatian)[2] Bosnia and Herzegovina declared its independence from Yugoslavia on 5.4.1992, this declaration was followed by a declaration of independence by the "Serbian Republic" ["Republika Srpska"] on 7.4.1992, comprising the territories of Bosnia and Herzegovina, which had a Serbian ethnic majority. The "Serbian Republic" also declared war against the Bosnian state with its Muslim ethnic majority, supported by Belgrade, the Yugoslav National Army [Jugoslovenska Narodna Armija, JNA] and paramilitary forces from Serbia. The war ended with the Dayton Accord signed on 14.12.1995, following first the diplomatic, then the military intervention of the United States and NATO, as well as successful military operations of Bosniak (Bosnian Muslim) and Croatian forces in Bosnia and Herzegovina.

The Dayton Accord re-established Bosnia and Herzegovina as a united state. It also installed a Peace Implementation Council (PIC) executing the international community's governance of Bosnia and Herzegovina (see Figure 6). This Council is composed of 55 countries and agencies and is to last until the country is deemed politically and democratically stable. It controls all levels of governance in Bosnia and Herzegovina and intervenes if this is found necessary. The executive bodies of PIC are a Steering Board and the High Representative for Bosnia and Herzegovina as the main actor on behalf of the international community.

Based on the Dayton Accord and the Constitution of Bosnia-Herzegovina, published as Annex 4 of the Accord, as well as subsequent national legislation, Bosnia and Herzegovina is composed of two "entities" (see Figure 6 and 7): the Federation of Bosnia and Herzegovina [Federacija Bosne i Hercegovine, FBiH][3] and the Serbian Republic [Republika Srpska, RS][4]. This was later complemented by the neutralized District of Brčko [distrikt Brčko][5], which is subject to direct jurisdiction of the state and comprises territories of both entities. The District is not a third entity and is therefore indicated in Figure 7 by a hatched area, which extends beyond the border between the two entities.

At Annex 4, Article I, Paragraph 3, under item "Composition [of the state]" the Dayton Accord states: "Bosnia and Herzegovina shall consist of the two Entities, the Federation of Bosnia and Herzegovina and the Republika Srpska." This suggests that the two entities are not constituent republics of a confederation, but rather subdivisions of a federation, although this is not explicitly expressed.

---

2 According to the census of 1991 the proportion was 43.5% Muslims, 31.2% Serbs and 17.4% Croats.

3 Area 26,110 sq.km, 2,325,018 inhabitants (2006).

4 Area 25,019 sq.km, 1,479,634 inhabitants (2005).

5 Area 208 sq.km, 80,000 inhabitants (2006).

Figure 6: **Bosnia-Herzegovina's current administrative system**

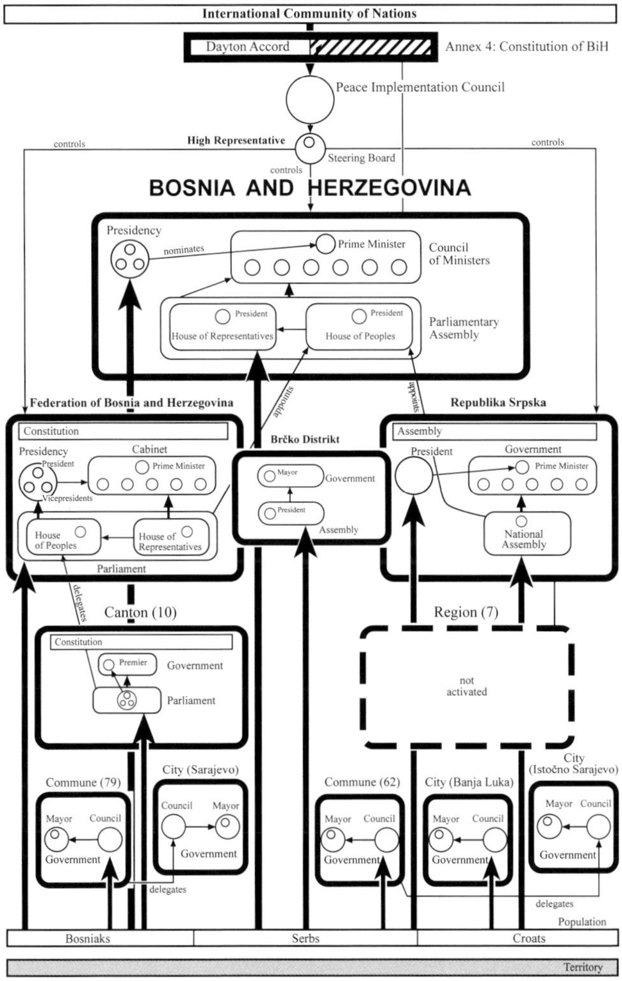

Source: Jordan 2010

The Constitution, on the other hand, specifically establishes the three nations as constituent elements of the state. According to estimates related to the years 2004 and 2005 (no population census has been carried out since 1991), the proportions between the Bosniaks (Muslims), Serbs and Croats at state level are 48:38:14%.[6] They are

[6] Calculations based on an estimate for the Federation of Bosnia-Herzegovina, published by Federal Office for Statistics [Federalni zavod za statistiku] 2004, an estimate for the Serbian Republic by Josipovič 2005 and an extrapolation for the whole state published by the Statistics Office of Bosnia and Herzegovina [Agencija za statistiku Bosne i Hercegovine] 2005.

proportionally represented in all state authorities and every single nation is endowed with veto rights. Since 2001 all three nations are also constituent nations of each of the two entities.

Figure 7: **Entities, cantons and communes in Bosnia-Herzegovina**

Source: Jordan 2010

The Constitution assigns the (confederate) state competencies in the following areas (University of Minnesota, Human Rights Library 2008):

- foreign policy;
- foreign trade policy;
- customs policy;

- monetary policy;
- international financial obligations of governmental institutions;
- immigration;
- refugee and asylum policy;
- criminal law enforcement in cases affecting both entities and several nations;
- relations with Interpol, establishment and operation of common and international transportation systems;
- regulation of inter-entity transportation;
- air traffic control.

The Constitution defines the competencies of the entities as follows (UNIVERSITY OF MINNESOTA, HUMAN RIGHTS LIBRARY 2008):

- external relations with neighbouring states consistent with the sovereignty and territorial integrity of Bosnia and Herzegovina,
- national security,
- civil justice,
- agreements with states and international organizations with the consent of the Parliamentary Assembly.

Every citizen of Bosnia and Herzegovina also has an entity citizenship and vice versa. The borders between the entities are clearly marked, but not controlled. A customs authority as well as a separate postal system exists in each of the two entities. The armed forces of both entities, the Army of the Federation [Vojska Federacije Bosne i Hercegovine] and the Army of the Serbian Republic [Vojska Republike Srpske], were officially merged in 2005.

The Constitution of Bosnia and Herzegovina establishes the following institutions at state level (see Figure 6)[7]:

The Presidency [predsjedništvo Bosne i Hercegovine] is composed of three members, each belonging to one of the three nations. They alternate in chairing the Presidency every 8 months. They are elected for a four-year term by the electorate of their respective national group. The Presidency represents the state at the international level, is responsible for foreign policy, nominates the Prime Minister [predsjedatelj vijeće ministara] and also proposes the annual budget to the Parliamentary Assembly upon the recommendation of the Council of Ministers [vijeće ministara].

The Council of Ministers [vijeće ministara] is confirmed by and answers to the House of Representatives [predstavnički dom/zastupnički dom], the larger of the two

[7] In the case of Bosnia and Herzegovina, the administrative structure of the state level is discussed here by way of exception, because it is precisely this, which helps to illustrate the special features of the sub-national administrative structure.

chambers of the Parliamentary Assembly. Its chair is the Prime Minister, who appoints the ministers. The Council of Ministers conducts the business in all the affairs mentioned as state competencies above.

The Parliamentary Assembly [parlamentarna skupština Bosne i Hercegovine] is a bicameral legislative body composed of the House of Representatives [predstavnički dom/zastupnički dom] and the House of Peoples of Bosnia and Hercegovina [dom naroda Bosne i Hercegovine]. The House of Representatives has 42 members elected by universal, secret and equal vote. 28 members come from the Federation and 14 from the Serbian Republic. The House of Peoples has 15 members who are not elected, but appointed by the parliaments of the entities. They are composed of 5 Bosniaks, 5 Serbs and 5 Croats. Their main task is to ensure that no law is passed by the House of Representatives unless all three nations agree on it. In practice this regulation has proved to be an obstacle to efficiency at the state level and it is certainly a major reason why real power only rests with the state level to a minor extent.

The **Federation of Bosnia and Herzegovina** [Federacija Bosne i Hercegovine, FBiH], which is predominantly bi-national (Bosniak/Croatian) by population structure, but (since 2001) formally also tri-national[8], is based on the Constitution as of 30.3.1994 (with several amendments). This Constitution defines an institutional pattern for the Federation level that very much reflects the state level, i.e., it has also a presidency, a cabinet and a bi-cameral parliament.

The Presidency [predsjedništvo], the supreme representation of the Federation, is composed of a President [predsjednik] and two Vice-Presidents [potpredsjednik], who must belong to different national groups and are elected for a four-year term by the House of Peoples [dom naroda].

The Cabinet [vlada] is appointed by the Presidency and approved by the House of Representatives [predstavnički dom]. It consists of 16 ministers, who are appointed by the Prime Minister [premijer] according to national quotas (8 Bosniaks, 5 Croats, 3 Serbs). The Prime Minister tends to be a Bosniak.

The Parliament's [parlament Federacije Bosne i Hercegovine] first chamber is the House of Representatives [predstavnički dom] with 98 members elected for four years by universal popular vote. The second chamber is the House of Peoples [dom naroda] composed of 57 members, of which 17 are Bosniaks, 17 Croats, 16 Serbs and 7 "Others". They are delegated for four years by the cantonal parliaments [skupština kantona]. Their national delegate clubs elect the three members of the Presidency (the Bosniak club the Bosniak member, etc.).

---

[8] According to an estimate related to 31.12.2003, the proportion between the national groups in the Federation is 72.6% Bosniaks, 21.8% Croats, 4.6% Serbs and 1.0% others (FEDERALI ZAVOD ZA STATISTIKU 2004).

The Federation is administratively subdivided into 10 self-governing **cantons** [kanton/županija], which correspond to the NUTS-3 level of the EU classification (see Figure 6, 7 and Table 2). Each of these cantons has its own constitution, courts of justice, police forces, and legislative as well as executive competencies. In addition, they execute tasks on behalf of the Federation (delegated competencies). They collect taxes, supervise and co-ordinate the activities of their communes [opština/općina] and cities [grad].

Table 2: **Cantons of the Federation and their national majorities (31.12.2003)**

Canton	Majority	Canton	Majority
Bosansko-podrinjski kanton	99% Bosniaks	Zapadno-hercegovački kanton/ Zapadno-hercegovačka županija	99% Croats
Unsko-sanski kanton	94% Bosniaks	Posavskikanton/Posavska županija	83% Croats
Tuzlanski kanton	91% Bosniaks	Hercegbosanska županija/Livanjski kanton/Zapadnobosanski kanton	79% Croats
Zeničko-dobojski kanton	84% Bosniaks	Srednjobosanski kanton/ Srednjobosanska županija	58% Bosniaks, 39% Croats
Sarajevski kanton	80% Bosniaks	Hercegovačko-neretvljanski kanton	50% Croats, 46% Bosniaks

Source: FEDERALI ZAVOD ZA STATISTIKU FBiH 2004

In practice, the cantons are the most powerful administrative layer in the Federation. They exceed the state as well as the federation level. This is partly due to their predominantly mono-national structure, which means blocs are rarely formed for national reasons. While five cantons have a distinct Bosniak and three a distinct Croat population majority, only two are close to having an ethnic equilibrium (Central Bosnian Canton [Srednjobosanski kanton/Srednjobosanska županija], Herzegovian-Neretvan Canton [Hercegovačko-neretvljanski kanton]) (FEDERALI ZAVOD ZA STATISTIKU FBiH 2004). Only in the latter two cantons, do cantonal laws and decisions have to be approved by the delegates of both national groups (see Table 2).

The guiding principle for the definition of cantons was obviously the ethnic structure, while aspects of historical identities and functional coherence only played a secondary role.

Self-government in the cantons is executed by the one-cameral cantonal parliament [skupština kantona], which is elected for a four-year term by universal popular vote. A president [predsjednik] and two vice-presidents [potpredsjednik] are elected from among its members, who have to belong to different national groups. If a canton is practically mono-national, only one vice-president is appointed. The delegates do not only establish parties, but also form national clubs. The presidency proposes the prime minister of the cantonal government to the cantonal parliament, which, in turn, appoints the ministers of his government and nominates them for approval by the parliament.

The cantons are again subdivided into 3 to 13 self-governing **communes** [opština/općina], in total 79 (see Figure 6 and 7). In size (NUTS-4) and function they do not differ very much from the large communes in Communist Yugoslavia. However, boundaries have frequently been redrawn. Some new communes have emerged and communes that are split by a border that runs between two entities are governed in two parts.

The communes have a communal council [opštinko vijeće/općinsko vijeće] elected for a term of four years. The council in turn elects the communal government [opštinka uprava/općinska uprava] and the mayor [načelnik].

By Federation law it is possible that at least two communes agglomerate to a city [grad] under the precondition that one commune has at least 30,000 inhabitants or a central settlement has at least 10,000 inhabitants. So far, only four communes (Stari Grad, Centar, Novi Grad, Novo Sarajevo) in the urban region of Sarajevo have used this opportunity by joining to form the City of Sarajevo [Grad Sarajevo]. This means that they maintain all their communal functions and authorities, but delegate 7 members each into the city council [gradsko vijeće] of Sarajevo, which in turn elects a city government [gradska uprava] and a lord mayor [gradonačelnik]. The city exercises coordinating functions and operates facilities, which are in the common interest of its constituent communes.

According to estimates, the **Serbian Republic** [Republica Srpska, SR] is 91% Serbian by nationality (Josipovič 2005), but since 2001 it acknowledges Serbs, Bosniaks as well as Croats as its constituent nations. It is based on the Constitution as of 28.2.1992 with several amendments. This Constitution defines Sarajevo as the capital, but since 1998 *de facto* all supreme authorities of the Republic are located in Banja Luka.

First of all, this is the uni-cameral National Assembly [narodna skupština] as the principal instrument of self-government (see Figure 6). It is composed of 83 delegates elected by universal popular vote for a term of four years. A President [predsjednik] and two vice-presidents [potpredsjednik] are elected from amongst the delegates. The Government [vlada] answers to the National Assembly.

The President of the Republic [predsjednik republike] and his deputy are also elected by direct popular vote, and, in this case, for a term of five years. They have to stand together on the same ticket. The President is the supreme representative of the Republic, nominates the Prime Minister [predsjednik vlade] and the President [predsjednik] of the Supreme Court [ustavni sud], calls elections of the National Assembly and has the right to pass emergency decrees in special circumstances. Not only the direct democratic legitimacy, but also the fact that he is not part of a collective body combining several nations, places the President of the Serbian Republic in a much stronger position than the President of the Federation.

The Republican Law on Territorial Organization and Local Self-Government adopted in 1994 and amended in 1999 (No. 35/99) defines 7 regions [regija], into which the whole territory of the Republic is subdivided. So far they have not been activated, i.e. they have no active authorities and no functions and are consequently not depicted in Figure 7. These regions are Banja Luka, Doboj, Bijeljina, Vlasenica, Sarajevo-Romanija (Sokolac), Foča and Trebinje.

The local administrative level (NUTS-4) is subdivided into 63 self-governing communes [opština/općina], two of which are cities [grad]. One city (Istočno Sarajevo), is composed of several communes (Kasindo, Lukavica, Istočni Stari Grad, Pale, Sokolac and Trnovo), while the city of Banja Luka consists of just one commune and has the same competencies as "normal" communes. Istočno Sarajevo, on the other hand, functions in the same way as the City of Sarajevo on the other side of the entity border.

As is the case in the Federation, the local administrative level of the Serbian Republic corresponds very much to the communal structure of federal Yugoslavia. The small number of changes compared to the Yugoslavian period also took place more or less in parallel in the two entities.

Communes have a communal council [skupština opštine/skupština općine] elected for a term of four years, a communal government [opštinska uprava/općinska uprava] and a mayor [načelnik opštine/načelnik općine]. In a city [grad], these bodies are named *skupština grada, gradska uprava*, and *gradonačelnik*, respectively.

The **District of Brčko** [distrikt Brčko], has the status of a neutralised zone within the territory of both entities, and is directly subordinated to the state. As institution of self-government it has an Assembly [skupština distrikta Brčko BiH], which is composed of 29 delegates elected for a term of four years. The Assembly elects the Government [vlada] and a Mayor [gradonačelnik].

It is obvious that this four-tier administrative system (with a fifth tier in Sarajevo) is extremely complicated and also expensive. As it is also strictly based on national proportionality including veto rights for individual national groups making it possible to obstruct and block any decision, it favours mono-national situations and thus promotes national segregation, which is already far advanced due to war and flight. The confederate state level is particularly affected by obstruction, while – with the exception of the local level – the mostly mono-national Serbian Republic as one of the entities works best in relative terms, as do those cantons within the Federation, which are also largely mono-national.

6 Montenegro [Crna Gora]

6.1 Cultural and administrative traditions

Montenegro's statehood can be traced back to Serbian principalities in the Early and High Middle Ages (Doclea, Zeta), when the territory of modern Montenegro was in fact a cornerstone of Serbian culture and state-building. From the 13th century onward its Adriatic coast was at least influenced, partly also controlled by Venice. During the 15th century the Ottoman Empire acquired supremacy over the Montenegrin hinterland, without extending the military occupation across the entire territory.

The Venetian presence along the coast and the Byzantine/Serbian/Ottoman shaping of the hinterland have had a strong and lasting impact on cultural identities. This division was not lessened by subsequent developments, but instead it was accentuated: When Austria took over most of the coastal fringe from Venice in 1797 and kept it (with a short interruption) until 1918, it conserved the prevailing cultural and social climate. In the mountainous hinterland a small Montenegrin principality with Cetinje as its capital achieved formal autonomy from the Ottoman Empire in 1852. The Berlin Congress of 1878 enlarged it considerably, also awarding it the southern section of the coast and made it formally independent. In 1910 Montenegro acquired the status of a Kingdom, after the Balkan Wars (1912/1913) it shared the Sandjak of Novi Pazar [Novipazarski sandžak] with Serbia, and acquired southwestern parts of Metohija (including Pejë/Peć and Gjakovë/Đakovica) as well as narrow strips along the Albanian border.

Montenegro's full integration into the Kingdom of Serbs, Croats and Slovenes after World War I was not a problem, since, in the 19th century, Montenegro had developed the identity of a second Serbian state populated by the same ethnic majority group and sharing the same denomination.

Tito-lead Second Yugoslavia which, unlike the First Yugoslavia, did pay heed to the equilibrium between the Southern Slavonic nations, adopted, for this very purpose, a federal structure consisting of autonomous constituent republics with the corresponding Southern Slavonic titular nations. Montenegro was given the position of one of six constituent republics with the state nation "Montenegrins". Just like the other constituent nations it was subdivided at the local level into large self-governing communes [opština]. Montenegro had 20 of these at the time of the disintegration of Yugoslavia.

6.2 Developments after 1991 and the current administrative-territorial system

During the time of the Second Yugoslavia, the Montenegrins had also merely perceived themselves as a separate state nation, but not as a separate cultural nation. Their Serbian national identity proved itself after the disintegration of Communist Yugoslavia, when they alone remained loyal to Serbia, continued to exist as federative constituent republic of rump-Yugoslavia and participated in all of its military and political activities.

A more distanced attitude did not take hold until the late 1990s, encouraged by the government of Milo Đukanović, when it consolidated to a quest for independence and ultimately found expression, amongst others, in a separate unit of currency, in a position of neutrality during the Kosovo conflict and in the friendly reception offered to Albanian refugees from the Kosovo.

At the instigation of and through the mediation offered by the EU, which initially took a sceptical stance towards Montenegro's independence, the Federal Republic of Yugoslavia (merely consisting of Serbia and Montenegro) was converted to the State Union of Serbia and Montenegro [Srbija i Crna Gora] on 4.2.2003. Union institutions would only have been responsible for foreign policy, legislation and defence. However, even these functions could not be executed, because joint institutions were either never installed, or not filled with appointed officials. *De facto*, Montenegro acted like an independent state. Following a referendum, Montenegro achieved independence formally on 3.6.2006.

The new Constitution dated 22.10.2007 designates Montenegro [Crna Gora] as the official state name without the prefix "Republic" and Montenegrin [Crnogorski], both in Cyrillic and in Latin script, as the official language, though Serbian, Bosnian, Croatian and Albanian can also be used in official matters. Podgorica is named as capital city [glavni grad], and Cetinje, the historical capital, is defined as residence [prijestonica].

Few changes have been made to the subdivision of the country into **communes** [opština] compared to the Yugoslavian era. Only the former commune Ivangrad was split into two in 1991 (Andrijevica and Berane), augmenting the number of communes from 20 to 21, with an average size of 658 sq.km and an average of 29,000 inhabitants (NUTS-4) (see Figure 8).

The new Constitution defines the communes as the basic units of the administrative-territorial system, and allows for the possibility to establish additional levels of administration. The Constitution further concedes that the communes can define their own statutes, but states that its communal authorities are to be the assembly [skupština] and the president [predsjednik], and that they are to be financed through self-generated revenues as well as by transfers from the state budget.

Figure 8: **Montenegro's subdivision into communes [opština]**

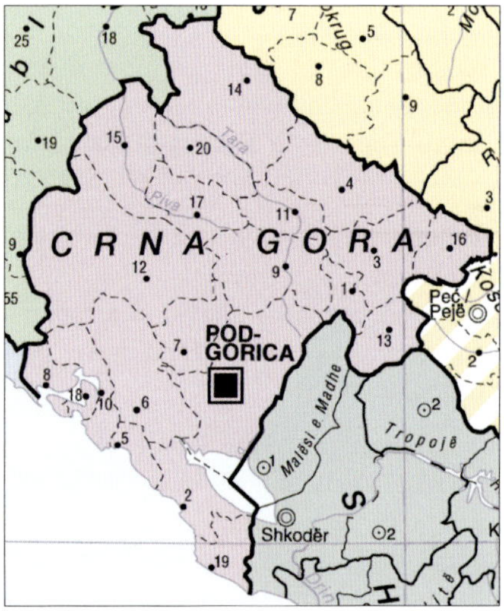

Source: Jordan 2010

The Law on Local Self-Government as of 2003 (No. 42/2003) with its amendments (Nos. 28/2004, 75/2005, 13/2006), defines the tasks of the communes and their individual bodies in greater detail. According this law the assembly is elected for a term of four years and it elects a president [predsjednik] from among its ranks (see Figure 9). The president of the commune [predsjednik opštine] is also elected by direct popular vote, and he serves for a term of five years. He can have one or more vice-presidents [potpredsjednik] and he represents the commune. A communal office [opštinska uprava] headed by a civil servant [glavni administrator] functions as an executive board.

The communes are further subdivided into 368 **local associations** [mjesna zajednica, MZ], which help to channel local interests, but have no elected bodies (see Figure 9).

There is no regional level of administration in Montenegro. This is mainly due to the large communes and the small size of the country. No other significant reasons can be determined. Considering this, the territorial administrative system of Montenegro is decentralized to an appropriate extent.

Figure 9: **Montenegro's current administrative system**

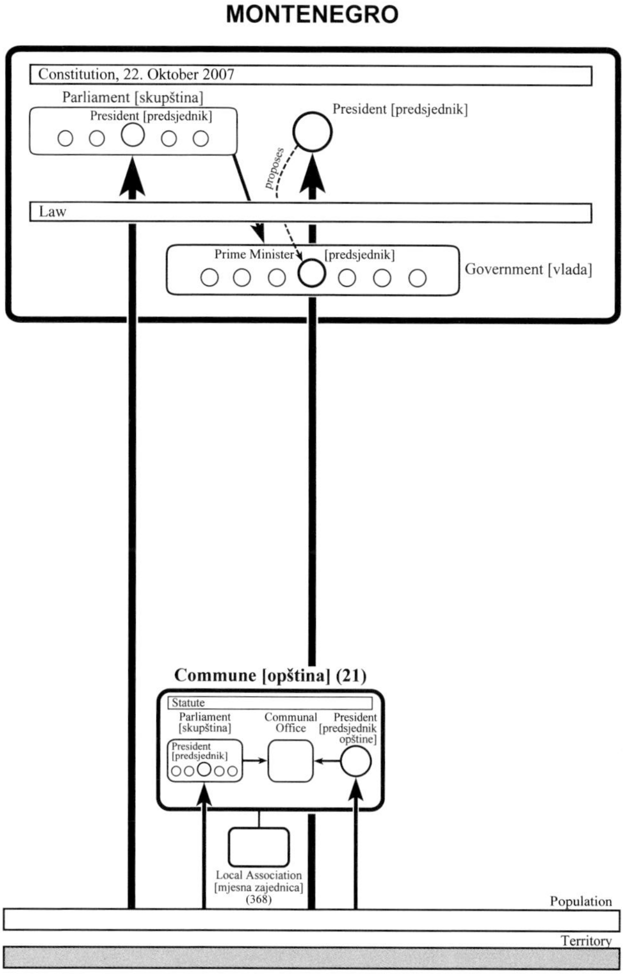

Source: Jordan 2010

7 Albania [Shqipëri]

7.1 Cultural and administrative traditions

Most of the territory of modern Albania stood under the centralist system of Ottoman rule from the 15th century until 1912. During this time, however, it never belonged to one common administrative unit of the Ottoman Empire, but was always distributed across several administrative units. After the First Balkan War (1912), when the Ottoman Empire was forced to make a significant retreat from Europe, and nation states emerged in the territories of its former dominion, the Albanians succeeded in establishing their own state, with the support of several of the great powers. Along the lines of unitarian nation states and of the French model of central government, from the very beginning, this state only featured units of deconcentrated state administration at the subnational administrative levels.

This did not change after World War II, even though the Communist regime in Albania had emerged from a partisan movement – just as in Yugoslavia, but in contrast to all other European Communist states – and initially followed a grass-roots democratic orientation. But in the dispute between Tito and Stalin (1948), the Albanian Communist Party chose to side with Moscow. This meant that, in contrast to the Self-Governing Socialism of Yugoslavia, Albania continued to follow a Stalinist and thus centralist path and it consequently remained one of the most rigid political systems in the Communist bloc until the end.

During this time, the country was structured into 26 districts [rrethi] at the regional level and small communes [komuna] at the local level. Neither of these had self-government.

7.2 Developments after 1991 and the current administrative-territorial system

Following the political turmoil during the years up until 1997 and a period of domestic calming, the Albanian administrative system was not completed until 2000. Since then, it has been a three-tier system with 12 regions [prefekturë or qark] at the upper regional level (NUTS-3), 36 districts [rrethi] at the lower regional level (NUTS-4) since 1995, and 309 (rural) communes [komuna] and 65 towns [bashkia] at the local level (NUTS-5) (see Figure 10). Towns and communes are further subdivided into a large number (approx. 2,900) of villages or urban wards.

The 12 **regions** (see Figure 11) are endowed with indirect or delegated self-government. Their councils are not elected by the region's population, but rather consist of delegates of the communes and towns (who are, in fact, elected).

The 36 **districts** (see Figure 11) represent deconcentrated state administration. They implement the directives issued by the state and by the regions in their respective territories (Hoxha 2007).

Only the **local level** (communes and towns) is self-governing. Both the councils and the mayors are elected directly by the population.

The lack of self-government at both regional levels can be led back to reasons that are generally applicable to Southeast Europe. Additionally, it can be explained above

Figure 10: **Albania's current administrative system**

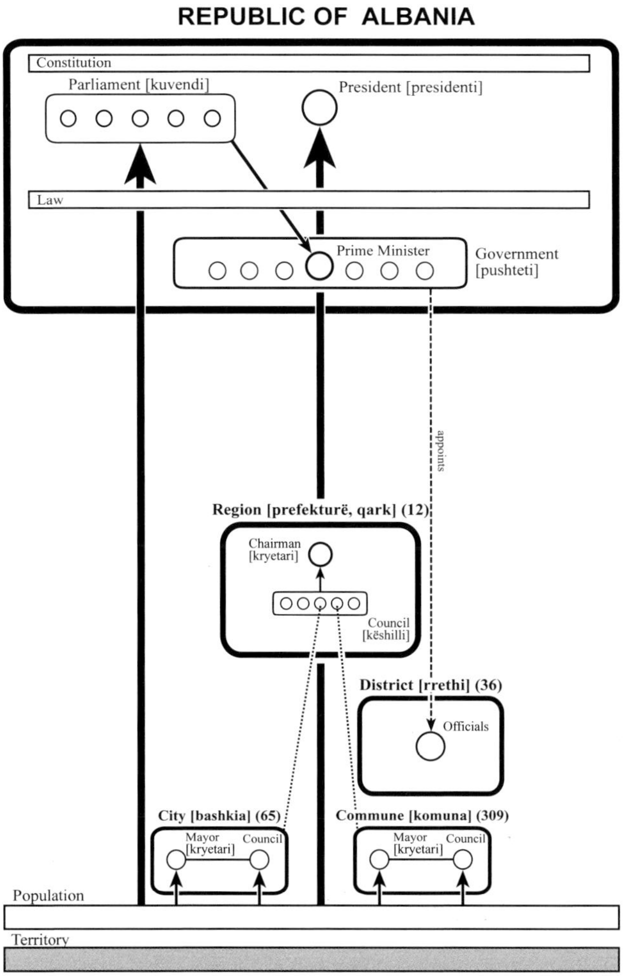

Source: Jordan 2010

all by the fact that the state does not wish to support the prevailing and pronounced clan structure, which has its own legal systems, by allowing self-government.

Respect for ethnic minorities presumably also plays a part. While these are small according to official figures (1989: 2%, Instituti i Statistikës 1991), experts estimate that they may account for approximately 10% (Bërxholi et al. 2003) and suggest that they would affirm their identity in greater numbers in a minority-friendly climate (particularly Aromunians, Roma, Greeks).

Figure 11: **Albania's subdivision into regions [prefekturë or qark] and districts [rrethi]**

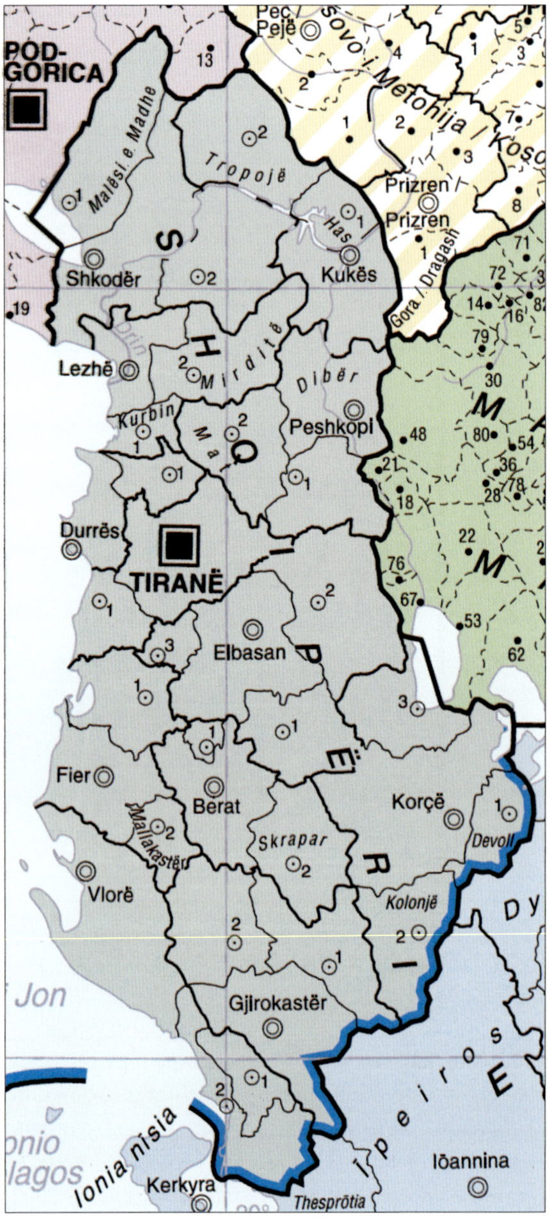

Source: JORDAN 2010

8 Conclusions

Figure 12: **Synopsis**

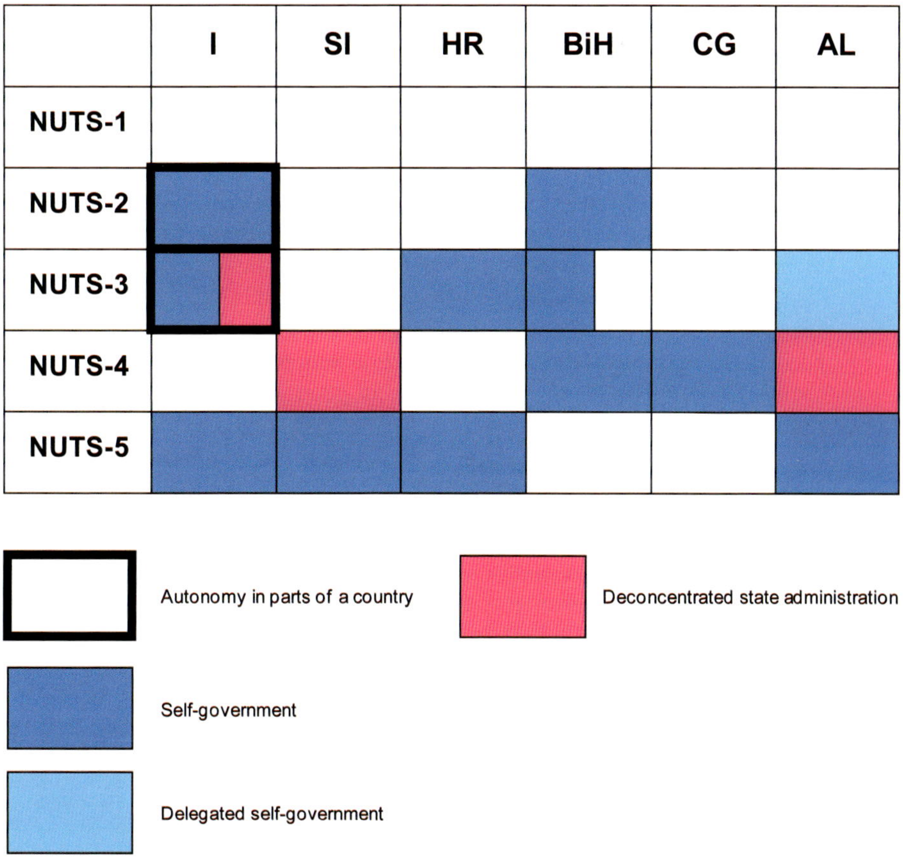

The findings mentioned above as well as the synopsis shown in Figure 12, suggest the following conclusions:

- The **local administrative level** (NUTS-5; in Bosnia-Herzegovina and Montenegro NUTS-4) is endowed with self-government. This self-government has a longer tradition in Italy, has in the successor states of Yugoslavia been established already during the Communist years, and was adopted by Albania very soon after the political turn-around. This expresses the early quest for democratisation "from the grass roots", but with the small size of the local units it only embraces political dimensions that do not pose a threat to the central government.

- The **regional administrative levels** (NUTS-2 to NUTS-4), on the other hand, are exclusively self-governed only in exceptional cases. Italy introduced self-governing regions at the NUTS-2 level in 1970. Where, as in Croatia and Bosnia-Herzegovina, this is the case in transformation countries, self-government is either endowed only with moderate competencies (Croatia) or it does not correspond to the ideal type of administrative regionalisation, but is rather a form of administratively supported and therefore solidified ethnic segregation (Bosnia-Herzegovina: entities on the NUTS-2 level and cantons at the NUTS-3 level in the federation). Slovenia and Montenegro have no regions.

  This deficit in the decentralisation process at the regional levels, in other words – with regard to a "real" administrative regionalisation – can be explained by administrative traditions, but beyond that also primarily by the poorly consolidated national identity and statehood. Against this background, different central administrations are keen to interpret various signs (ethnic and other minorities, pronounced regional identities, gravitational pull of foreign centres, socio-economic spatial disparities, etc.) as good reasons for demonstrating restraint in this matter.

- **Autonomies**, in the sense of partial territories of a state that are endowed with special competencies of self-government exist in the Italian share of the Adriatic space (Friuli-Venezia Giulia, Trentino-Alto Adige), but could not be established in the transformation countries of the Adriatic space, although regionalist movements (especially on Istria) were striving for them.

- **Administrative traditions** display some impact. In Slovenia, deconcentrated state administration at the lower regional administrative level (NUTS-4) follows (like in other East-Central European countries) the pattern of the Political Districts during the end phase of the Austrian-Hungarian Monarchy. The different approaches chosen by Croatia and Bosnia and Herzegovina can be partially (Croatia) or fully (Bosnia-Herzegovina) explained by the circumstances of war that prevailed in the 1990s. With the exception of Slovenia and Croatia, by the successor states of Communist Yugoslavia the self-governing large communes were retained at the lower regional level (Bosnia-Herzegovina, Montenegro). Slovenia and Croatia returned to small communes immediately after gaining independence, this being the structure that had existed there prior to the years of Communist Yugoslavia.

9 References

Ausschuss der Regionen (ed.) (2000), Ein Europa der Regionen und Städte: Strategien und Perspektiven für die EU-Erweiterung. Brüssel.

Bertić I. (ed.) (1987), Veliki geografski atlas Jugoslavije. Zagreb, SNL.

Bërxholi A., Doka Dh., Asche H. (ed.) (2003), Minoritete Etnike 2001. Ethnic Minorities 2001. Ethnische Minderheiten 2001. Unpublished map.

Borovac I. (ed.) (2002), Veliki atlas Hrvatske. Zagreb, Mozaik knjiga.

Budak N. et al. (eds.) (1995), Kroatien. Wien – Köln – Weimar, Böhlau.

Bufon M., Gosar A., Nurković S., Sanguin A.L. (eds.) (2006), The Western Balkans – A European Challenge. On the Decennial of the Dayton Peace Agreement. Koper.

Committee of the Regions (ed.) (1999), Preparing for EU Enlargement. Devolution in the First Wave of Candidate Countries. Brussels. = COR Studies E-4/99.

Europäische Kommission, Eurostat (ed.), http://epp.eurostat.ec.europa.eu/ (29.2.2012)

Federalni zavod za statistiku BiH (ed.) (2004), Procjena ukupnog broja prisutnog stanovništva po starosti, spolu i kantonima, 30.06.2004. godine. Sarajevo.

Foucher M. (ed.) (1998²), Fragments d'Europe. s.l., Fayard.

Grimm F-D., Friedlein G., Müller E. (1997), Central Place Systems in Central and Eastern Europe. In: Jordan P. (ed.), Atlas of Eastern and Southeastern Europe, Wien, No. 5.3-MO1.

Heilborn A. (1995), Istrien: Kroatiens Herz schlägt eigensinnig. Kroatiens größte Ferienregion und seine Regionalpartei IDS. In: Budak N. et al. (eds.), Kroatien. Wien – Köln – Weimar, Böhlau, pp. 391–410.

Instituti i Statistikës (ed.) (1991), Regjistrimi i Përgjithshem i Popullsisë e Banesave. Tiranë.

International Constitutional Law (ICL) (ed.), Italy – Constitution. http://servat.unibe.ch/icl/it00000_.html (29.2.2012)

ISTAT (ed.), http://www3.istat.it/ (29.2.2012)

Jordan P. (1992), Regionale Identität in Mitteleuropa im Hinblick auf die europäische Integration. In: Mitt. d. Österr. Geogr. Ges., 134, pp. 177–188.

Jordan P. (2001), Regional Identities and Regionalization in East-Central Europe. In: Post-Soviet Geography and Economics, 42, 4, pp. 235–265.

Jordan P. (2004), EU-Erweiterung und europäische Identität. In: Mitt. d. Österr. Geogr. Ges., 146, pp. 43–60.

Jordan P. (2004), Renaissance of Regionalism – Reaction to Globalisation and European Integration? In: Siwek T., Baar V. (eds.), Globalisation and its Geopolitical, Cultural, Economic and Ecological Context. Ostrava, pp. 13–22.

Jordan P. (2005), Major problems of administrative regionalisation and decentralisation in Central and Southeast Europe. In: Acta Universitatis Carolinae, Geographica XXXVIII, 2003, No. 1, Praha, pp. 141–155.

Jordan P. (2006), Administrative regionalisation in Southeast Europe – Slow progress due to strong regional identities and cultural minorities? In: Henkel R. (ed.), South Eastern European Countries on their Way to Europe. Geographical Aspects, pp. 39–59.

Jordan P. (2006), Ethnic Consciousness in Central and Southeast Europe. In: Jordan P. (ed.), Atlas of Eastern and Southeastern Europe, Wien, No. 2.9-G9.

Jordan P. (2010), Administrative Subdivision of Central and Southeast Europe 2007. In: Jordan P. (ed.), Atlas of Eastern and Southeastern Europe, Wien, No. 5.4-G10.

Josipovič D. (2006), Suitability of the Dayton Territorial Division for the Process of Integration of Bosnia and Herzegovina. In: Bufon M., Gosar A., Nurković S., Sanguin A.L. (eds.), The Western Balkans – A European Challenge. On the Decennial of the Dayton Peace Agreement. Koper, pp. 391–418.

Klemenčić M. (ed.) (1993), A Concise Atlas of the Republic of Croatia & of the Republic of Bosnia and Hercegovina. Zagreb, The Miroslav Krleža Lexicographical Institute.

Klemenčić M. (ed.) (1997), Atlas Europe. Zagreb, The Miroslav Krleža Lexicographical Institute.

Krallert R. (1970), Verwaltungsgebiete. In: Breu J. (ed.), Atlas der Donauländer. Wien, Deuticke, Table 251.

Lukan W., Trgovčević Lj., Vukčević D. (eds.) (2005), Serbien und Montenegro. Wien, LIT-Verlag.

Magocsi P.R. (2002^{2}), Historical Atlas of Central Europe. Toronto, Toronto University Press.

Marko H., Borić T. (1991), Slowenien – Kroatien – Serbien. Die neuen Verfassungen. Wien – Köln – Graz, Böhlau.

Paasi A. (1995), The institutionalization of regions: a theoretical framework for understanding the emergence of regions and the constitution of regional identity. In: Fennia, 164, 1, pp. 105–146.

Parlament Federacije Bosne i Hercegovine, http://www.parlamentfbih.gov.ba, accessed 13 January 2008.

Pickles J., Smith A. (eds.) (1998), Theorising transition: the political economy of transition in post-Communist countries. London – New York, Routledge.

Pusich Sc. M. (1996), The Case of Regionalism in Croatia. In: Hall D., Danta D. (eds.), Reconstructing the Balkans. A Geography of the New Southeast Europe. Chichester – New York – Brisbane – Toronto – Singapore, John Wiley & Sons, pp. 53–65.

Regan K. (ed.) (2003), Hrvatski povijesni atlas. Zagreb, The Miroslav Krleža Lexicographical Institute.

Republic of Slovenia, Constitutional Court, http://www.us-rs.si, accessed 7 January 2008.

Roggemann H. (1980), Die Verfassung der SFR Jugoslawien. Berlin, Berlin-Verlag.

Roggemann H. (ed.) (1999), Die Verfassungen Mittel- und Osteuropas. Berlin, Berlin-Verlag.

Sanguin A.L., Cattaruzza A., Chaveneau-Le Brun (eds.) (2005), L'ex-Yugoslavie dix ans après Dayton. Paris, L'Harmattan.

Slawisnki, I. (1989), Administrative Subdivision of Eastern and Southeastern Europe. In: Jordan P. (ed.), Atlas of Eastern and Southeastern Europe, Wien, No. 5.1-G1.

Slobodna Dalmacija, Split 23/8/2000.

Službeni list Crne Gore, http://www.sllrcg.cg.yu, accessed 13 January 2008.

Statistical Office of the Republic of Slovenia, http://www.stat.si/eng/index.asp, accessed 7 September 2010.

Statuti regionali, http://www.simone.it/statuti/index.htm (29.2.2012)

University of Minnesota, Human Rights Library, http://www1.umn.edu/humanrts/icty/dayton/daytonannex4, accessed 13 January 2008.

Vlada Federacije Bosne i Hercegovine, www.fbihvlada.gov.ba, accessed 27 July 2007.

Vrišer I. (1998), Središčna naselja in vplivna območja pomembnejših središč leta 1994. In: Geografski atlas Slovenije, ed. by Založništvo literature, Inšitut za geografijo, Geografski inštitut Antona Melika, Ljubljana, p. 306.

Weichhart P. (1999), Die Region – Chimäre, Artefakt oder Strukturprinzip sozialer Systeme? In: Brunn G. (ed.), Region und Regionsbildung in Europa. Konzeptionen der Forschung und empirische Befunde (= Schriftenreihe des Instituts für europäische Regionalforschungen, 1). Baden-Baden, pp. 25–43.

Werlen B. (1997), Sozialgeographie alltäglicher Regionalisierungen, vol. II. Stuttgart, Franz Steiner Verlag.

White G.W. (2000), Nationalism and Territory. Lanham – Boulder – New York – Oxford, Rowman & Littlefield Publishers, Inc.

Focus on Countries

Development of Regional Disparities in Slovenia

*Lučka Lorber, Maribor**

with 3 figures and 4 tables in the text

Content

Summary ... 97
1 Introduction ... 98
2 Historical summary ... 100
3 Sectoral structure of regional economies and regional disparities ... 101
4 Future directions ... 106
5 Conclusions ... 107
6 Bibliography ... 108

Summary

The paper presents a survey over regional disparities in Slovenia measured by Gross Domestic Product (GDP). Slovenian regions at the NUTS-3 level are compared with the Central Slovenian (statistical) Region [Osrednjeslovenska regija].

The paper focuses also on the spatial distribution of economic activities by regions and stresses the necessity to accelerate the economy as well as to increase competitiveness; also that regions must work hard to establish a good balance between stable economic development, structure adjustment and inflation management. It is supposed that this will be a long and arduous process aggravated by the international financial crisis.

The Slovenian regions' economic structure, determined by Gross Value Added (GVA), is slowly approaching the structure of developed economies with the importance

* Lučka Lorber, Assist. Prof. PhD; Department of Geography, Faculty of Arts, University of Maribor, Koroška cesta 160, SI-2000 Maribor, e-mail: lucka.lorber@uni-mb.si, http://www.ff.uni-mb.si

of agriculture and manufacturing decreasing and the importance of services increasing. However, financial and business services as well as technologically demanding sectors are growing too slowly in less developed regions.

Slovenia's basic development goal is to exceed the average economic development of the enlarged EU to be able to secure social security, faster development in all its regions and improve the environment – in other words to strive for a better quality of life and overall human development across the country.

1 Introduction

The paper researches into regional disparities in Slovenia by Gross Domestic Product (GDP) at the level of two NUTS-2 cohesion regions as well as of twelve NUTS-3 regions. The Nomenclature of Territorial Units for Statistics (Nomenclature des unités territoriales statistiques, NUTS) is the common European statistical classification of territorial units that was confirmed by the Parliament on May 26, 2003. The NUTS classification has three levels. By virtue of ES Regulation No. 1888/2005, the entire territory of the Republic of Slovenia has been classified as a NUTS-1 region and is subdivided into two NUTS-2 regions, while at the NUTS-3 level, Slovenia is subdivided into twelve regions corresponding to the precedent statistical regions. It was not until the ES Regulation No. 105/2007 as of January 1, 2008, that Slovenia was divided into the two cohesion regions at the NUTS-2 level.

Figure 1: **NUTS-2 and NUTS-3 regions in Slovenia**

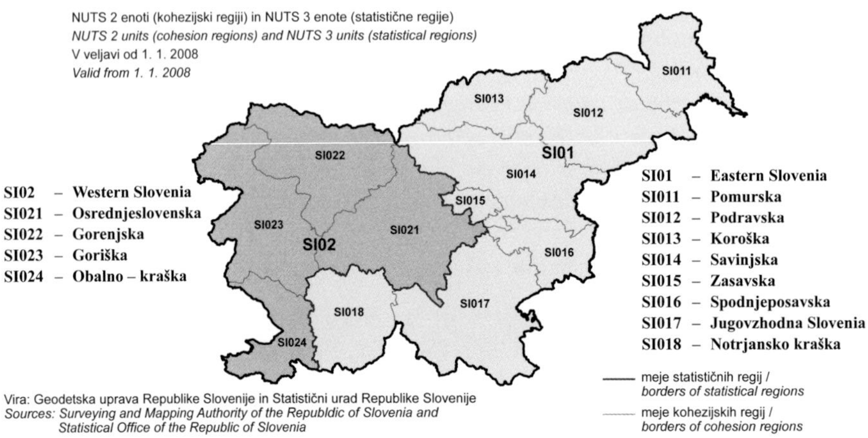

Source: SORS

The survey comprises the period 1995-2008, in which the transition of the Slovenian economy took place. Slovenia joined the European Union in May 2004 and introduced the Euro January 1, 2007. These events affected the economic development of Slovenia most decisively.

Significant regional differences in economic development were already pointed out as early as in 1969 in a collection of selected papers by a group of intellectuals ("The Full and the Hungry Slovenians" [Siti in lačni Slovenci]). Political circles responded to it by adopting legislation to promote less developed areas. The state allowed investments into infrastructure and the opening of new posts, particularly in labour-intensive industrial sectors with a lower Gross Value Added (GVA). But the results of these investments did not meet expectations and had no significant effect on lessening regional disparities. The trend towards emigration of younger, educated people to the better developed urban areas continued.

Transition and the period after independence generated a new economic situation that had a significantly deepening effect on regional disparities. First signs of crisis appeared in areas with a traditional structure of processing industries. The loss of the Yugoslavian market and an inability to adapt to the new market conditions resulted in a decline of traditional industry sectors, especially the labour-intensive.

For an in-depth analysis of regional disparities adequate statistical data were missing. The Statistical Office of the Republic of Slovenia (SORS) published the first data on regional GDP as late as in 1999 for the year 1996. It was only after 2000 that periodical regional statistical data (by SORS) and topical working papers treating regions in a more comprehensive way, also from the viewpoint of economic geography (by the Institute of Macroeconomic Analyses and Development, IMAD), were published. It is also one of the main strategic goals of the European Union (EU) to lessen regional disparities, both within individual member states as well as in border and contact areas (Bufon 2008) and the newly-established euroregions.

Although Slovenia is one of the European countries with the smallest regional disparities, those are present and even widening. The difference between the most and the least developed region in the country amounted to a 1:1.9 ratio in terms of GDP (Piry 2006) until the end of the millennium. It was in 2001, when this ratio exceeded 1:2 for the first time; and in 2008 it approached 1:2.2.

Characteristically enough for the majority of new EU member states, regional disparities were increasing faster due to a fast economic development based on extensive Foreign Direct Investment (FDI) inflow and a growing share of foreign banks in the new states' financial markets.

It is particularly interesting that a fast growth of GDP resulted everywhere in widening regional disparities. Many authors came to the conclusion that an increasing GDP means a smoothing of regional disparities in high-developed countries, while it means exactly the opposite for medium-developed countries. This is very true for Slovenia, where regional disparities widened during the period of the strongest economic growth. This is logical with regard to the fact that growth of the less developed regions should be much faster than growth of the most developed.

2 Historical summary

Disparities in development and well-being between individual regions have been a part of the history of mankind since the very beginning, when division of work and decision-making amongst the members of human society occurred. Earlier, they depended primarily on natural resources and individuals, whose decisions affected interpersonal relations.

Comprehensive and long-term changes, however, were caused by the Industrial Revolution. By means of the Southern Railway from Vienna [Wien] to Trieste, industrialisation reached Slovenian regions as well. New industrial centres began to develop fastly affecting demographic trends in the area.

Although a very small country of little more than 20,000 sq.km, Slovenia has regions with very distinct historical and cultural identities that are not only apparent in the cultural landscape, but also deep-rooted in the consciousness of the population. These identities (Carniola [Kranjska], Styria [Štajerska], Carinthia [Koroška], the Littoral [Primorsko], Prekmurje) have been founded by the lands of the Habsburg Empire existing from the Middle Ages (13th century) up to 1918. They express themselves a.o. by styles of architecture, dialects as well as ecclesiastical subdivisions (Jordan 2003).

Upon creation of the Kingdom of Serbs, Croats and Slovenes after World War I, the Slovenian regions, within the Austro-Hungarian Monarchy rather the less-developed, became the most developed regions of the new kingdom. During this period, industry was spatially concentrated in the form of a so-called "industrial crescent". The remaining areas were in economic decline and their demographic structure became unfavourable.

After World War II, a change in the economic system occurred and, following the model of the Soviet Union, state-induced industrialisation accompanied by the generation of a labour class was set as the utmost priority, which caused cities to grow fast. A negative attitude towards private agricultural production in association with forced collectivisation supported the depopulation of rural areas. These socio-economic processes resulted in growing regional disparities. In their work "Siti in lačni Slovenci" intellectuals warned of the inacceptable lagging behind of rural areas in comparison to the fast-growing urban centres as early as in 1969.

In his work "Spatial Influences of Slovenian Regional Policy" Janez Nared (2007) divided the post-war era into three periods. According to Nared the first period (1971-1991) of promoting less-developed areas began in the 1970s, when the government adopted the Act on Measures to Accelerate Development in Less-developed Areas of the SR of Slovenia (1971) thus beginning to implement an active policy in lessening regional disparities. The Act defined the criteria of defining less-developed areas and provided for instruments to improve the conditions given. The approach used was top-down, which in fact, during the first phase of moving labour-intensive sectors to rural areas, generated a lot of new jobs. At that time, however, the developed part of the global economy had already shifted to the post-industrial stage. The start of transition of the Slovenian economy coinciding with social changes in eastern European countries and Slovenian independence then revealed structural weaknesses of the economy and its unpreparedness for transition to market economy.

The second period (1991-1999) started with the adoption of the Development Promotion in Demographically Endangered Areas Act as an answer to a sharp deterioration of the demographic situation in Slovenia. When defining problem areas, economic criteria were discarded entirely and the process of defining was based on demographic indicators at the level of local communities and settlements. On the background of a lack of funding and an all but perfect strategy, such an approach was necessarily bound to fail.

According to European legislation, Slovenia's preparations for entering the EU called for a changed approach in solving regional disparities. Therefore, the Promotion of Balanced Regional Development Act, adopted in 1999, put regional policy on a completely new set of foundations. It asserted the principle of endogenity and partnership with the newly established institutional structure.

3 Sectoral structure of regional economies and regional disparities

Transition to market economy and the abandoning of the Socialist model of the economy resulted in significant shifts between economic sectors. The most affected during the crisis period at the beginning of transition were the industrially most developed regions, the Central Slovenian (statistical) Region [Osrednjeslovenska regija] SI021 in particular. They disposed over highly developed manufacturing activities in traditional labour-intensive branches on the one hand and technologically less demanding and energy-wasting production on the other.

The structure of the Slovenian economy has changed significantly since 1991 similar to other countries. The share of agricultural activities in GDP dropped by more than a half, i.e. from 5.7% of the GDP in 1991 to 2.5% in 2008. There was also a sharp decrease in the share of industry and construction; these activities were creating 44% of the GDP in 1991 and only 33.8% in 2010. There was, in contrast, a strong increase in the share of services, i.e. from 50% in 1991 to 63.6% in 2008.

In 1995, the GDP index of the Central Slovenian Region was 138 (Slovenia in total, SVN = 100), which means that the regional disparity factor was 1: 1.38. It reached the lowest value in 1997 and 1998, when it amounted to 1:1.37, while it was the highest in 2003, 2006 and 2007, when it totalled to 1:1.44. The average value of the relevant time period amounts to 1:1.404 – the absolute difference being 0.07.

The development of the Central Slovenian Region is based on a structure of GDP comparable with the most developed countries. For the year 2008, the share in GVA of agriculture is 1%, of industry 23.6% and of services 75.4%. Slovenia's capital city belongs to this region affecting its economic power. In the period 1995-1999, the share of the Central Slovenian Region in the overall Slovenian GDP amounted to 33.6% +/– 0.3%, between 2000 and 2004 it was 34.9 +/– 0.8 and in the period 2005-2008 as high as 36.1 +/– 0.2% (see Tables 1, 2 and 3).

Based on data for Slovenia in total (NUTS-1) and the cohesion regions (NUTS-2) compared to the best-developed NUTS-3 region, calculations show that Eastern Slovenia (SI01) had the best ratio in 1998, when it totalled to 1:1.61 (Western Slovenia – SI02 – 1:1.15 in 1997), and the worst in 2006 – 1:1.75 (Western Slovenia – SI01 – 1:1.20 in 2006) (see Figure 2). In other words: The difference between the minimum and the maximum distance of Eastern Slovenia (SI01) from the Central Slovenian Region as the best developed NUTS-3 region in Slovenia amounts to 0.14 (0.05).

Figure 2: **Regional disparities of Slovenia (NUTS-1, SVN) and of the NUTS-2 regions (SI01 and SI02) by GDP compared to the Central Slovenian Region (SI021)**

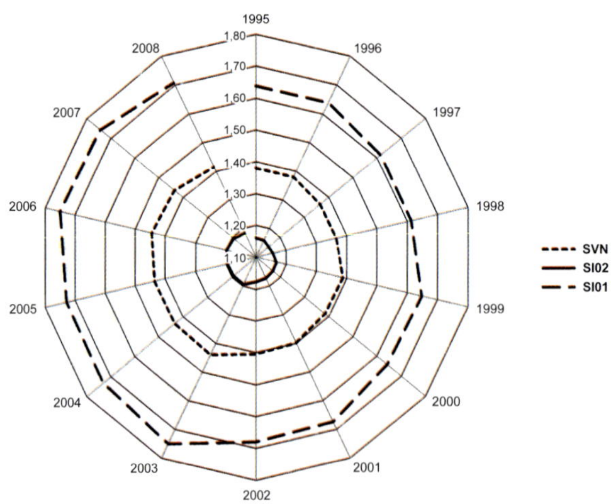

Source: SORS, author's own calculations

During the entire period 1995-2008, disparities between the two cohesion regions and the Central Slovenian Region (SI021) diminished (compared to SI01 by -0.02 and to SI01 by -0.01), most affected by the fall of GDP in 2008. This is due to the fact that the beginning of the depression was most reflected by the Central Slovenian Region (SI021) suffering the most from the stagnation of investments and stagnating works in the construction sector.

The NUTS-2 region Eastern Slovenia (SI01) comprises 61.5% (Western Slovenia – SI02 – 38.5%) of the Slovenian territory and hosts 52% (48%) of the overall population generating 44.3% (55.7%) of the GDP in 2008. Developmental disparities can be explained by the GVA structure by sectors, since Eastern Slovenia still holds 3.9% in agriculture (Western Slovenia 1.4%), 41.9% in industry (27.4%) and 54.2% (71.1%) in services.

Figure 3: **Changes in GVA by economic sectors at NUTS-1, -2 and -3 levels**

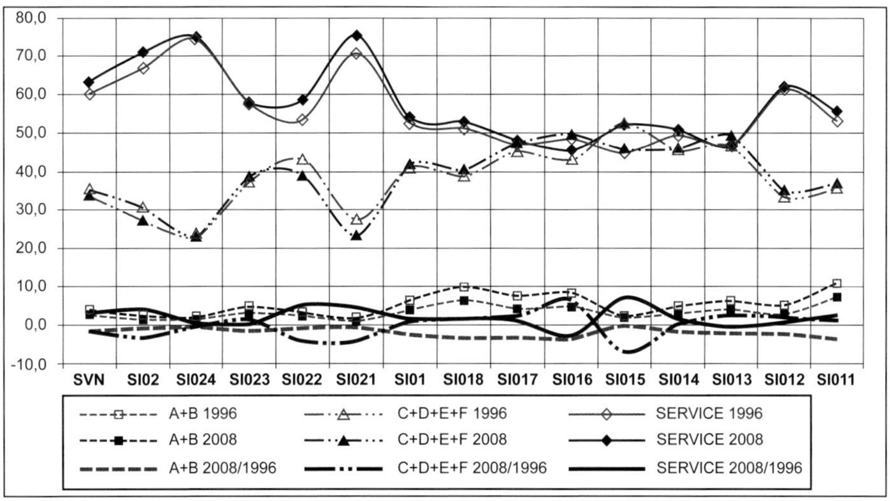

A+B – Agriculture, C+D+E+F – Industry and Construction

Source: SORS, author's own calculations

Industrial production remained at the same level as before independence as late as the year 2000. Most affected by the initial transition crisis were the industrially most developed regions, in particular the Drava Valley Region [Podravska regija] SI012. Characteristic for developed industrial regions in this period were highly developed manufacturing activities in traditional labour-intensive, energy-wasting and technologically less demanding branches (LORBER 2005).

Official data on GVA by regions and economic activities have been made available only since 1995 and are so far available up to the year 2008. We divided this period into three time sets, the first comprising the years 1995-1999. During this time, the Development Promotion in Demographically Endangered Areas in the Republic of Slovenia Act was in force (in force actually between 1991 and 1999).

Table 1: **Change of the regional disparity factor compared to the previous year (1996-1999)**

	SVN	*SI02*	*SI024*	*SI023*	*SI022*	*SI021*	*SI01*	*SI018*	*SI017*	*SI016*	*SI015*	*SI014*	*SI013*	*SI012*	*SI011*
1996	0.00	0.00	**-0.01**	**-0.01**	0.00	0.00	0.00	**-0.01**	0.01	0.00	0.01	0.02	0.00	**-0.01**	0.00
1997	**-0.01**	**-0.01**	0.01	**-0.02**	**-0.04**	0.00	**-0.02**	**-0.04**	**-0.05**	**-0.05**	**-0.02**	**-0.02**	**-0.01**	**-0.02**	**-0.01**
1998	0.00	0.01	0.00	0.02	0.01	0.00	**-0.01**	**-0.01**	**-0.02**	**-0.07**	0.02	0.01	**-0.01**	0.00	0.02
1999	0.02	0.01	0.04	0.01	0.06	0.00	0.04	0.07	0.03	0.07	0.04	0.03	0.03	0.01	0.11

Source: SORS, author's own calculations

It is characteristic for this period (see Table 1) that regional disparities between statistical regions were rather low (ratio 1995-1998 1:1.85), while they increased rapidly in 1999 up to the ratio of 1:1.96. Except the year 2003, 1999 was the only year when none of the regions reduced its backlog compared to the leading Central Slovenian Region (SI021). As a sum of the whole period, backlogs compared to the Central Slovenian Region were diminished only in three regions, i.e. in Southeast Slovenia [Jugovzhodna Slovenia] (SI017), the Lower Sava Valley Region [Spodnjeposavska regija] (SI016) and the Drava Valley Region (SI012). These regions disposed over the most developed industry and were the first to start restructuring traditional industrial activities. In this period, only one region, the Mura Valley Region [Pomurska regija] (SI011) exceeded the limit of +0.10 by +0.12; all other regions remained below 0.05.

Table 2: **Change of the regional disparity factor compared to the previous year (2000-2004)**

	SVN	*SI02*	*SI024*	*SI023*	*SI022*	*SI021*	*SI01*	*SI018*	*SI017*	*SI016*	*SI015*	*SI014*	*SI013*	*SI012*	*SI011*
2000	0.00	0.00	0.00	0.01	0.00	0.00	**-0.01**	**-0.04**	**-0.01**	**-0.03**	0.07	0.01	**-0.07**	**-0.02**	0.03
2001	0.01	0.00	0.03	0.01	0.00	0.00	0.03	0.04	0.01	0.02	0.12	0.05	0.03	0.03	0.02
2002	0.00	0.01	0.00	0.03	0.02	0.00	0.01	**-0.01**	0.03	0.02	0.06	**-0.01**	0.05	**-0.01**	0.03
2003	0.04	0.01	0.05	0.07	0.06	0.00	0.07	0.10	0.05	0.14	0.10	0.06	0.10	0.05	0.08
2004	**-0.01**	0.00	0.00	**-0.01**	0.02	0.00	**-0.02**	0.01	**-0.04**	**-0.02**	0.00	**-0.02**	0.00	**-0.02**	**-0.01**

Source: SORS, author's own calculations

The second period, between 2000 and 2004, was a time of intensive preparations for Slovenia's EU access. To overcome the weaknesses of the preceding regional policy and for the sake of an approximation to European guidelines, the Promotion of Balanced Regional Development Act was adopted in 1999. This Act meant an entirely new foundation and introduced endogenous development as a means of solving regional issues.

An analysis of the period from the adoption of the Act to Slovenia's access to the EU shows that despite a good Act, disparities were not lessening; quite the opposite, the period was the most turbulent one (see Table 2).

In 2000, five of the eight NUTS-3 regions of Eastern Slovenia (NUTS-2) reduced their backlog compared to Slovenia's leading region SI021, the Carinthian Region [Koroška regija] (SI013) most of all, while in 2001 and 2003 none of them did so and in 2004 as many as six of the regions reduced it. In this period, average GDP growth at the state level was higher resulting in an overall widening of regional disparities due to a stronger growth in the most developed regions. The region to widen its backlog least was the Drava Valley Region SI012 (+0.03), while the region to do it the most was the Sava Region [Zasavska regija] SI015 (+ 0.35), where the coal mines were closed down. The limit of 0.10 was also exceeded by the Gorica Region [Goriška regija] SI023 (+0.11), the Lower Sava Valley Region SI016 (+0.13), the Carinthian Region SI013 (+0.11) and the Mura Valley Region SI011 (+0.15).

Regional disparities in 2000 were 1:1.989 and grew by 2004 up to the ratio of 1:2.118, which was mainly a result of the fast development of the Central Slovenian Region and the structure of GVA by economic sectors. The majority of industrially developed regions widened their distance to the leading region during this period due to the fact that restructuring the production into producing more demanding products with higher added value was not fast and efficient enough. The Drava Valley Region (SI012) is an exception, since it was one of the first to overcome economic problems owing to the fact that the structure of its industrial sector was founded on traditional industrial sectors whose prevailing market was common Yugoslavia (Lorber 2008).

The third period corresponds to the time after Slovenia's access to the EU (see Table 3). During this period the economy was growing extremely fast. GDP growth was based on rapid increase of exports and structural changes in industry, where production of medium- and high-level products gained at the expense of labour-intensive production. It is characteristic for this period that the negative trend of growing regional disparities stopped and as many as six regions reduced their gap to the leading region, most successfully the Lower Sava Valley Region SI016 (-0.07), the Coastland-Karst Region [Obalno-kraška regija] SI0124 (-0.05), the industrially developed Southeast Slovenia (SI017), the Carinthian Region SI012 (-0.04) and the Savinja Region [Savinjska regija] SI014 (-0.03). Backlog grew the most in the Sava Region (SI015), namely by as much as +0.14.

Table 3: **Change of the regional disparity factor compared to the previous year (2005-2008)**

	SVN	***SI02***	*SI024*	*SI023*	*SI022*	*SI021*	***SI01***	*SI018*	*SI017*	*SI016*	*SI015*	*SI014*	*SI013*	*SI012*	*SI011*
2005	0.00	0.00	0.02	**-0.01**	0.00	0.00	0.00	0.03	**-0.01**	**-0.05**	0.03	**-0.01**	**-0.03**	0.02	0.04
2006	0.01	0.01	0.00	0.01	0.03	0.00	0.02	0.04	0.00	0.05	0.06	0.02	0.06	**-0.01**	0.05
2007	0.00	**-0.01**	**-0.03**	**-0.01**	**-0.01**	0.00	**-0.01**	**-0.02**	**-0.01**	0.00	0.05	0.01	**-0.01**	**-0.02**	0.00
2008	**-0.02**	**-0.01**	**-0.04**	**-0.01**	**-0.01**	0.00	**-0.03**	0.00	**-0.02**	**-0.07**	0.00	**-0.05**	**-0.02**	**-0.03**	**-0.02**

Source: SORS, author's own calculations

An analysis of the whole examined period (see Table 4) shows that the worst breakdown occurred in the Sava Region (SI015), where the backlog compared to the Central Slovenian Region (SI021) increased by 0.55. Second ranks the Mura Valley Region (SI011) with an increase of 0.34. In the whole period from 1995 to 2008, only the industrially developed Southeast Slovenia (SI017) with its pharmaceutical and automobile industry as well as its well-performing energy sector, and the Carinthian Region (SI012), which was the only to start comprehensive restructuring immediately after 1991, when the largest decrease of GDP occurred (LORBER 2010), lessened their distance to the leading region, namely by 0.03 points.

Table 4: **Change of the regional disparity factor compared to the previous year (1995-2008)**

	SVN	***SI02***	*SI024*	*SI023*	*SI022*	*SI021*	***SI01***	*SI018*	*SI017*	*SI016*	*SI015*	*SI014*	*SI013*	*SI012*	*SI011*
Average 95- 08	0.04	0.02	0.07	0.09	0.14	0.00	0.07	0.16	**-0.03**	0.01	0.55	0.10	0.12	**-0.03**	0.34

Source: SORS, author's own calculations

4 Future directions

Janez NARED (2007) presents a comprehensive analysis of the conditions in his "Spatial Influences of Slovenian Regional Policy" and conceives a directed polycentric development of cities as an opportunity for better regional development. David BOLE's (2008) "Economic Transition in Slovene Cities" is logically associated with this idea. The paradigm of Postfordism can sufficiently explain economic transition and its main results – the de-industrialisation and tertiarisation of urban space. Polycentricism in the urban region is a possible solution to alleviate the emerging unsustainable spatial patterns that are direct outcomes of economic transition (Bole 2008).

These considerations can be applied to transitional processes of NUTS-3 regions. Polycentric strengthening of cities based on the paradigm of endogenity could generate a creative environment for further development. Local communities should use an interdisciplinary approach to search for advantages and opportunities both at the local and the regional level. They should also attract young, professionally trained co-operators who could, having elaborated proper development programmes, apply for European cohesion funds as well as solicit for FDI stakeholders. Only a critical analysis of the current conditions and a wide scope of new development programmes based on natural and human resources can assure appropriate restructuring of the existing local and regional economy.

In the past years the main focus was laid on improving infrastructure, which – due to a lack of investments into small and medium-sized enterprises – actually deepened regional disparities. In order to improve the sectoral structure, GVA and investments into Research and Development (R&D) will have to increase significantly. In the year 2008 the ratio of investment into R&D between Western and Eastern Slovenia was 71.3:28.7 as a percentage of Slovenia in total.

5 Conclusions

Regional disparities between Slovenian NUTS-3 regions are the result of structural inadequacy of regional economies. As data show, only two regions exceed the average of Slovenia: Central Slovenian Region and Coastland-Karst Region. These statistical regions have a sectoral structure of the economy similar to developed countries. All other regions have problems, larger or smaller. Most endangered are border regions and regions lacking adequate transport links to the motorway network. Contrary to other new states, Slovenia had a reserved attitude towards FDI and a liberalisation of the banking system. Considering that it entered transition with the highest GDP by Purchasing Power Parities (PPPs) and also due to its smallness, Slovenia was divided into two NUTS-2 regions, which facilitate its drawing on European cohesion funds, since Eastern Slovenia reaches less than 75% GDP in PPPs of the EU-27 average, which is the limit when drawing from European funds.

In 2009 Slovenia fell into a deep economic crisis. Rapid growth after EU access was based on rapid growth of export and cheap money, which promoted excessive growth in building of homes, business and sports facilities on a mortgage basis. In 2009 the breakdown of the building industry began, which affected also building materials and equipment industry. Access to money became extremely difficult practically over night. Difficulties of large building companies affected their subcontractors, which resulted in a large number of bankruptcy processes of small enterprises.

This time of recession should be used to implement distinct structural economic changes which will enable creating and growth of high-quality jobs. This means that the labour market will have to become more flexible and that educational reforms will have to be implemented. Restructuring of the public sector is supposed to be a priority to ensure social cohesion, which is the European Union's global advantage in the context of quality of life and development of democracy.

By consistent implementation of regional integration processes and changing priorities regarding European structural resources, a network of European economic power centres will develop, which will be able to reduce regional disparities using their multifunctional influences.

The current crisis, paradoxically, may provide more political space to make these kinds of changes possible, given the widely shared experience of severe economic insecurity of all relevant actors in society.

6 Bibliography

Bole D. (2008), Economic Transition in Slovene Cities. Ljubljana, Založba ZRC.

Bufon M. (2008), Na obrobju ali v osredju? Slovenska obmejna območja pred izzivi evropskega povezovanja (= Knjižnica Annales Majora). Koper, Univerza na Primorskem, Znanstveno-raziskovalno središče, Založba Annales: Zgodovinsko društvo za južno Primorska.

European Parliament, Directorate General Internal Policies of the Union (ed.) (2007), Regional disparities and Cohesion: What strategies for the future, Study. http://www.europarl.europa.eu/hearings/20070625/regi/study_en.pdf

Institute of Macroeconomic Analyses and Development (IMAD) (ed.), http://www.umar.gov.si/en/zapisi/?no_cache=1

Jordan P. (2005), Major Problems of Administrative Regionalisation and Decentralisation in Central and Southeast Europe. In: Acta Universitatis Carolinae, Geographica, XXXVIII, 1, pp. 141–155.

Lorber L. (2005), Regional development problems of Podravje. In: Podravina (Samobor), 4, 8, pp. 107–120.

Lorber L. (2008), Sloweniens Weg von einer Agrargesellschaft zum postindustriellen Staat. In: Volker A. (ed.), Slowenien: Transformationen und kleinräumige Vielfalt (= Natur – Raum – Gesellschaft, 5), pp. 186–206. Frankfurt am Main, Institut für Humangeographie.

Lorber L. (2010), Socio-economic trends in contemporary Central and Eastern Europe: the case of Slovenia. In: Acta Univ. Palacki. Olomouc, Geographica, 41, 1, pp. 35–49.

Nared J. (2007), Spatial Influences of Slovenian Regional Policy. Ljubljana, Založba ZRC.

Piry I. (2006), Vpliv programov predpristopne pomoči EU na razvoj obmejnih območij Slovenije v obdobju 1994-2004. In: Dela 25, pp. 109–121.

Rotar J. , Forstnerič F. (eds.), (1969), Siti in lačni Slovenci. Maribor, Založba Obzorja.

Statistical Office of the Republic of Slovenia (SORS) (ed.), http://www.stat.si/eng/index.asp

Re-defining Slovenian Touristic Regions

Anton Gosar, Koper/Capodistria[*]

with 8 figures and 2 tables in the text

Content

Summary 109
1 Introduction 110
2 The frame 112
3 Tourism strategies and tourism regions 115
4 Conclusion 124
5 Bibliography 124

Summary

Twenty years ago, the post-Socialist transition and civil war in wider parts of Yugoslavia resulted in a widespread discussion on future tourism development and priorities. Slovenia has, since becoming a nation state, produced three tourism development strategies within which regional characters were bundled into diverse packages as tourism destinations. This paper examines the different ways Slovenia's territory was subdivided into selective units for tourism purposes. A wider socio-economic and geo-political frame is observed as "tourism destination sub-regions" have been created. The physical landscape and character, and even the natural and cultural heritage elements, are playing an increasingly weak role in the definition of contemporary touristic regions. Tourism products promoting experience, entertainment and adventure as well as human-made attractions (including cultural events and events based on tradition) are the primar decision maker(s) in contemporary attempts to characterize specific macro-, meso- or micro- touristic regions.

[*] Anton Gosar, Prof. PhD., Department of Geography, Faculty of Humanities, University of Primorska, Titov trg 5, SI-6000 Koper/Capodistria, Slovenia; e-mail: anton.gosar@hs.upr.si

1 Introduction

Tourism is a profit-making economy. According to BUTLER's model of the lifecycle of a tourist destination (BUTLER & ARAMBERI 2005), to overcome saturation and increase profits, a change in the supply part of the economy is needed. This could be achieved through several ways of action; one often-used method is related to the restructuring and to the re-vision of the geographic size or general features of the destination. The purpose of defining and re-defining geographic regions for tourism purposes – thus spacious areas/places of outstanding and/or unique attraction(s) – is therefore to characterize attractive area(s) and, as result, receive economic benefits by pinpointing and designating the site of the attraction. In such geographically wider or narrower (newly) defined regions the natural, historical, cultural and human resources, out of which one or more tourism products could be produced, are rediscovered and/or re-invented. The new tourism products could than subsequently initiate a follow-up regionalization, where specific elements of nature, culture and/or human-made attractions become the core of promotion and subsequently profit.

Countries by themselves are "touristic destinations" and therewith touristic regions – as by their own territorial sovereignty, history, language, law, natural and cultural heritage, etc. The ITB Berlin [Internationale Tourismus Börse] and similar events in London, Milan [Milano], and elsewhere are events, where close to 200 countries world-wide express their own "destination" characters as nation states. They tend to draw attention by summarizing their own promotional characteristics in single sentences. Most often the country's natural, people's cultural, history's outstanding and citizen's warm attitudes/characters, as well as hidden (regional) treasures are addressed (Table 1). Promotional slogans tend to change in regard to politics and/or trends within the tourism supply and demand spheres. In the contemporary tourism world, traditional attractions related to history and outstanding places of nature and culture tend to be replaced by eco-awareness slogans, by experience/adventure provisions, or by friendly cultural endowment.

In this contribution we will concentrate on the strategy of tourism development and tourism regionalization in the Alps-Adriatic geographic area of Central and Southeast Europe, in particular on Slovenia. Tourism attractions of this area have been elaborated on maps and in discussion within the Atlas of Eastern and Southeastern Europe (JORDAN & SCHAPPELWEIN et al. 1999). The attempt to point out attractive places in a wider/broader European area is rather unique. Namely, governments of nation-states and provinces/regions normally would stimulate and financially support scientific research and promotional materials which would concentrate on territory under their sovereignty. Now, countries and provinces of Central and South East Europe are digging into the material discussed above ("International Tourism Attractions in Central and Southeast

Europe"), select relevant features, and form new promotional strategies which often result in revised strategies and/or (inner-state) touristic regions.

Table 1: **Selection of tourism promotional nation-state advertising**

	Country	***Slogan***
1	Albania	A New Mediterranean
2	Aruba	One Happy Island
3	Belize	Mother Nature's Best Kept Secret
4	Canada	Keep Exploring!
5	Croatia	Mediterranean As it Once Was
6	Ecuador	Life at its Purest
7	Egypt	Where It All Begins
8	France	Rendez-Vous En France
9	Germany	Affordable Hospitality
10	Grenada	Rhythms of Spice
11	Hong Kong	Best Place, Best Taste
12	Hungary	A Love for Live
13	Italy	Much More
14	Maldives	Sunny Side of Life
15	Montenegro	Wild Beauty
16	New Zealand	100% Pure
17	Slovakia	Little Big Country
18	Slovenia	Sunny Side of the Alps
19	Spain	Smile! You are in Spain
20	Switzerland	Get Natural!

In the context of the discussion, we have registered that, within nation states, provinces tend to point out their outstanding features as well. In Slovenia's neighboring Austrian Carinthia [Kärnten], slogans tend to be extra- and introverted: "Carinthia – The Land of Waters", "Carinthia – Holidays spent with Friends", and – recently – "Carinthia – The Joy of Life"; in the neighboring Styria [Steiermark] two recent slogans were noticed: "Styria – The Green Hearth of Austria" and "Love Wonders through Styria". In the Italian Friuli-Venezia Giulia the official slogan points out the fact to "Be Guest of Unique People" and in the Croatian Istria [Istra] the slogans calls for "Mediterranean being a Perfect Holiday". Therewith provinces (Länder, regione, županije) are already circling up the tourist region (= destination) being equal to the administrative, political designation.

Provincial trans-boundary concepts are rare. Instead, Central-European nation states' cross-border tourism regions tend to be numerous. (Sadly, they remain often just a political torso, with no added value for the peripheral, border regions.) The positive example of the alpine three-border area of Austria, Italy and Slovenia has been elaborated on several occasions (Moritsch 1998, Gosar 2005, Zimmermann 1998). The almost two decades long attempts (1984-1999) to bring this "destination" on the world map of tourist regions through Winter Olympics failed, but the character of a unified tourist region remained. Along with several cross-border tourism products ("Europeus Sine Finibus", "The White Waters of the 3Borders", "The Diner of Three Cultures", etc.) the promotional naming of the area, developed for the two bids to organize the event, namely "Senza Confini" (Without Borders), continues to exist.

2 The frame

The answer for the trend of (several) re-defining(s) of Slovenian tourist regions is narrowly linked to the disintegration of Yugoslavia and the political and societal changes (from Communism to democracy and from a central-planning economy to the globalized market economy). Regarding tourism trends, three major time-frames are to be distinguished:

(1) Slovenia as province (= Socialist republic) of Yugoslavia;
(2) Slovenia as a sovereign nation-state (Republic of Slovenia) on the edge of Europe's instability area;
(3) Slovenia as member of the European Union, the Euro-zone and the Schengen space.

Slovenia was within Yugoslavia (until 1991) characterized as a tourism transit area/province. Tourism visits have concentrated on the Mediterranean coast of which Slovenia had just 2.2%. But the airline (Adria Airways) and travel agencies (including their duty free shops at border crossings), with its headquarters in Slovenia, participated heavily in the Yugoslav tourism economy – by some estimates with close to 43% (Mihalič 1995). According to international visits in 1988, Slovenia was ranked third among the six Yugoslav republics (13.8% of bed-nights, 1.13 million visitors).

As the disintegration of Yugoslavia turned into a long-lasting military confrontation (Croatia, Bosnia and Herzegovina, Serbia and Montenegro), Slovenia's tourism struggled for survival on the edge of regional instability in the Western Balkans. International visits in 1998 were a mere 23.7% of the number of tourists registered 10 years before. In 2004, Slovenia was accepted as member of the European Union and NATO, in 2007 the country joined the Schengen Space by eliminating border-control posts towards EU member states (and by strengthening the EU outer border), and – in the same year – the Euro (€) was introduced as the national currency. By 2008 international visits finally overrode the number of tourists from 20 years ago: 1.77 million foreign visitors have been registered, among which Italians (21.2%), Germans (11.0%), Austrians (10.9%) and Croatians (6.0%) prevailed (Statistični urad Republike Slovenije 2008).

According to CIGALE (2010), the reason to visit Slovenian touristic regions, resorts and municipalities is highly linked to (1) the outstanding recognition of the resort/region, (2) the accessibility of the place, (3) the major highway network, and (4) the touristic product (which is within the sphere of traditional tourist interest). In this sense, the following types of municipalities are ranked according to foreign tourist visits: (1) mountain resorts, (2) Ljubljana, the capital, (3) non-specified touristic resorts, (4) seaside resorts, (5) health resorts, (6) other localities (STATISTIČNI URAD REPUBLIKE SLOVENIJE 2008). In relation to this fact, we can conclude that Slovenia is mostly known internationally by its mountainous (alpine) environments (see Figure 1). If we add domestic tourism travels, mountainous environments would still prevail, immediately followed by health and seaside resorts (Table 2).

Table 2: **Tourist arrivals and overnight stays by types of tourist resorts (in 1,000)**

Resort type		***1998***		***2002***		***2006***		***2008***	
	All	Visits	*Stays**	Visit	*Stays**	Visit	*Stays**	Visit	Stays*
Mountain resorts		441	1,443	605	1,824	607	1,790	663	1,947
Ljubljana, the capital		141	313	214	437	351	636	372	707
Non-specified resorts		265	532	372	798	380	765	434	895
Seaside resorts		370	1,663	520	2,010	523	1,925	546	1,992
Health resorts		340	1,884	501	2,359	596	2,550	633	2,651
	Intern.								
Mountain resorts		185	657	393	1,245	423	1,276	459	1,384
Ljubljana, the capital		116	259	195	404	334	608	353	676
Non-specified resorts		166	360	287	594	297	572	342	688
Seaside resorts		160	624	280	1,035	293	1,022	305	1,053
Health resorts		93	507	196	850	248	970	266	1,018

*bed-nights

(Source: STATISTIČNI URAD REPUBLIKE SLOVENIJE 2008)

At this point it should be noted that the division of 64 settlements into six categories of tourism towns – according to resort locality and relief characteristics (mountain, seaside) and/or touristic domain (the capital, health resort, non-specified resort, other localities) – is performed solely at the level of the national statistical office (Statistični urad Republike Slovenije, SURS) and has little to do with the country's geographic divisions, tourism strategies or touristic regionalizations performed by other institutions (see Figure 2). But it is a good indicator of recognition of Slovenia's touristic supply by foreign and domestic tourists.

Figure 1: **Slovenia: Major physiographic regions**

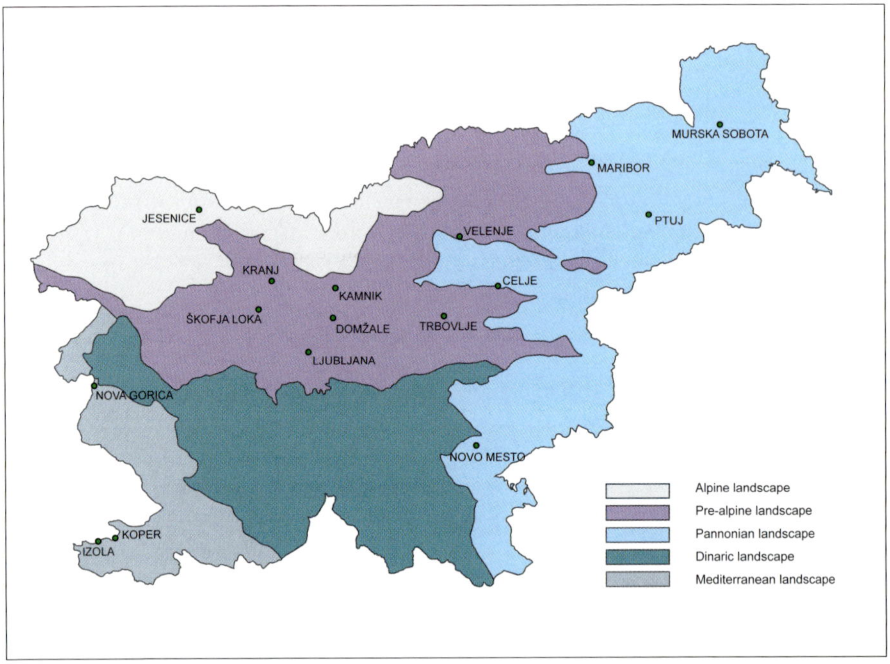

Source: PERKO et al. 1995

Figure 2: **Major tourist resorts**

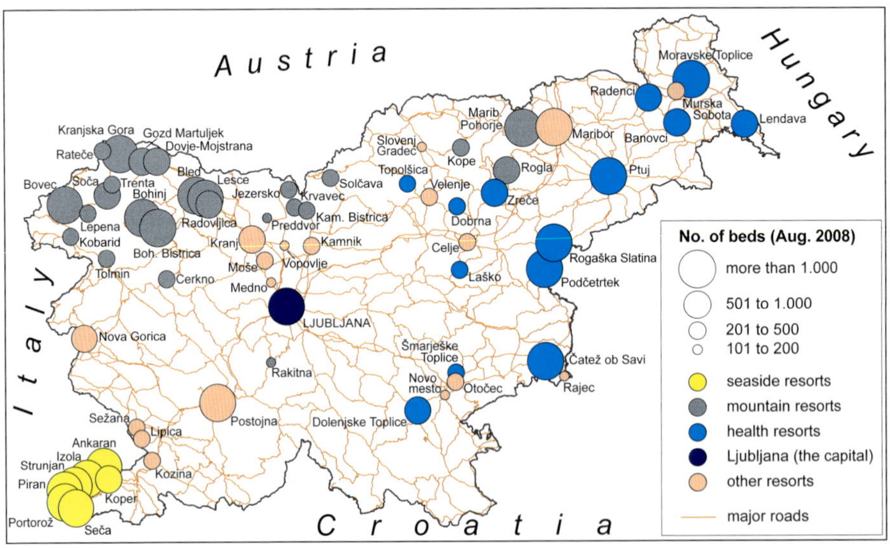

Source: STATISTIČNI URAD REPUBLIKE SLOVENIJE 2008

3 Tourism strategies and tourism regions

In Slovenia the first regionalization devoted to/for tourism was written 45 years ago; the next was published about 20 years later. Two have followed. Authors of the first regionalization could be identified as geographers, whereas the subsequent regionalization attempts have all had the imprint of economists. Whereas the beginner produced a regionalization aimed to place Slovenian tourism supply within the Yugoslav frame, the follow-up regionalizations were meant to give orientation to the restructuring tourism sector after the disintegration of the federal state and proclamation of Slovenia's independence. This work from the mid-1990s was accompanied by a precise and knowledgeable strategy, the basic purpose of which was to overcome burdens of the isolation during the continued instability in the Balkan neighborhood.

Registered regionalization attempts for tourism purposes, in conjunction with adequate tourism strategies, to be discussed are:

(1) Slovenia's Touristic Regions, 1965
(2) Tourism Development Strategy, 1993
(3) Slovenian Tourism Strategy, 2002
(4) Slovenian Tourism Development Plan and Directions, 2007

Geography offered substantial groundwork for the strategies and regionalization in progress. In particular, the territory of the state was thoroughly analyzed since independence. Notable are the following publications: the National Atlas of Slovenia (Fridl et al. 1995), Slovenia – the Tourist Guide (Gosar & Jeršič 1999), Relief of Slovenia (Perko & Orožen Adamič 1995), The Township Gazetteer of Slovenia (Orožen Adamič et al. 1995), Slovenia: People and Places (Perko & Orožen Adamič 1998).

Slovenia had, within the former federation, a substantial autonomy in politics and economy and had even developed its own policy of promotion. The "tourism destination" of the Socialist republic of Slovenia was clearly recognizable within the Yugoslav frame. Slogans like "We, people are tourists" [Turizem smo ljudje] and the slogan with an outstanding geographic touch "Slovenia – on the sunny side of the Alps" [Slovenija – na sončni strani Alp] were established in the 1980s and had had no equivalent in other provinces of Yugoslavia. Since independence in 1991, under the umbrella of the Slovenian Tourism Organization (STO) three slogans have characterized the "touristic destination" of the young nation state: "Slovenia – the Green Piece of Europe" (1994), "Slovenia Invigorates" (2002) and, finally "I Feel S**LOVE**nia" (2007). "Slovenia – the Green Piece of Europe" indicated the geographic fact of Slovenia's 61% forestlands; since the slogan was launched in times of the worst military confrontation in the nearby Croatia, some experts speculate on the intended promotional word-play "peace" vs. "piece".

3.1 Slovenia's Touristic Regions (1965)

Slovenia's territory was subdivided on principles of evaluating natural and cultural heritage sites for tourism purposes in the 1960s. Several authors (ŽAGAR 1976, PLANINA & MIHALIČ 1985, JERŠIČ 1978) have challenged the initial regionalization by KOKOLE (1965), but not one single author questioned the initial four geographic regions as major "tourist destinations": the European (south-eastern) Alps, the Pannonian/Danubian flatlands and hills, the karstic ridge of the Dinaric Alps, and the Mediterranean coastal zone (see Figure 3). Basic regionalization criteria aimed at attracting tourists were based on natural appearance and character. Physical geography was the lead segment of regionalization. Tourism destinations have been formed accordingly (KOKOLE 1965):

- Alpine Slovenia ["Visokogorje"]
  - Julian Alps [Julijske Alpe] and western Karawanken [Karavanke]
  - Eastern Karawanken and Kamnik-Savinja Alps [Kamniške in Savinjske Alpe]
- Pre-Alpine Slovenia ["Predalpski svet"]
  - Breginj nook
  - Cerkno and Škofja loka highlands
  - Ljubljana basin
  - Posavje highlands
  - Celje basin
  - Podravlje highlands and Pohorje
- Dinaric karst ["Dinarsko-kraško ozemlje"]
  - Karstic plains
  - Suha krajina
  - Pivka
  - Brkini and valleys of Podgrad
  - Vipava valley
  - Kras
- Pannonian/Danubian edge [„Panonsko obrobje"]
  - Drava lowlands and hills
  - Slovenske gorice
  - Mura lowlands and Goričko
- Koper seacoast ["Koprsko primorje"]
  - Coastal (Adriatic) plains
  - Istria's hilly hinterland [Šavrini].

Figure 3: **Slovenia: Major tourism regions**

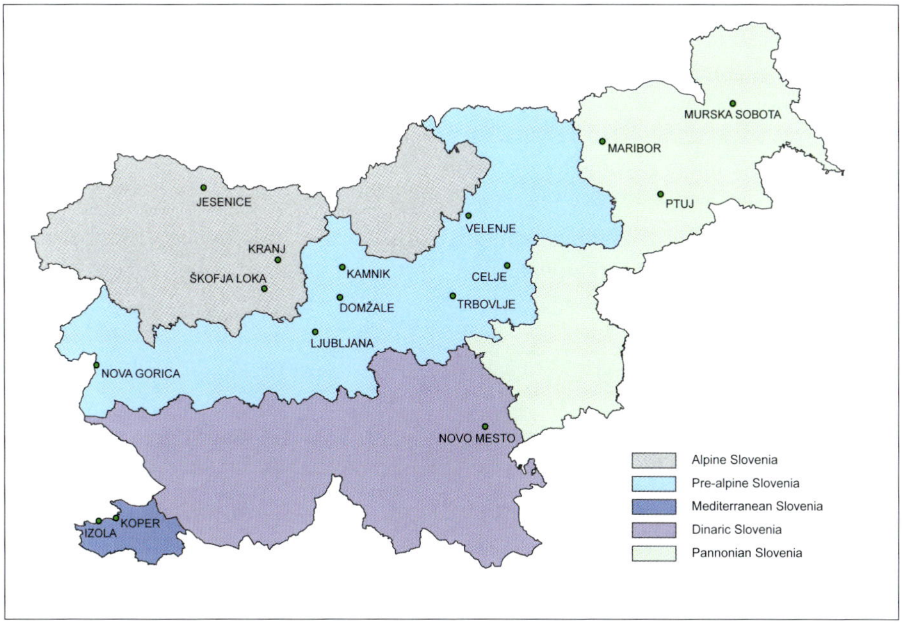

Source: Kokole 1965

3.2 Tourism Development Strategy (1993)

Slovenia's independence called for the re-drawing of tourism policies. The nation state's border in the East and South, towards Croatia, suddenly eliminated the once very lively exchange of knowledge, services, products and financial transactions of the tourism sector of the economy within Yugoslavia. At the same time, it separated for several years areas of military confrontation from the peaceful part of Europe (with the exception of the 10-day war – June/July 1991 – on Slovenian territory). The geo-political situation initiated the first tourism strategy ever developed for the territory of Slovenia (Sirše et al. 1993, Sirše 1995). This initial development strategy distinguished between five "tourism subjects" (see Figure 4):

(1) The Coast and the Karst,
(2) The Mountains and Lakes
(3) The Natural Health Resorts,
(4) The Rural Countryside,
(5) The Historic Towns.

Likewise, the strategy identified several "tourism products" ["turistični proizvodi"] – like biking, skiing, gambling, etc. The strategy warns readers that "tourism subjects" ["turistična področja"] should not be mixed up with "tourism regions" [turistična območja] – despite the fact that some of the naming has geographic connotation. "Tourism subjects" are namely, according to the authors, spheres of activity and should be perceived as destinations in a broader sense of understanding. Within named spheres of activity, initiation of specific tourism products could take place – namely, according to natural and cultural features (= heritage) of the related geographic area.

It must be noted that the geopolitical situation and this strategy of the 1990s, and to some extent related regionalization, in the initiation stage gave wings to the "watering places", mineral and thermal resorts of Slovenia. Tourist visits in "watering places" doubled: in 1988 17.5% and in 2008 34.1% of all bed-nights registered have been made in health resorts (Horvat 2010).

Figure 4: **Slovenia: Tourism regions according to Tourism Development Strategy**

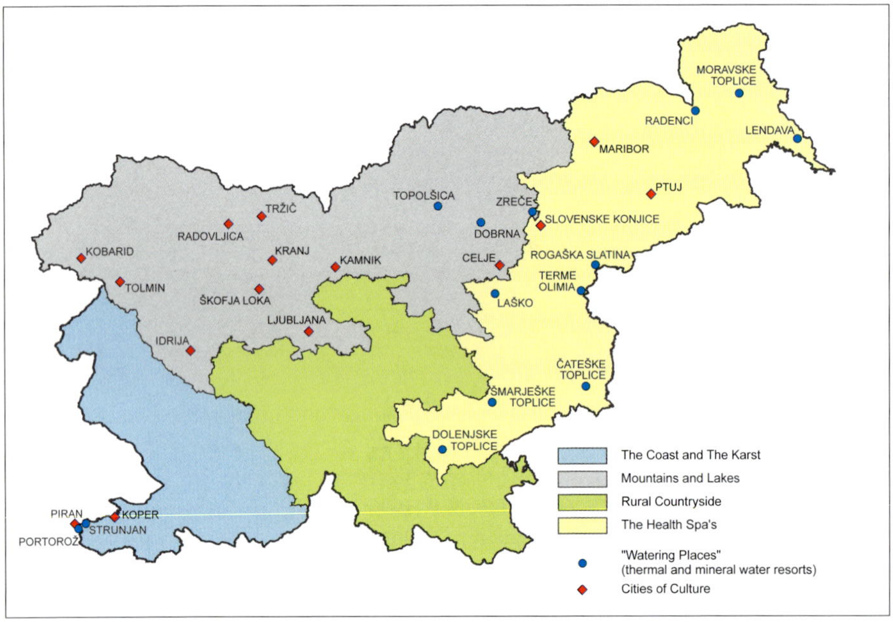

Source: Sirše et al. 1993

3.3 *Strategy of the Slovenian Tourism (2002)*

At the dawn of the 21st century, the first move to break the rule of identifying "touristic regions" with geographic setting was made by an economist, whose basic idea was to subdivide Slovenia by its leading "brand-name" tourism destinations ["blagovne znamke"] – like Portorož/Portorose, Kranjska Gora, Bled, Radenci, Nova Gorica, Ljubljana, etc. – and to point out the importance of the touristic experiences, adventures and entertainment in the contemporary tourism economy (KOVAČ 2002). In accordance with this idea, KOVAČ put Slovenia under the umbrella of 32 Local Tourism Organizations (LTO, now RDO – Regional Destination Organization) – as suggested in the previous strategy – and placed their headquarters in leading tourist resorts (see Figure 5).

Further, KOVAČ's strategy initiated tourism research beyond the classical 3S (sun, sand and sea) segment. In accordance with directions set above, along with his 3A (activity and adventure tourism), 3E (rural, responsible and eco-tourism) and 3D (experience and entertainment tourism) he foresaw (just) 3 major geographic spheres "the Sunny Alps", "the Green Mediterranean" and the "Mysterious Karst" worthwhile to promote.

To reach the goal set by KOVAČ, the Slovenian Tourist Board (STO) accepted the proposal of Imago Slovenia, a consultant firm, to switch its promotional activity from the slogan "Slovenia – The Green Piece of Europe" to "Slovenia Invigorates" and to oversee six promotional segments: "Invigorate your Senses", "Invigorate your Imagination", "Invigorate your Passion", "Invigorate your Body", "Invigorate your Soul", "Invigorate your Drive" (STO 2004). Geography was moved to the periphery of interest, while the visitor's motives have been put into the foreground of advertisement. Micro-

Figure 5: **Slovenia: Casino' Resorts and its regional development area, 2002**

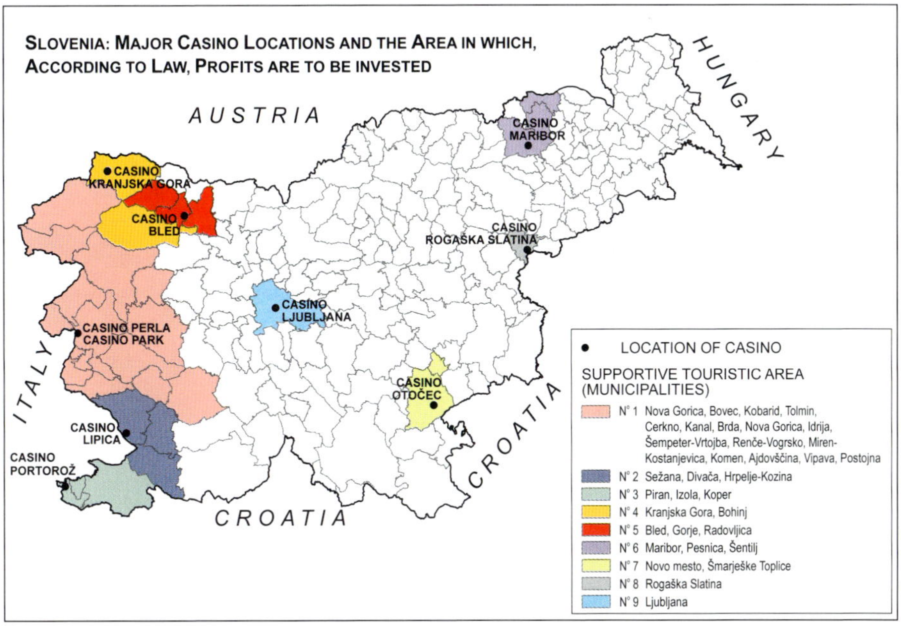

centers of tourism (most often well-known resorts) responsible for the development of a larger tourist region were created. According to law, even gaming enterprises have had their own share of responsibility for the region of their existence.

3.4 Development plan and directions of Slovenian tourism (2006)

After Slovenia's inclusion in EU political and financial structures, discussion flamed up within the tourism sector of the economy about the relatively small scale of the nation state's space. The fact that in transit towards Croatia millions of tourists remain on four lane highways and crisscross Slovenia in a couple of hours, without being acquainted with the country's specifics, produced the idea of re-routing tourists off highways. The product "Byways are More Attractive than Highways" along with the phrase "Let's take the next exit" were born. Diverse geographic regions now have intermingled with each other in 6 north-south/south-north highway (better: byway) directions. New "subjects of tourism" and tourism regions have been created. The following touristic regions, based on geographic, historic and cultural heritage have set foot (STO 2005) (see Figure 6):

- Emerald Route (from the sources of the Soča River to innumerable green treasures)
- Wind Route (to the mysterious Karst and the Adriatic Sea)
- Amber Route (on the trail of our ancestors)
- Sun Route (through the warm region of wine and healing waters)
- Peddler Route (from all corners of the world to the white birches)
- Gold horn Route (with a view of Alps and lakes)

In 2006 researchers at Turistica – College of Tourism, Portorož/Portorose (University of Primorska) concluded that efforts to recognize the "destination Slovenia" have not been sufficient and that the existent tourism strategy needs to be enriched with changes in the supply-side of the economy. In their strategy they have pointed out that the exclusive geostrategic position of the nation state can be a burden and opportunity at the same time. The gateway character of the country could be linked to the European cores of tourism (Venice [Venezia], Salzburg, Vienna [Wien], …), to meetings and exhibits of particular branches, and at the same time to the promotion of specific features of Slovenia (even to tourists in transit). Entertainment, including casinos and wellness programs, in particular on 87 mineral and thermal water locations, should become the identity mark of Slovenia. Tourism products must be linked to already established attractions – like to thematic paths and biking routes, as well as to enology tourism and vine routes. The supply side of tourism should be (re-)arranged to the expectation of the 3 leading cultures visiting (50% +): the Italians, the Germans and the Austrians (URAN & OVSENIK 2006).

Figure 6: **Slovenia: Tourism regions according to tourism product "Byways are More Attractive than Highways"**

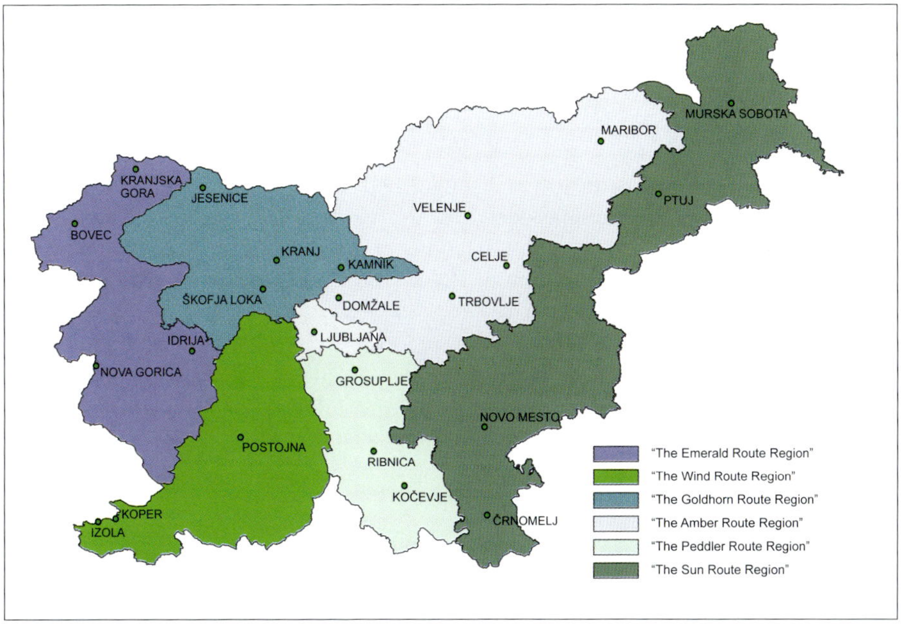

Source: STO 2005

3.5 Tourism's diverse contemporary regionalization

In the follow-up implementation of the above discussed strategy by the Slovenian Tourist Board's development plans and directions ["Razvojni načrt in usmeritve slovenskega turizma"] tourism products have become the lead element in tourism promotion and in the creation of contemporary touristic regions. Geography has been regarded only as a general environmental factor to be considered and partly, on a small scale in specific socially/historically related contexts, for example in conjunction with gastro- and enological features (= products).

Authors of the 2006 tourism strategy implementation (VESENJAK & RAVNIKAR 2007) have deliberated on two issues:

(A) the national tourism product ("Slovenia 4U")

(B) the regional tourism products ("Slovenia Diverse")

Within frame A (national tourism product) nine sets of activity spheres (not to be identified with any geographic macro-region) have been identified:

- "Slovenia Adventure" – activity rich leisure
- "Slovenia Nature" – countryside holidays
- "Slovenia Culture" – town and country experience
- "Slovenia Culinary" – food and wine tasting
- "Slovenia Balance" – health and wellness programs
- "Slovenia Meetings" – business travels
- "Slovenia Life" – gaming and gambling
- "Slovenia Prestige" – special event holidays
- "Young People's Slovenia" – youth tourism

Within frame B, regions are to be distinguished on the product bases. The gastronomy tourism product, for example, identifies 24 regions (see Figure 7). Every single region's typical dish is described and locations of taste advertised – like for example for region 17 – the "Culinary Region of Rovte, Idrija and Cerkno": *Typical dishes of the region (idrijski žlikrofi, smukavc, zelševka, etc.) may be also tasted in the following restaurants: Kmečki hram Fortuna and Kos in Idrija and in Kendov dvorec hotel in Sp. Idrija that was built in the 14th century; Kendov dvorec in Sp. Idriji, full of relics of the past, continues with preserving the rich culinary tradition in the way how the ancient local dishes are being prepared in the "nouvelle cuisine" style.* (STO 2009)

Figure 7: **Slovenia: Culinary regions**

Source: STO 2009

Further deliberations among authors of the tourism strategy No. 4 (2006) resulted in the conviction that some tourism products could be promoted and experienced only on a geographic micro-scale, where certain historic environments, traditions and social/cultural knowledge exist. The forthcoming Slovenian tourism strategy No. 5 (2012) would again put the importance of the geographic frame forward. Namely, the Official Gazette of the Republic of Slovenia just recently stated that "the tourist regions are geographically rounded up areas of one or more municipalities which offer defined touristic services and/or tourism products in their entirety and are therefore becoming travel destinations of tourists." (Republika Slovenija 2011).

According to diverse sources, 15 to 23 tourism regions (Slovenia info 2010, Kos Grabnar 2010) have been identified (from West to East; the endonyms of regions are in brackets, see Figure 8): The Adriatic Coast [Obala]; The Adriatic Karst [Primorski Kras]; The Karst of Inner Carniola [Notranjski Kras]; Gorizia and the Vipava Valley [Goriška-Vipavska]; The Isonzo Valley [Posočje]; The Ribnica-Kočevje area [Ribniško-Kočevsko]; Ljubljana and surroundings [Ljubljana z okolico]; The area of Škofja Loka [Škofjeloško]; Kranj and surroundings [Kranj z okolico]; The Upper Sava Valley [Zgornje Savsko]; Bela krajina; Central Lower Carniola [Osrednja Dolenjska]; The Mid-Sava Valley [Zasavje]; The Lower Sava Valley [Posavje]; The Sotla Valley [Obsotelje]; Celje and surroundings [Celje z okolico]; The Upper Savinja Valley [Zgornjesavinjsko]; The Lower Drava Valley [Spodnje Podravje]; The Dravinja Valley [Dravinjsko]; Carinthia [Koroška]; Maribor and surroundings [Maribor z okolico]; The Hills of Prlekija [Prlekija]; The Lowlands and Hills of Prekmurje [Prekmurje].

Figure 8: **Slovenia: Regions of typical touristic products**

Source: Slovenia info 2010

4 Conclusion

Slovenia is among some rare countries of the world where national tourism development strategies are produced and refurbished. Since publication of the first regionalization for tourism purposes in 1965 (within Yugoslavia), Slovenian researchers and tourism managers have developed several strategies. Some just placed directions for the proper identity of Slovenia as tourist destination; others have considered heritage as "tourism subjects" on nation state's micro-scale level and produced adequate regionalizations.

The first strategy and regionalization, made for the young nation state in 1993, had to consider the consequences of the disintegration of Yugoslavia and had to pin-point tourism products which had potentials in this, naturally and culturally very diverse European country. The growth in visits to the "watering places" of Slovenia has, for example, proven right to the development directives of the strategy.

The physical landscape and character, and even the natural and cultural heritage elements are playing an increasingly weak role in the definition of contemporary touristic regions. Tourism products promoting experience, entertainment and adventure, as well as human-made attractions (including cultural events and events based on tradition), are the primary decision maker(s) in contemporary attempts to characterize specific macro-, meso- or micro-regions of tourism.

5 Bibliography

BUTLER R., ARAMBERI J. (2005), Tourism Development: Issues for a Vulnerable Industry: Aspects of Tourism. Chichester, Chanel View Publ.

CIGALE D. (2010), Značilnosti turističnega oiska slovenskih občin glede na državni izvor turistov. In: Geografski vestnik – Geographical Bulletin, 82, 2, pp. 9–24.

FRIDL J., KLADNIK D., OROŽEN ADAMIČ M., PERKO D., ZUPANČIČ J. (eds.) (1995), Geografski atlas Slovenije. Ljubljana, Geografski inštitut Antona Melika ZRC SAZU.

FRIDL J., PERKO D. (2006), Slovenija. Ljubljana, Rokus.

GOSAR A. (2005), The Cross-Border Bricklaying Concept in the Alpen-Adria Region. In: Tourism Analyses, 10, 1, pp. 65–78. (http://www.citeulike.org/journals)

GOSAR A., JERŠIČ M. (1999), Slovenia – the Tourist Guide. Ljubljana, Mladinska knjiga.

HORVAT U. (2010), Health resorts and their importance for the development of less developed areas in Slovenia. In: Revija za geografijo, 5, 1, pp. 147–159.

JERŠIČ M. (1978), Bewertung des Naturraumpotentials für den Gesellschaftsbedarf an Hand von Beispielen aus Slowenien. In: PAK, M. (ed.), Socialnogeografski problemi obmestnih in obmejnih območij (= Geographica Slovenica, 8). Ljubljana, pp. 159–163.

JORDAN P., SCHAPPELWEIN K. et al. (1999), International Tourism Attractions in Central and Southeastern Europe [1:3,000,000]. In: JORDAN P. (ed.), Atlas of Eastern and Southeastern Europe. Stuttgart, Borntraeger.

KOKOLE V. (1965), Slovenske pokrajine in turizem. In: Geografski obzornik, XII/1-2, XIII/1-2. Ljubljana, Geografsko društvo Slovenije.

KOS GRABNAR J. (2010), Predlog členitve Slovenije na turistične pokrajine in območja. In: Delovni zvezek SDE, 10. (http://www.sdeval.si/attachements/184_SDEDZ_Turist_regionali%20 (14.05.2009)

KOVAČ B. et al. (2002), Strategija slovenskega turizma 2002-2006. Ljubljana, Ministerstvo za gospodarstvo, Vlada Republike Slovenije.

MIHALIČ T. (1995), Tourism and Warfare: the Case of Slovenia. In: PIZAM A., MANSFELD Y. (eds.), Tourism, Crime and International Security Issues, pp. 231–246. Chichester, John Wiley & Sons.

MORITSCH A. (1998), Ursachen und Folgen der politischen Teilung in den Alpen – das Beispiel Dreiländereck = The Causes and Consequences of Border Settings in the Alps – the Case of the "Dreilaendereck/Tre Confini/Tromeja". In: Dela, 13, pp. 189–200.

OROŽEN ADAMIČ M., PERKO D., KLADNIK D. (1995), Krajevni leksikon Slovenije. Portorož, DZS.

PERKO D., OROŽEN ADAMIČ M. (1995), Relief Slovenije. Ljubljana, Znanstveno raziskovalni center SAZU.

PERKO D., OROŽEN ADAMIČ M. (1998), Slovenija: pokrajine in ljudje. Ljubljana, Verlag.

PLANINA J., MIHALIČ T. (1985), Razvoj in dejavniki turističnega povpraševanja. Ljubljana, Inštitut za ekonomska raziskovanja.

REPUBLIKA SLOVENIJA (ed.) (2011), Zakon o spodbujanju razvoj turizma (ZSRT). In: Uradni list, ULRS 2011, 2. (http://www.uradni-list.si/1/objava.jsp?urlid=20042&stevilka=73)

SIRŠE J. (1995), The New Strategy for the Development of Tourism in Slovenia. In: Revue Tourism, 50, 2, pp. 18–22.

SIRŠE J., STROJ-VRTAČNIK I., POBEGA N. (1993), Strategija razvoja slovenskega turizma. Ljubljana, IER – Inštitut za ekonomska raziskovanja.

SLOVENIA INFO (ed.) (2010), Turistične destinacije (http://www.slovenia.info/si/turisticne-destinacije.htm?destinacije=0&lng=1)

SLOVENSKO DRUŠTVO EVALVATORJEV (ed.) (2010), Predlog členitve na turistične pokrajine in območja. http://www.sdeval.si/attachements/184_SDEDZ_Turist_regionali%20 (14.05.2009)

STATISTIČNI URAD REPUBLIKE SLOVENIJE (ed.) (2008), Statistical Yearbook: Tourism: Tourist Arrivals and Overnight Stays by Types of Tourist Resorts. Ljubljana, pp. 429–430.

SLOVENIAN TOURIST BOARD (STO) (ed.) (2004), Slovenija poživlja! Slovenia invigorates! Slowenien belebt! Tržna kampanija ob vstopu v EU (http://www.slovenia.info/pictures%5Cpress%5Catachments_1%5C2004%5C06-07_TURIZEM_397.pdf)

SLOVENIAN TOURIST BOARD (STO) (ed.) (2005), Byways are more attractive than highways. NEXT-EXIT. Ljubljana (promotional material). Ljubljana.

SLOVENIAN TOURIST BOARD (STO) (ed.) (2007), Strategija trženja slovenskega turizma. Ljubljana, Hosting svetovanje d.o.o.

SLOVENIAN TOURIST BOARD (STO) (ed.) (2009), Culinary Regions of Slovenia (Janez Bogataj) (http://en.slovenskifestivalvin.si/radost/winegastronomy/about-gastronomy/culinary-regions/)

URAN M., OVSENIK R. (2006), Razvojni načrt in usmeritve slovenskega turizma 2007-2011. In: UP Turistica, Portorož.

VESENJAK P., RAVNIKAR D. (2007), Strategija trženja slovenskega turizma 2007-2011. Ljubljana, Slovenska turistična organizacija.

ZIMMERMANN F.M. (1998), Das europäische Raumentwicklungskonzept als Grundlage für grenzüberschreitende Kooperationen = The European Concept of Spatial Development as the Base for Transborder Cooperations. In: Dela, 13, pp. 225–235.

ŽAGAR M. (1976), Turistični potenciali Slovenije. In: Geografski obzornik, 23, 1-2, pp. 3–14.

Wine Tourism as a Development Factor of the Primorska Wine Region

Simon Kerma*, Koper/Capodistria*[*]

with 1 figure and 4 tables in the text

Content

Summary 127
1 Introduction 128
2 The Primorska wine region and its four wine districts 130
3 Wine tourism in the Primorska wine region 132
4 Conclusion 137
5 Bibliography 138

Summary

The paper deals with the Slovene wine region of Primorska and its four wine districts (the Brda Hills [Brda], the Vipava Valley [Vipava], the Karst Plateau [Kras] and Slovene Istria [Slovenska Istra]) in the context of wine tourism. The Primorska wine region (one of three in Slovenia) has developed a traditionally important viticulture, a relatively intensive production of typical grape varieties and in some cases also a distinct entrepreneurial spirit, which consequently reflects itself in the development of wine tourism and the region. Although in total characterised by the beneficial influence of the Mediterranean, Primorska is a relatively heterogeneous (wine) region. Its four wine districts could be defined as wine micro-regions with their own identities and

* Simon Kerma, PhD. Candidate, Department of Geography, Faculty of Humanities, University of Primorska, Titov trg 5, SI-6000 Koper/Capodistria, Slovenia; e-mail: simon.kerma@fhs.upr.si

more or less distinct conditions for wine growing. Comparative analysis reveals some major differences related to wine tourism offer and development strategies.

1 Introduction

"The great thing about wine tourism is that every wine region is a new experience waiting to happen, with its own wines, its own history, its own landscapes, and its own culture." (SOMMERS 2008, p. 259)

We can refer to one of many definitions and describe wine tourism as visiting vineyards, wineries, wine festivals and other wine events, with wine tasting and/or experiencing the attributes of a wine region being the dominant motivating factors for visitors (HALL et al. 2000). GETZ & BROWN (2006) consider wine tourism – simultaneously – as a form of consumer behaviour, a strategy of local development and marketing local wines, especially by selling them directly to consumers. According to SHOR & MANSFELD (2009), wine tourism is a type of special interest tourism conducted in wine districts where vineyards and wineries abound. TOMLJENOVIĆ (2009) points out – in the context of wine tourism development in the Mediterranean space – that wine tourism is one of the more lucrative products and of extreme importance for many of the Mediterranean destinations.

Slovenia is an integral part of the Mediterranean geographical and cultural area with a long and rich viticultural tradition as well as well-developed tourism attractions. This is even more so with the Primorska region in the Southwest of the country.

Development of wine tourism in Slovenia has for almost 20 years (since 1992) been based on wine tourist routes in all three wine regions (Podravje, Posavje and Primorska) implemented by the Ministry of Agriculture, Forestry and Food. Despite this fact, wine tourism along wine routes, although considered an important feature for both tourism and wine producers, has received little attention by researchers – with some rare exceptions focusing on wine tourism marketing and brand name development (BOJNEC & JURINČIČ 2006a, BOJNEC & JURINČIČ 2006b), on the role of wine consortiums in wine marketing and wine tourism development (JURINČIČ & BOJNEC 2006), marketing of wine tourism as a territorial product (BOJNEC, JURINČIČ & TOMLJENOVIĆ 2007), and some case studies of selected wine regions and districts (e.g. BOJNEC, JURINČIČ & TOMLJENOVIĆ 2006, JURINČIČ & BOJNEC 2009).

The aim of this paper is to provide an analysis of the supply side of wine tourism in the Primorska wine region by highlighting each of its four wine districts. The Primorska wine region, in fact, is just a frame of its four wine districts, subregions or micro-regions, which have developed their own and recognized (in some cases also institutionally supported) identity[1]. A comparative perspective will be employed to

[1] For regional identity see Anssi PAASI (2003).

identify similarities and differences of strategies/approaches related to wine tourism development.

At first a brief description of the subregions is presented including some basic information on current viticulture. This is followed by the results of an analysis of selected elements of wine tourism supply and promotion, wine events and other activities including visits.

Figure 1: **Primorska wine region in the Southwest of Slovenia**

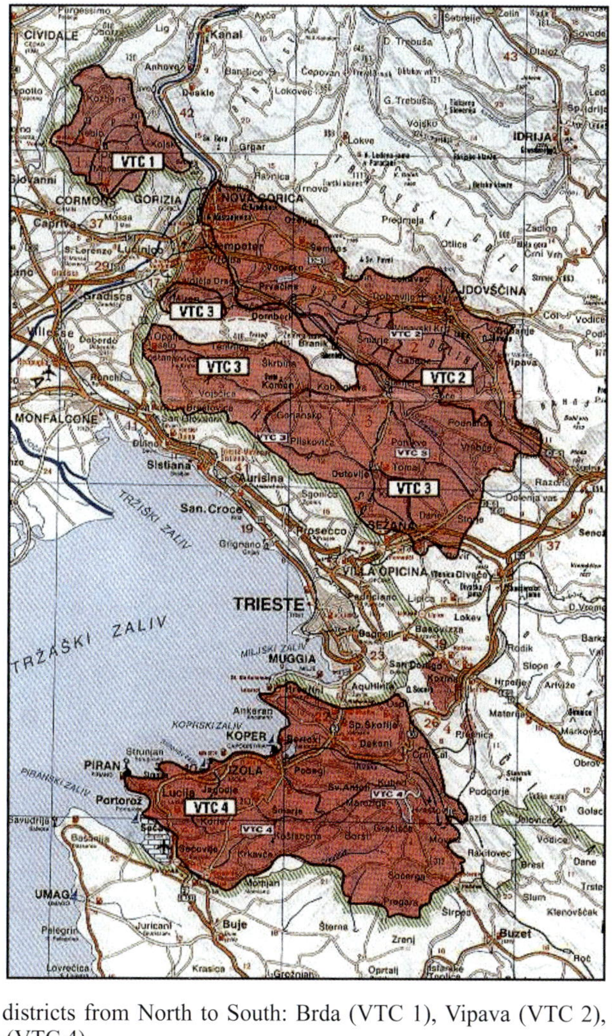

The four wine districts from North to South: Brda (VTC 1), Vipava (VTC 2), Kras (VTC 3), Slovenska Istra (VTC 4).
Source: Ministrstvo za gospodarstvo Republike Slovenije, Direktorat za turizem 2007

2 The Primorska wine region and its four wine districts

The Primorska wine region is situated in the Southwest of Slovenia and includes the wine districts Brda Hills [Brda], Vipava Valley [Vipava], Karst Plateau [Kras] and Slovene Istria [Slovenska Istra]). The southern part of the region extends to the Adriatic Sea and the Istrian peninsula up to the border with Croatia. Towards the West it borders Italy, to the East and North it is limited by the harsh continental climate of higher hills and plateaus (see Figure 1).

According to Jancis Robinson (2006) Primorska has made great progress in wine quality since the early 1990s and is today the most appreciated Slovene wine region. The region is known for dry extract wines with a very complex structure and full taste. The Primorska wine region produces the majority of Slovenia's best reds.

In comparison to the other two (continental) wine regions of Slovenia, Primorska is in total characterised by the beneficial influence of the Mediterranean climate. It has lots of sunny days, is warm, in summertime also hot, but still with a considerable amount of precipitation. An occasional biting northeast wind (locally called *burja*) is also typical for the region, as well as mineral-rich soils. The influence of the sea can be felt in all parts of the region, but the mix of these general characteristics (with specific human responses to the environment) is different for each particular wine district. In fact, Primorska is quite a heterogeneous wine region. Its four wine districts could be defined as wine micro-regions with their own identities and more or less distinct conditions for wine growing.[2]

The Brda Hills in the Northwest at the border with Italy (VTC1 in Figure 1) are an area with approximately 6,000 inhabitants in one municipality and recognised as the most developed and esteemed wine district in the country. Soils consist mostly of marl, shale and sandstone in alternation (flysch). The Hills are very prone to erosion, so most of the vineyards must be terraced. They are best known for their matured red and white blends, but the local (regional) brand is definitely based on Rebula (Ribolla).

The Vipava Valley (VTC2 in Figure 1) is proud of its native wine specialities Zelen and Pinela. It is surrounded by higher karst plateaus. The climate is submediterranean to continental. There is enough rainfall and the soils are relatively rich, but this is the area most influenced by the cold and dry burja that sweeps down from the Northeast drying the soil and even eroding the top layer.

Kras (*Carso* in Italian, VTC3 in Figure 1) is unique in many aspects. Its typical karstic landscape made it the scientific term for similar land forms around the world. The relatively inhospitable surface with a lack of groundwater offers unfavouarble conditions for vegetation. The soil is terra rossa *(jerina* in Slovene*)*, a characteristic red

[2] The subdivision of the Slovene wine regions is based on ecological and physical-geographical factors important for growth and development of wine and influencing the character of wines (Rajher 1997, Škvarč & Brdnik 2011).

earth, a product of limestone decay. The climate is harsh with frequent lasting droughts in summer and cold winters aggravated by burja, which dries the land. Terra rossa and burja are of fundamental importance for the production of the famous red wine Teran (Terrano) and the dried ham Pršut (Prosciutto).

Slovenska Istra (VTC4 in Figure 1), administratively composed of the three coastal municipalities of Koper/Capodistria, Izola/Isola and Piran/Pirano and a minor part of the municipality of Hrpelje-Kozina, is most distinctively influenced by the Mediterranean (the Adriatic Sea), though these influences slowly weaken towards the hilly hinterland of the area. However, the climate is mild, and the soils are mostly derived from flysch. The grapes of this area are the earliest to ripen of all the districts. Among wines the extremely popular Refošk (Refosco) and Malvazija (Malvasia) prevail. The later seems to be, surprisingly, one of the very rare common denominators for wine tourism promotion of the Primorska wine region.

In the Primorska wine region several (local and global) white and red grape varieties are cultivated. White varieties prevail in the Brda Hills and the Vipava Valley, whereas the red represent more than 50% in Kras and Slovenska Istra. Vintagers from Primorska mostly produce varietal wines, although some white cuvees are typical as well (Škvarč & Brdnik 2011).

Table 1: **Selected data for viticulture in Slovenia, Primorska and its wine districts, 2009**

Country, region and districts	*Number of wine-growers*	*Vineyards' total size (ha)*	*Grape production (in 1,000 kg)*	*Wine production (in 1,000 l)*
Slovenia	27,890	16,590	79,263	54,833
Primorska	4,604	6,718	41,236	28,418
Brda	834	1,906	13,677	9,540
Vipava	1,781	2,437	14,410	9,922
Kras	898	635	3,418	2,448
Slovenska Istra	1,091	1,740	9,730	6,509

Source: Ministrstvo za kmetijstvo, gozdarstvo in prehrano Republike Slovenije, Agricultural Institute of Slovenia 2010

According to official data of registered grape and wine production, Primorska obviously dominates among the three wine regions in Slovenia. Only one sixth of all Slovene vintagers are from Primorska, but they cultivate 40% of the total area of vineyards and provide 52% of the total grape and wine production in the country (see Table 1). Table 1 also shows that the most productive wine district is Brda, where the structure of holdings is the most favourable among the four wine districts.

3 Wine tourism in the Primorska wine region

We proceed now to wine tourism in the broader context of regional development in each of the four wine districts of Primorska. We are therefore interested in the touristic offer of wine tourist routes, traditional wine-related festivals and events that (wine) tourists can visit and the actual number of visitors recorded as well as visits to the four largest wine cellars in the region. In the context of district promotion, we take into account the role of different players (tourist information centres, wine associations and consortia, individual vintagers, etc.). For this purpose we conducted some structured interviews with competent representatives to get relevant information.

It is evident that in Slovenian development plans wine tourism (still) does not occupy the position that it probably deserves, although most of the documents stress its potential for local or regional development. The authors of the "Development Plan and Policies of Slovene Tourism", e.g., conceive wine tourist routes, an already developed segment of tourism, as one of the key elements of an authentic tourist offer, that should, however, be more intensively integrated into an integral tourist product of the tourist destinations (Uran & Ovsenik 2006).

No more specific suggestions can be found in the Regional Development Programme of South Primorska 2007-13 (RDA South Primorska 2006), which is rather general and proposes only a clustering of supply with markets by promoting the wine route offer.

The Regional Development Programme (RDP) of North Primorska 2007-13 (RDA North Primorska 2006b) is much more specific, when it stresses the big potential of wine tourism, especially in connection with excellence in tourism (Priority 2) and the promotion of sustainable tourism development, with two bigger projects planned (the museum of wine culture in the Brda Hills and the reconstruction of an old wine cellar in Vipava in connection with the establishment of the museum of winegrowing of Slovenia).

The development of wine tourism is by all means directly connected to rural development. Even though the cover document of the Republic of Slovenia's Rural Development Programme 2007-13 (Ministrstvo za kmetijstvo, gozdarstvo in prehrano Republike Slovenije 2007) disregards wine tourism completely, its importance is recognized in all local or regional strategies (rural development programmes), which include the areas of the wine districts analysed (RDA North Primorska 2006a, RDC Koper 2008, ROD Ajdovščina 2008, TDC Kras and Brkini 2008). All these documents stress the importance of enhancing viticulture and wine-producing farms together with the development of complementary tourism supply along wine tourist routes.

Table 2: **Wine tourist routes (WTR) in the Primorska wine region and their tourist offers**

Name of WTR (district)	*No. of wineries**	*Wineries with accommodation*	*Typical wines, attractions and tourist offer*
Briška WTR (Brda)	61	15	Traditional wines: Rebula, Pikolit and "Sauvignonasse" (ex Tocai Friulano); extensive assortment of high quality wines; sale of succulent fruits (especially cherries), promotion of local dishes at tourist farms, creative cuisine; several cultural-historical attractions (old villages, churches and castles); many traditional events, sport and cultural activities, arts and wine festivals; slogan: 'Land of invigorating moments' Web: no official WTR internet promotion, useful info available at http://www.brda.si/en/
Vipavska WTR (Vipava) Lower valley Upper valley	127	11	Traditional wines: Zelen, Pinela and Rebula (all whites), among 25 varietal wines; one of the biggest WTRs in Slovenia, well signposted; orchards (peaches), tourist farms, wine cellars and "osmice" with home-made and locally produced food and drinks; lots of natural and cultural sights, castles, churches and monasteries, handicrafts, traditional festivals etc.; various sports activities (cycling, flying, gliding); slogans: 'The wine, born to the sun and wind' / 'There's more than meets the eye!' Web: lower Vipava: www.novagorica-turizem.com/; upper Vipava: http://www.ra-rod.si/stara/vvc/index.htm
Kraška WTR (Kras)	155	16	Traditional wines: Teran (red), Malvazija and Vitovska grganja (white); variety of other wines produced in smaller quantities; unique landscape (karst formations, caves, etc.) with typical villages; rich natural and cultural heritage (i.e. the Škocjan caves – UNESCO world heritage site, the Lipica horse stud, beautiful Štanjel and Pliskovica); lots of small wine-cellars and "osmice" offering home-made wine, spirits, liqueurs and typical food (dry-cured meat, "štruklji", "jota"), honey, etc.; agrotourism and sports-related activities (horse-riding, cycling, hiking, jogging); no particular slogan; 'the land of Teran and Pršut' Web: www.vinskacestakras.si
Istrska WTR (Slovenska Istra)	59	4	Traditional wines: Refošk, Malvazija, Yellow Muscat, Cipro (Red Muscat) and a good selection of other recognized varieties; urbanized coastal destination (old towns of Koper/Capodistria, Izola/Isola and Piran/Pirano), Portorož/Portorose, hotels, casinos, congresses, festivals, fairs and other events; Venetian heritage, tradition of saltpans and fishery in the coastal part, handicrafts, viticulture and olive oil production in the hinterland; village feasts ("šagre") and "osmice", small wine-cellars (open wine) and some excellent family wine-producers; typical Istrian cuisine based on olive oil, seafood, dried and smoked meat, truffles, pasta "fuži", minestrone "bobiči", etc.; general tourism slogan for the region: 'Enjoy!' Web: http://www.vinskacesta.com/

Source: Tourist information centres of Brda, Koper/Capodistria, Nova Gorica, Sežana and Vipava.

*Only those included in the WTR.

Surprisingly, the Briška WTR (Brda) is not on the web. It is, however, signposted in the field (as others). Its offer includes the most (due to the size of the district) and best (with vintagers) accommodation facilities. It is very homogenous (a single municipality!) offering a wide range of tourist attractions, events and activities. Wine is part of every event, but the Cherry Festival is the best known and visited of all.

The Vipavska WTR (Vipava) is divided into the Lower and the Upper Vipava Valley, which causes coordination problems between the tourist information centres of the two parts. They have their own specifics, e.g., Zelen and Pinela are more characteristic for the Upper Vipava Valley. But the tourist offer improves continually, although accommodation offered by vintagers is still too scarce. A very positive factor that could help strengthen wine tourism is the School of Viticulture and Enology in Ajdovščina (as a part of the University of Nova Gorica).

The Kraška WTR (Kras) is perhaps advertised best – by an up-to-date web page and catalogues. The offer is really diverse; practically every vintager, also those producing nothing more than house (open) wine, participates. Very important is the authentic local enogastronomic offer, which is both traditional ("osmice") and innovative (e.g. Terra Carsus, the Slovene-Italian project of young chefs).

Istrska WTR (Slovenska Istra) has despite its undeniable potential fallen behind in development and upgrading its offer, which is based on typical Istrian wines, olive oil and cuisine together with its characteristic Mediterranean landscape. The biggest problem is a non-defined status of trustees and consequently uncoordinated management of the three coastal municipalities. The district's webpage is out of date, but the major problem is, that there are virtually no accommodation facilities in the countryside with vintagers and other farmers.

The authors of local and regional rural development plans share the opinion that WTRs represent the backbone of rural development, but need to be upgraded by authentic events and festivals. They consider it extremely important to establish a regular control system of suppliers, which due to the non-defined status of trustees still doesn't work as it should.

It has, however, also to be said that many suppliers are rather passive when it comes to participating, e.g., in seminars focusing on the improvement of the tourist offer. Local authorities and tourist organizations as well as vintagers' associations are to motivate suppliers by awarding them, offering advice as regards maintenance of buildings and outdoor areas as well as trade mark design and offering administrative support with tenders for development funds, etc. This seems all the more necessary, since for most vintagers wine growing is not the main activity, but merely adds to the family income.

Authorities are also to feel responsible for the promotion of WTRs, to provide tourist offices and agencies with up-to-date information on the tourist offer. It is also vital to combine the WTR offer with other forms of the tourist offer in the countryside,

Table 3: **Important (traditional) wine-related events by wine districts of the Primorska wine region**

Wine district	*Wine-related events (feasts, festivals, fairs, celebrations etc.)*	*Estimated number of visitors in 2010*	*Characteristics*
Brda	"Spring, Nature and Wine"; "Brda and Wine"; "Rebula and Olive Oil Festival"; "Wine Day"; "Dreams in Medana – Book and Wine Festival"; Saint Martin's Day	30,000	Combination of high quality festivals for professionals and wine lovers and traditional mass events; special promotion of Rebula and olive oil. Other events (art, culture, sports) from March to November – all including wine. Best known is the Cherry Festival in June.
Vipava	"The Noble Heritage of Slovenia: Festival of Wines"; "The Taste of Vipava: Festival of Wine and Culinary"; "Day of the Open Cellars"; "Plutovina – plutovino – plutoviva"; "B'ndimska kvaternica"; "Vipavska trgatev" – vintage time festival; Saint Martin feasts; Wine cellars of the Vipava Valley between Saint Martin's Day and Christmas	25,000	Lots of small and bigger events from early spring till late fall, some noble festivals emphasising local grape varieties, wine and food. Most visited and popular is a vintage time festival including the contest for the wine queen. Very popular are also *osmice* and open wine cellars between Saint Martin's day and Christmas.
Kras	"Br'stovska Kolosmica"; "In the Heart of the Land of Teran"; "One Karst, a Thousand Tastes - Wine Festival"; "Festival of Teran and Prosciutto"; Saint Martin's Festival	20,000	Most popular and visited is the Festival of Teran and Prosciutto in August, when the Queen of Teran is elected. Very popular are also the traditional *osmice*.
Slovenska Istra	"Tasting of Wine and Olive Oil"; "Women and Wine"; "Malvazija - the Mediterranean Noble Taste"; "Feast of Flowers, Wine and Olive Oil"; "Feast of Refosco"; "From the Winemaker to the Olive Oil Maker"; "Days of Fish, Wine and Olive Oil"; Saint Martin's Festival and feasts	40,000	The Mediterranean character of the events is reflected by combining wine with olive oil, e.g. with "Mayor's Wine and Olive Oil Award". Bigger festivals take place in summer and are thus well visited by seasonal tourists. Local feasts in the countryside ("šagre", "osmice"). To Refošk and Malvazija two special festivals in spring are devoted. Also a wine queen contest.

Source: Interviews with organizers and/or staff of local tourist information centres

e.g., by organizing daytrips or longer travel packages. At the moment, only some local tourist agencies are independently developing and marketing the big potential of WTRs.

Traditional events related to wine are an important part of a quality tourism offer in the region. As can be seen in Table 3, this offer is quite diversified and locally specific, yet in some aspects quite similar, since it is based on similar traditions and customs (grape-harvesting, festivities on Saint Martin's Day, established promotional strategies like open cellars, wine queens, etc.).

While data on visits to all (or the majority of) wine cellars are not available, we have collected data on the biggest four wine cellars in the Primorska wine region (one for each wine district).

Table 4: **Visits to the four biggest wineries in the Primorska wine region in 2010**

Wine district	*Winery*	*Number of visitors**	*Percentage of foreign visitors*	*Country of origin***
Brda	Goriška Brda Wine Cellar	12,000	*25*	UK, Italy, Belgium
Vipava	Vipava 1894	1,500	*35*	Italy, Austria, Germany
Kras	Vinakras	2,500	*35*	Austria, Germany, Italy
Slovenska Istra	Vinakoper	10,000	*47*	Germany, Austria, Italy

*Approximate number of visitors with guided tours and wine-tastings;

**Countries in the order of visitor numbers

Source: Interviews with the staff of each winery

As can be seen from Table 4, the Goriška Brda Wine Cellar and Vinakoper stand out by tourist visits. These two wineries are among the biggest in Slovenia, according to production and recognition. In the past few years they have both been investing a lot into the promotion of their trademarks, by skilfully incorporating the typical elements of regional identity.

While Vinakras, in size quite smaller than the previous two, receives the expected number of visitors, this is most certainly not true for Vipava 1894, which is a winery of the same category as Goriška Brda Wine Cellar and Vinakoper. According to the management, the number of visitors constantly declined in recent years. Reasons are the new motorway making it easy to bypass Vipava and to proceed to Nova Gorica and

Brda, the termination of the Vipava 1894-Postojna Cave connection, but most of all the serious lack of promotion of the winery as an integral part of the Vipava Valley tourist destination.

4 Conclusion

To summarize the main results of this preliminary study (to be followed by in-depth research), we can describe the Primorska wine region as versatile and heterogeneous on the one hand and internally poorly connected and uncoordinated on the other. One of the reasons for the latter is the fact that Primorska is not an administrative unit (due to the lack of administrative units at the regional level in Slovenia) and also statistically and in development plans divided into Southern and Northern Primorska. The Primorska wine region differs significantly from the other two Slovenian wine regions (Podravje and Posavje) due to its Mediterranean character, which positions it much closer to the neighbouring Friulian wine regions DOC Collio, DOC Friuli Isonzo and DOC Carso.

The heterogeneity of the Primorska wine region expresses itself also in its four wine districts (Brda, Vipava, Kras and Slovenska Istra). Despite being situated in close neighbourhood, they are quite distinct and have their own identities based on specific microclimatic, relief and pedologic conditions, on history and specific human responses to the environment. This distinctness is reflected by the conditions for wine growing and the characteristic grape and wine varieties, but also by different kinds of wine-tourism. But even the districts are all but homogeneous, especially the Vipava Valley with its lower and upper sections, mainly due to administrative fragmentation into several municipalities.

The Brda wine district belonging entirely to one municipality has an advantage in this respect and is also the most developed Slovene wine region. This reflects itself also in wine tourism. According to Jurinčič & Bojnec (2009) we can classify Brda as belonging to the third (maturity) stage of the wine tourism destination life-cycle, whereas the other three wine districts still correspond to the second (developing) stage.

Wine tourist routes are an important element of wine tourism development (or rural development in general) in all wine districts of the Primorska wine region. However, there are still some shortcomings that limit greater efficiency. Yet we witness a high quality tourist offer in these wine districts, especially in connection with traditional (and some innovative) wine-related events. The offer is diversified and locally specific, yet in some aspects quite similar, since it is based on similar traditions and customs.

Wine festivals and events are in general well visited. The majority of visitors, however, especially of traditional events, are locals and daily visitors rather than (wine) tourists. An exception is to some extent Slovenska Istra, where the higher number of visitors is the result of summer tourism, which is also reflected by the higher number of foreign visitors to the Vinakoper winery. According to some organizers, there are even too many wine-connected events and competition for visitors is strong. But certainly, only original and authentic events will prosper also in the future.

It will anyway be necessary to carry on in-depth research on motives and impressions of tourists visiting the Primorska wine region.

5 Bibliography

BOJNEC Š., JURINČIČ I. (2006a), Marketing and brand name development: wine and wine tourism. In: PODNAR K., JANČIČ Z. (eds.), Contemporary Issues in Corporate and Marketing Communications: Towards a Socially Responsible Future, pp. 252–254. Ljubljana, Fakulteta za družbene vede.

BOJNEC Š., JURINČIČ I. (2006b), Wine regions, brand name, and wine tourism marketing: the Slovene Istria. In: TSARTAS P., CHRISTOU E., SIGALA M. (eds.), In search of excellence for tomorrow's tourism travel and hospitality: proceedings, pp. 25–28. Thessaloniki, The University of the Aegean.

BOJNEC Š., JURINČIČ I., TOMLJENOVIĆ R. (2006), Wine growing areas and wine tourism in Slovenia and Croatia. In: FACULTY OF TOURISM AND HOTEL MANAGEMENT (ed.), Tourism & hospitality industry 2006: new trends in tourism and hospitality management: congress proceedings: 18th Biennial International Congress, May 03-05, 2006, pp. 588–604. Opatija, Faculty of Tourism and Hotel Management.

BOJNEC Š., JURINČIČ I., TOMLJENOVIĆ R. (2007), Marketing of wine tourism as a territorial product. In: BOJNEC Š. (ed.), Managing global transitions: globalisation, localisation, regionalisation (International Management Conference), pp. 1075–1082. Koper, Faculty of Management.

GETZ D., BROWN G. (2006), Critical success factors for wine tourism regions: a demand analysis. In: Tourism Management, 27, pp. 146–158.

HALL C.M., SHARPLES L., CAMBOURNE B., MACIONIS N. (2000), Wine Tourism around the World. Butterworth, Heinemann.

JURINČIČ I., BOJNEC Š. (2006), The role of wine consortiums in wine marketing and wine tourism development in Slovenia. In: MULEJ M., REBERNIK M., KROŠLIN T. (eds.), STIQE 2006: proceedings of the 8th International Conference on Linking Systems Thinking, Innovation, Quality, Entrepreneurship, and Environment, Maribor, Slovenia, 28-30 June, 2006, pp. 81–86. Maribor, Faculty of Economics and Business, Institute for Entrepreneurship and Small Business Management.

JURINČIČ I., BOJNEC Š (2009), Wine tourism development: The case of wine district in Slovenia. In: Tourism, 57, 4, pp. 435–448.

MINISTRSTVO ZA GOSPODARSTVO REPUBLIKE SLOVENIJE, DIREKTORAT ZA TURIZEM (ed.) (2007), Strategija razvoja zidaniškega turizma. Ljubljana.

MINISTRSTVO ZA KMETIJSTVO, GOZDARSTVO IN PREHRANO REPUBLIKE SLOVENIJE (ed.) (2007), Program razvoja podeželja Republike Slovenije za obdobje 2007-2013. Ljubljana.

MINISTRSTVO ZA KMETIJSTVO, GOZDARSTVO IN PREHRANO REPUBLIKE SLOVENIJE, AGRICULTURAL INSTITUTE OF SLOVENIA (eds.) (2010), Poročilo o stanju kmetijstva, živilstva in gozdarstva v letu 2009. Pregled po kmetijskih trgih. Kmetijski inštitut Slovenije. Ljubljana.

PAASI A. (2003), Region and place: regional identity in question. In: Progress in Human Geography, 27, 4, pp. 475–485.

RAJHER Z. (1994), Korenine slovenskega vinogradništva. In: PRUNK J. et al. (eds.), Vodnik po slovenskih vinorodnih okoliših, pp. 10–22. Ljubljana, Založba Grad.

ROBINSON J. (2006), The Oxford companion to wine. Oxford, Oxford University Press.

RDA NORTH PRIMORSKA (ed.) (2006a), Razvojni program podeželja občin Šempeter – Vrtojba, Brda in Miren – Kostanjevica 2007-2013. Regional Development Agency of North Primorska. http://www.sempeter-vrtojba.si/?vie=gds&id=20081002123 608 (15.2.2011).

RDA NORTH PRIMORSKA (ed.) (2006b), Regionalni razvojni program Severne Primorske 2007-2013. Regional Development Agency of North Primorska. http://www.prc.si/dokumenti (15.2.2011).

RDA SOUTH PRIMORSKA (ed.) (2006), Regionalni razvojni program Južne Primorske 2007-2013. Strateški in izvedbeni del programa. Regional Development Agency of South Primorska. http://www.rrc-kp.si/programi/76 (15.2.2011).

RDC KOPER (ed.) (2008), Lokalna razvojna strategija za območje občin Koper, Izola in Piran. Regional Development Centre Koper. http://www.las-istre.si/akti-in-dokumenti (15.2.2011).

ROD AJDOVŠČINA (ed.) (2008), Lokalna razvojna strategija za območje Zgornje Vipavske doline in Komenskega Krasa (občine: Ajdovščina, Komen in Vipava) za programsko razvojno obdobje 2007-2013. ROD Development Agency. http://www.las-razvojpodezelja.si/ (15.2.2011).

SHOR N., MANSFELD Y. (2009), Between wine consumption and wine tourism: Consumer and spatial behaviour of Israeli wine tourists. In: Tourism, 57, 4, pp. 381–403.

SOMMERS B.J. (2008), The geography of wine: how landscapes, cultures, terroir, and the weather make a good drop. New York, Plume.

ŠKVARČ A., BRDNIK M. (2011), Vinorodna dežela Primorska. Kmetijsko gozdarski zavod Nova Gorica. http://www.kvz-ng.si/panoge/vinogradnistvo (10.2.2011).

TDA KRAS AND BRKINI (ed.) (2008), Razvojni program podeželja Krasa in Brkinov za območje občin Divača, Hrpelje-Kozina in Sežana za obdobje 2007-2013. Territorial Development Agency of Kras and Brkini. http://www.ora.si/las.php (15.2.2011).

TOMLJENOVIĆ R. (ed.) (2009), Wine tourism in Mediterranean. In: Tourism, 57, 4, pp. 361–500.

URAN M., OVSENIK R. (2006), Development plan and policies of Slovene tourism 2007-2011. Ljubljana, Ministry of the Economy.

Regional Economic Development of Central Croatia in the Transition Period

Jelena Lončar, Zoran Stiperski, Zagreb*

with 8 figures and 6 tables in the text

Content

Summary 141
1 Introduction 142
2 Demography 144
3 Economic activities 147
4 Employment 150
5 Industry 152
6 Economic subjects 154
7 Gross Domestic Product (GDP) 156
8 Conclusion 157
9 Bibliography 157

Summary

In the last decade of the 20th century the process of transition initiated decisive changes in the former Communist countries of Europe. They affected also Croatia and will be documented and explained in this article by the example of Central Croatia [Srednija Hrvatska]. The region of Central Croatia consists of eight counties [županije] and the City of Zagreb [Grad Zagreb] and is economically the most developed part of Croatia. Nevertheless, significant socio-economic disparities exist also in this region

* Jelena Lončar, PhD., Zoran Stiperski, Prof. PhD., both University of Zagreb, Faculty of Science, Department of Geography, Marulićev trg 19/II, HR-10000 Zagreb, Croatia; e-mail: jloncar@geog.pmf.hr;zstiper@geog.pmf.hr

– its north-western part is the most developed, whereas its southern and south-eastern areas are the least developed, owing to the effects of aggression against Croatia during the Homeland War (i.e. Croatia's war for independence) as well as less success in economic restructuring.

1 Introduction

Today, Croatia is by functional criteria divided into the macro-regions Zagreb, Split, Rijeka and Osijek. They are further divided into smaller regions. The Zagreb region including the City of Zagreb [Grad Zagreb], had already a significant role when it was the centre of the Socialist Republic of Croatia (within former Yugoslavia), but this role became even more significant in independent Croatia. Compared to the Zagreb Region all other regions are peripheral, although some are more developed than others.

Figure 1: **Counties in Croatia and Central Croatia**

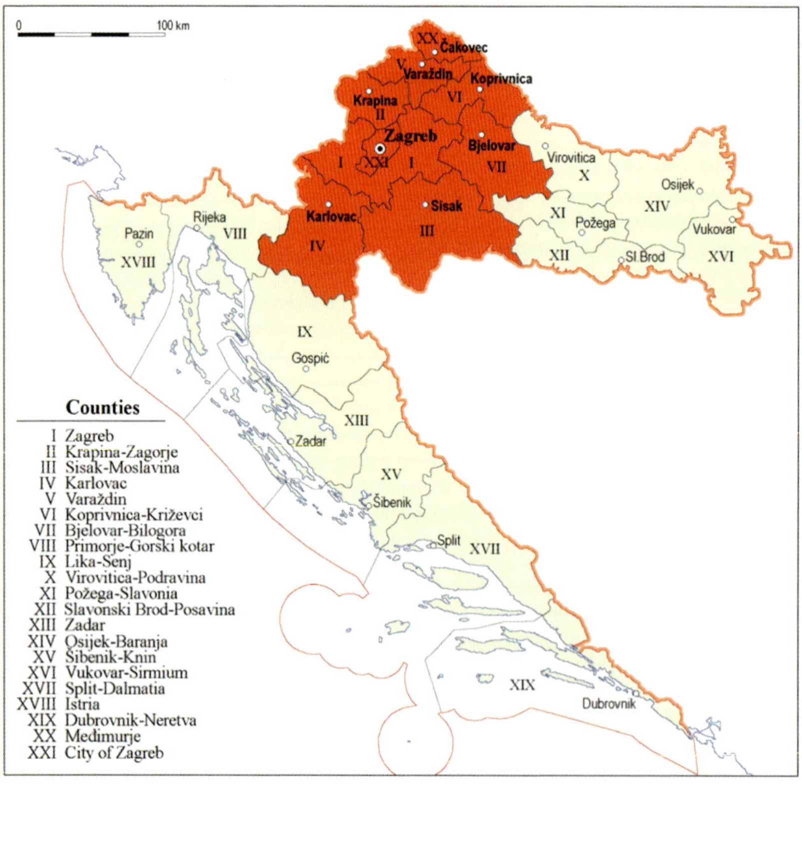

Central Croatia [Središnja Hrvatska], as its name suggests, has a central position in Croatia and lies at the interface of several larger European landscapes: the central Danubian Basin, the Alps and the Dinaric mountain range. The role of the entire macro-region is enhanced by the metropolitan structure of Zagreb. The impact of Zagreb is so big that Central Croatia corresponds in fact to the Zagreb macro-region in the functional sense (ROGLIĆ 1974).

Central Croatia is the key area of Croatia, both in respect to its geographical location in the country as well as to its role in economy. Due to its exceptional importance in transportation and economy it is also Croatia's most densily populated area. With a surface of 19,380 km^2 and 2,119,193 inhabitants (2001) Central Croatia makes up for 34% of Croatia's territory and 48% of its population.

Central Croatia is delimited in the West by Slovenia, in the North by the Drava and Mura rivers, in the East by the peri-Pannonian area and in the South by Bosnia-Herzegovina (MAGAŠ 1998). It is composed of nine counties [županije] (see Figure 1 and Table 1), i.e. the Zagreb County [Zagrebačka županija], the Krapina-Zagorje County [Krapinska-zagorska županija], the Sisak-Moslavina County [Sisačko-moslavačka županija], the Karlovac County [Karlovačka županija], the Varaždin County [Varaždinska županija], the Koprivnica-Križevci County [Koprivničko-križevačka županija], the Bjelo-var-Bilogora County [Bjelovarsko-bilogorska županija], the Međimurje [Međimurska županija] and the City of Zagreb [Grad Zagreb].

Table 1: **Cities, municipalities and settlements by counties in Central Croatia**

County	*Cities*	*Municipalities*	*Settlements*
Republic of Croatia	123	423	6,759
Counties of Central Croatia	44	163	2,614
Zagreb	8	26	697
Krapina-Zagorje	7	25	423
Sisak-Moslavina	6	13	456
Karlovac	5	16	649
Varaždin	6	22	301
Koprivnica-Križevci	3	22	264
Bjelovar-Bilogora	5	18	323
Međimurje	3	21	128
City of Zagreb	1	0	70

Source: DRŽAVNI ZAVOD ZA STATISTIKU 2001

2 Demography

In the inter-census period 1991-2001, Central Croatia was the only part of the country with overall population growth. Its main reason was urban growth of the City of Zagreb, but growth was also due to the fact that Central Croatia had the smallest share of territory occupied during the war in the early 1990s. However, if we exclude the City of Zagreb, Central Croatia suffered from population decrease like other parts of Croatia. According to LUKIĆ (2009), out of 3,398 settlements in Central Croatia 2,796 (82.3%) displayed demographic regression. This accounted for 81.8% of the surface area and 28.3% of the total population. Depopulation affected 83.3% of all rural and 8.9% of all urban settlements in Central Croatia.

Population density (Table 2, Figure 2) in 2001 had also declined in all counties except Zagreb County and the City of Zagreb compared to 1991. And the population change index (i.e. population change 1991-2001 compared to 1991) in Central Croatia for the period 1991-2001 was the highest in the City of Zagreb and the lowest in the Sisak-Moslavina County. The highest reduction in the number of inhabitants

Table 2: **Surface area, population and population density in the counties of Central Croatia in 1991 and 2001**

County	***Surface (km²)***	***Share in the surface area of Croatia***	***Population 1991***	***Population density***	***Population 2001***	***Population density (inhabitants/km²)***
Zagreb	3,077	*5.44*	282,989	91.2	309,696	100.7
Krapina-Zagorje	1,230	*2.18*	148,779	120.9	142,432	115.8
Sisak-Moslavina	4,445	*7.86*	251,332	56.5	185,387	41.7
Karlovac	3,625	*6.41*	184,577	50.9	141,787	39.1
Varaždin	1,260	*2.23*	187,853	149.0	184,769	146.6
Koprivnica-Križevci	1,735	*3.07*	129,397	74.5	124,467	71.7
Bjelovar-Bilogora	2,638	*4.66*	144,042	54.6	133,084	50.4
Međimurje	730	*1.29*	119,866	164.2	118,426	162.2
City of Zagreb	640	*1.13*	777,826	1,215.3	779,145	1,217.8
Central Croatia	19,380	*34.27*	2,226,661	114.8	2,119.193	109.34

Source: NEJAŠMIĆ 2008

Figure 2: **Population density in the counties of Central Croatia in 1991 and 2001**

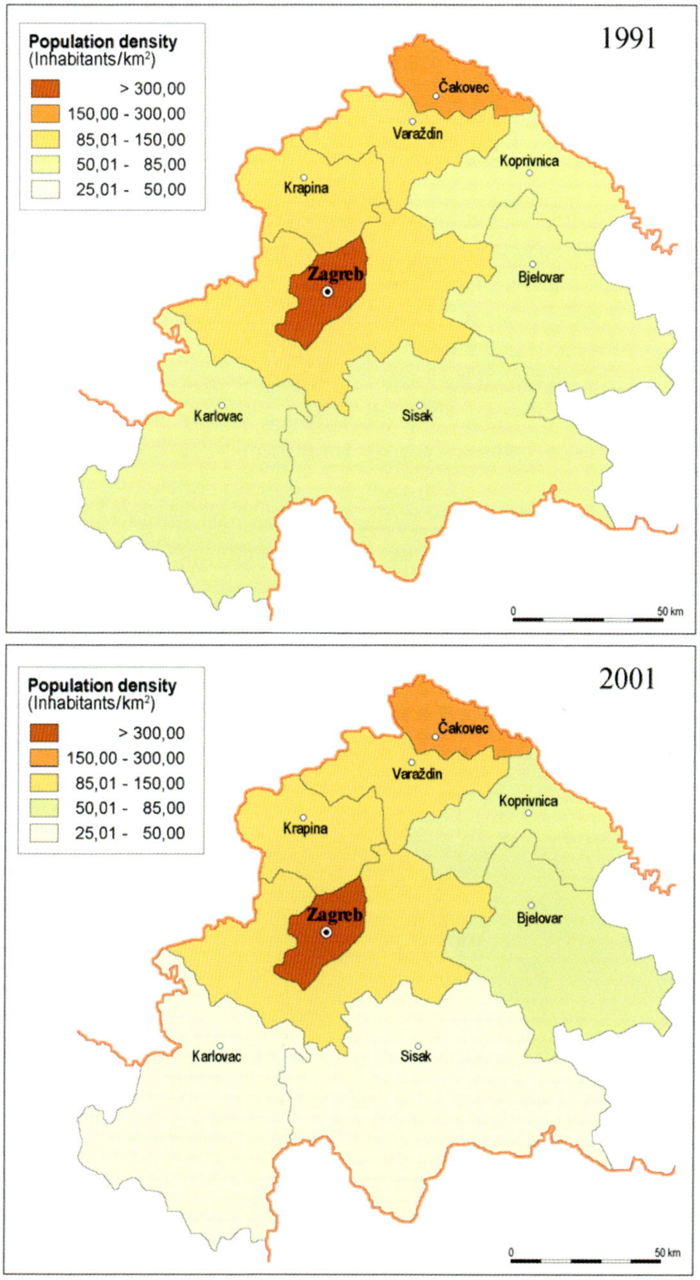

Source: NEJAŠMIĆ 2008

occurred in municipalities and towns from which the Serbian population departed, while additional factors of population decrease in Central Croatia were continued – economically motivated emigration, negative natural population development and seriously aggravated economic circumstances. The decrease was partly compensated by immigration of several thousand Croats from Bosnia-Herzegovina, Vojvodina and Kosovo.

The strongest population increase in Central Croatia occurred in the zone surrounding the City of Zagreb, primarily along its western and eastern ends. Between 1961 and 2001 in as many as 21 settlements around Zagreb the number of inhabitants increased 2.5 to 5 times as a result of suburbanisation that began in the 1960s. Until the 1960s the strongest concentration of population was in the city core (Lukić 2009). Suburbanisation was promoted by lower municipal costs and lower land prices.

Therefore, Central Croatia can be described as the "demographic-economic basis of Croatia, with a stable rhythm of population growth" (Friganović 1992, p. 55).

When analysing the demo-geographic situation in Central Croatia, it is important to take into account also the share of economically active population, since it indicates human resources. Labour force or economically active population consists of employed and unemployed persons, classified according to their economic activity. Usually there

Table 3: **Population by activity in the counties of Central Croatia 2001**

County	*Active population (total)*	*Active population (%)*	*Persons with income*	*Dependent population*
Zagreb	144,406	*46.30*	73,756	91,534
Krapina-Zagorje	69,480	*48.78*	33,587	39,365
Sisak-Moslavina	75,951	*40.97*	53,157	56,279
Karlovac	62,295	*43.94*	43,377	36,115
Varaždin	81,828	*44.29*	50,060	52,881
Koprivnica-Križevci	57,127	*45.90*	29,213	38,127
Bjelovar-Bilogora	63,963	*48.06*	30,855	38,266
Međimurje	61,302	*51.76*	23,173	33,951
City of Zagreb	356,186	*45.71*	208,833	214,126

Source: Državni zavod za Statistiku 2009

are two sources of statistical indicators on employment or unemployment: (1) data on registered unemployed persons, collected and processed by employment offices, and (2) indicators from labour force surveys (ARS), mostly conducted by statistical agencies and based on a methodology that has been harmonised with regulations and instructions of the International Labour Organisation and the European Office of Statistics (Eurostat) (Bejaković 2003).

The overall activity rate, i.e. the share of active persons in the total population of Central Croatia in 2001 amounted to about 46%, which is only slightly above the national average (Lukić 2009). There were 1,952,619 active persons in entire Croatia in 2001, of which 1,553,643 had some kind of occupation.

In Central Croatia, the largest share of active persons in the total population could be documented in Međimurje (51%) owing to a larger share of young people, followed by Bjelovar-Bilogora County as well as Krapina-Zagorje County (both 48%). Sisak-Moslavina County had the lowest share of active persons in the total population (40%). Shares of this size are, however, poor compared to other European countries, were they use to amount at the average to about 60-70%. Even more disturbing is the fact that all counties had a large share of dependent population, e.g. in the City of Zagreb as many as 214,000.

3 Economic activities

Economic developments in the period 1990-2000 were overshadowed by the negative consequences of war. These consequences included considerable war casualties, accompanied by high costs of transforming the centrally-planned into a market economy. War against Croatia influenced the fact that from 1990 to 1994-95 Croatia experienced negative growth rates.

Agriculture and commerce enjoyed already a developed private sector at the beginning of the 1990s, so that soon after the start of transition these two sectors accounted for about 50% of all firms. Industry, however, had been dominated by public ownership in over 80% of all cases, and negative growth rates in several successive years indicated certain problems in privatisation. Since planned economies had been shut off from the world market, they were also not affected by its price mechanisms.

Later, from 1991 to 2001, due to war events and a polarized development, differences in the concentration of work potential arose resulting in regional disparities. Such differences manifested themselves also in the number of employed persons in various counties (Pejnović 2004).

Data analysed in this section refer to the number of employees in specific economic branches important for Central Croatia, i.e. industry, transportation, agriculture, construction, commerce and financial services. The finance sector is especially important for the City of Zagreb, which has a leading role in this branch, not just in Central Croatia, but also at the national level.

In 1991, a total of about 610,000 persons were employed by legal entities (firms) in Central Croatia, and the City of Zagreb was the major location of employment in all economic branches. Over a half of all persons employed by legal entities worked in Zagreb city. Among the other counties, the largest numbers of employed persons were registered in Sisak-Moslavina County, followed by the Varaždin and Karlovac counties.

As regards activities, industry and mining had the largest numbers of employed persons in all counties. The largest number of employees in the industrial sector was registered in the City of Zagreb, followed by the Sisak-Moslavina and Varaždin counties.

As a sum of all counties of Central Croatia, in 1991 244,040 persons were employed in the industrial sector, which made up a third of all persons employed by legal entities in the examined area. This also confirms the importance of industry for this area.

The second largest by employees in 1991 was the commerce sector with slightly less than 68,000, most of them in the City of Zagreb and in the Sisak-Moslavina and Karlovac counties. Construction ranked as the third sector, in which 53,000 persons were employed in 1991. It was followed by financial and other services.

Figure 3: **Share of employed persons by the counties of Central Croatia in some economic sectors 1991**

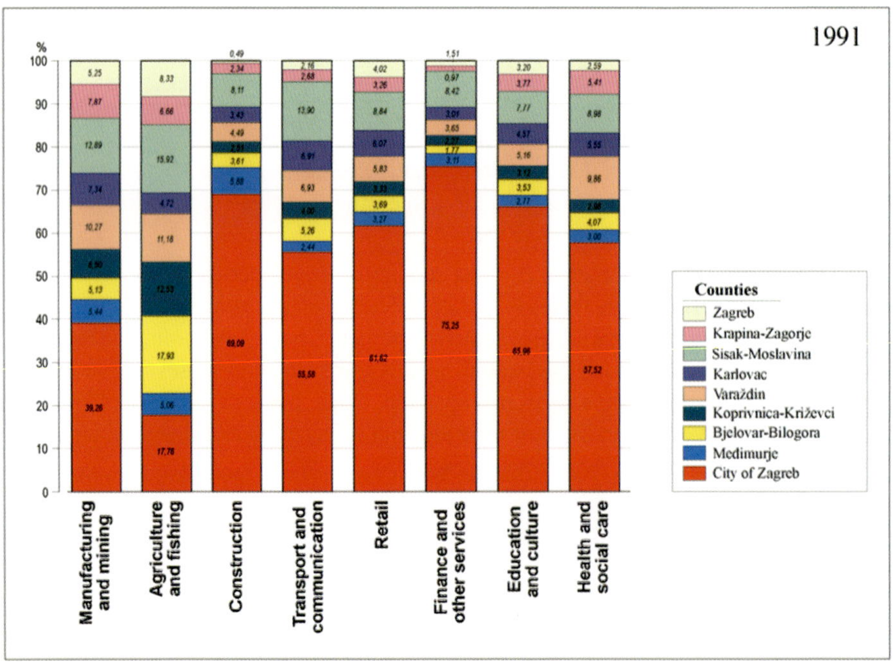

Source: Državni zavod za Statistiku 1994

When we consider the share of employed persons in various counties in Central Croatia in 1991 in all activities except agriculture (Figure 3), the City of Zagreb has a prevalent role, especially when financial services, construction, education, cultural activities and commerce are taken into account. In these economic sectors the share of the City of Zagreb is more than 70% or 60%, respectively.

In 2007, the number of persons employed by legal entities (firms) in Central Croatia amounted to 651,000, and most of them were employed in the City of Zagreb and in the Zagreb County. As in 1991, the largest number was employed in the processing industry, followed by wholesale and retail trade as well as by repair work on motor vehicles and motorcycles and items for personal and household use. These two economic branches taken together had in 2007 almost 280,000 employees. Construction was in third place according to the number of persons employed by firms, but had already three times less employees in Central Croatia than the processing industry.

When analysing the share of employed persons by counties and economic activities in 2007 (Figure 4), we can see that by far the largest share of employed persons is documented for the City of Zagreb in the sectors financial mediation, wholesale and

Figure 4: **Share of employed persons in Central Croatia in some economic sectors 2007**

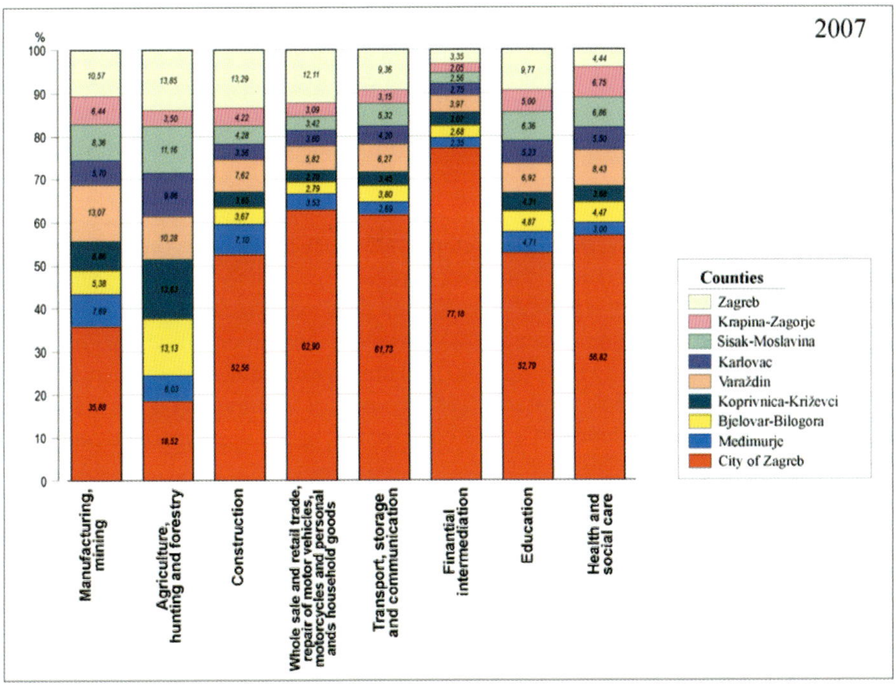

Source: Državni zavod za Statistiku 2008

retail trade and in transportation, warehousing and communications. In comparison to 1991, the share of the City of Zagreb in construction employment fell by 17%. When we observe Zagreb County in relation to 1991, we find that employment had increased in all examined economic branches, whereas the share of employed in the Sisak-Moslavina County has fallen. Most stable remained the shares of employed persons in agriculture and processing industry (not including the City of Zagreb).

4 Employment

Adaptation to new business conditions as well as the collapse of the COMECON and subsequent loss of export markets are frequently regarded as the main reasons of unemployment in transition countries (Dujšin 1999). Transition brought a shift from a system that guaranteed employment security to another one in which the threat of losing employment is a constitutive part of the business cycle. Likewise, transition implied attachment to the mechanisms of the global market and thus resulted also in new threats to job security.

As regards unemployment, Central Croatia, as one may expect, is to the highest degree linked to trends on the national level. This can be explained by the fact that this link is closest with industrial regions. Furthermore, in Croatia regional input affects unemployment more than in some countries that have recently entered the European Union (EU) (Botrić 2003).

From 1997 to 2002, the decrease in employment in Croatia has brought its activity rate to the level of Mediterranean countries (Greece, Spain, Italy), which is about 7% below the EU average. In this period privatization continued, with a slower increase of new jobs in the private sector. Around 2000, however, the number of newly employed people increased significantly (almost by 40% in three years), although three quarters of them received only fixed-term contracts. Such temporary employment is more flexible, yet more insecure for employees. Croatia corresponds in this respect to a trend in the EU (Matković 2003).

From 1989 to 1996 the largest decrease in employment had occurred in metallurgy, machine construction and in the textile industry. In this period, moreover, the number of individual farmers decreased to a half. From 1993 on job creation, mostly in the private sector, has significantly countered the loss of jobs. After the end of the war in 1995, a normalisation of the labour market created new jobs and let the share of employed persons increase, mainly outside the public sector (Matković 2002).

Since in the pre-transition period practically no workers were dismissed, the structure of unemployed persons was at that time very specific: most unemployed people were young or seeking their first employment. At the start of the period, i.e. in 1990, the share of young unemployed people (up to 29 years of age) amounted to about 66%, and at its end (2001) it was still high amounting to 42%. In the total number of young unemployed, women had a share of 53.4%.

Fortunately, among young people without jobs temporary unemployment prevails. Unqualified and semi-skilled workers wait for work about 12 months, qualified workers for about 7 months, people with secondary school education about 9 months, people with higher professional qualifications about 6.5 months, and persons with university degrees approximately 5 months (VLADA REPUBLIKE HRVATSKE).

In the period 1991-2001, all Central Croatian counties documented an increase in the share of unemployed (Table 4, Figure 5). This was especially evident in the Sisak-Moslavina, Karlovac and Bjelovar-Bilogora counties due to the difficult economic situation in these areas during the Homeland War. In other counties the increase was smaller and ranged around 1-4%.

Table 4: **Share (%) of unemployed in the total population of counties, 1991 and 2001**

County	*1991*	*2001*
Zagreb	*3.9*	*6.4*
Krapina-Zagorje	*5.0*	*6.1*
Sisak-Moslavina	*4.4*	*10.7*
Karlovac	*5.4*	*11.4*
Varaždin	*3.6*	*6.6*
Koprivnica-Križevci	*3.1*	*6.9*
Bjelovar-Bilogora	*3.9*	*10.5*
Međimurje	*3.3*	*6.6*
City of Zagreb	*4.7*	*6.5*

Source: DRŽAVNI ZAVOD ZA STATISTIKU 2009

Figure 5: **Share (%) of unemployed in the active population of counties in 2001**

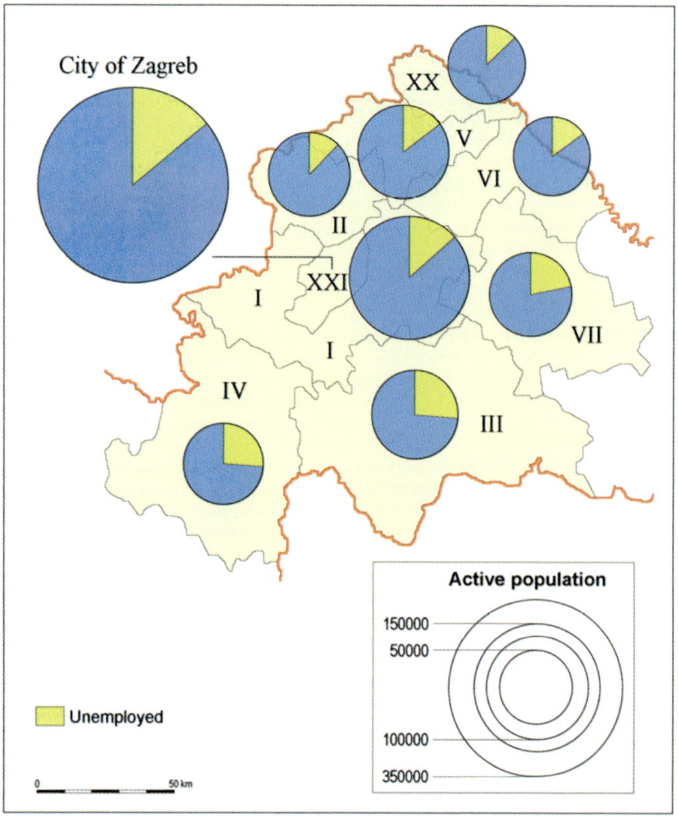

Source: Hrvatski zavod za zapošljavanje 2009

5 Industry

Industry is also today one of the main forces in any economy. But industry in the EU is no longer based on labour-intensive activities, and its adjustment resulted in a growth of unemployment. This applies especially to textile and clothing industry (Teodorović & Buturac 2006).

In Croatia in 2009 around 274,000 people were employed in industry, and this number is the result of numerous changes that occurred in the industrial sector since the end of the 1980s. The number of industrial employees in Croatia increased until 1987 and then declined. If we assume that the year 2000 had an employment index of 100, the index was at 236 in 1987 and at only 113 in 1997. This decline continued also later – down to an index value of 88 in 2006.

Figure 6: **Annual rates of change of industrial production, 1990-2002**

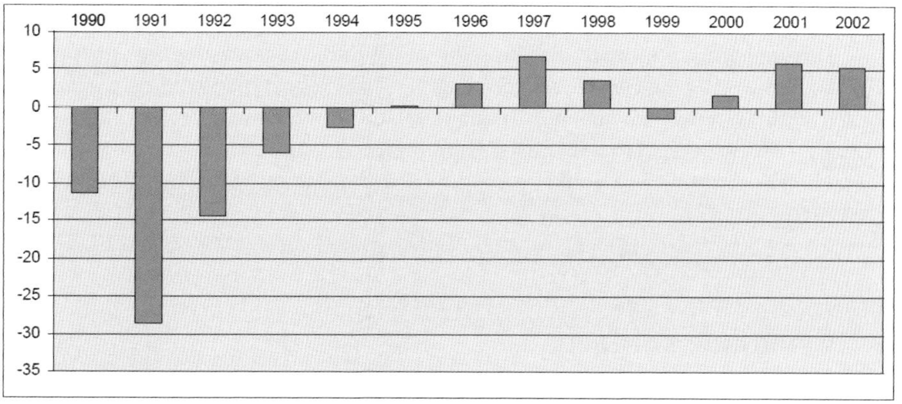

Source: Hrvatska gospodarska komora 2009

As regards value of production, the most significant increase of all industrial branches was achieved by printing/publication activities – as much as 258%. A duplicating was realised in the production of motor vehicles and other means of transportation, in recycling works and in metal industry. It was precisely metal industry that had experienced a large fall of production after 1987, but some segments of this branch were renewed and thus significantly increased their production later. The largest reduction occurred in clothing and leather industries as well as in the production of office machinery and computers (Stiperski 2007).

As regards industrial productivity, it doubled in the first decade of the 21th century compared to the 1980s. Productivity still decreased in the early 1990s, since industrial production declined faster than industrial employment. The lowest productivity was reached in 1991, when the index fell to only 61 (2000 = 100). During the 1980s productivity had been on a level of 71 to 76, and from 1991 it constantly increased, so that the index for 2005 was 142.

Central Croatia in its entirety is a region in which the processing industry is largest compared to all other activities. The most significant industrial areas are linked to leading urban centres and their urbanised regions. Among several industrial areas the following stand out: the wider area around Zagreb, then Karlovac, Sisak (and Petrinja), Kutina and Ivanić-Grad. In these industrial areas in 2007 over 115,000 people were employed, i.e. 64% of all industrial employees in Central Croatia. Besides, also Međimurje-Upper Podravina, Varaždin, Čakovec and Koprivnica are important industrial areas in Central Croatia (Magaš 1998).

Due to war events, but also due to the deindustrialization process, production and the number of industrial firms has significantly been reduced in comparison with the pre-war period. The faster rate of deindustrialization reduced the level of utilisation of local resources, both natural and manpower resources, which led to major regional differences in development. In this process, smaller counties and towns clearly lagged behind (LOKIN et al. 2007).

The county exceptionally standing out in Central Croatia as regards the number of industrial firms is the City of Zagreb. Zagreb is the largest industrial core in Central Croatia with the great advantage of being situated in the central part of the country (STIPERSKI 1991). Second to the City of Zagreb rank the Zagreb and Varaždin counties, where industrial production could be continued without interruption by war events.

6 Economic subjects

The number and quality of economic subjects is an important factor and indicator of economic development. In this section economic subjects in Central Croatia in selected branches are analysed: agriculture/forestry, processing industry, construction, wholesale and retail trade, real estate transactions, rentals and business services (see Figure7). These activities were chosen, since by numbers of employees and firms they

Figure 7: **Share of economic subjects by counties of Central Croatia in selected branches in 1998**

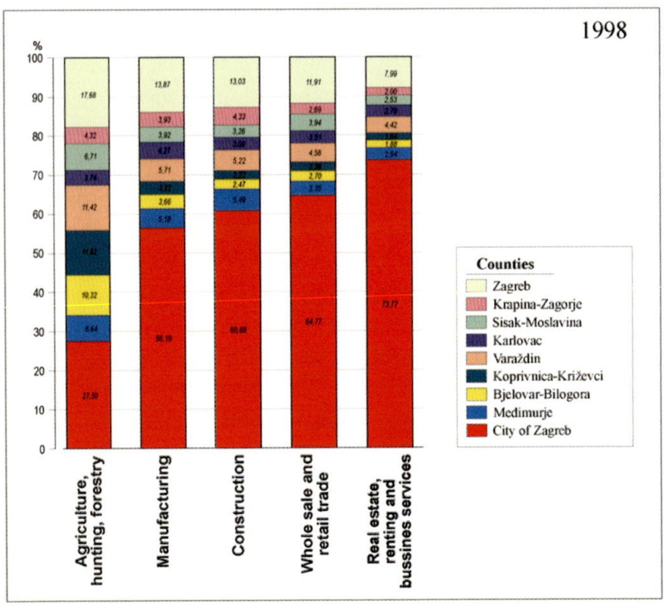

Source: DRŽAVNI ZAVOD ZA STATISTIKU 1998

are the most important in Central Croatia. When all activities are taken into account (not only the before-mentioned), Central Croatia documented in 1998 95,558 economic subjects. The largest number was located in the City of Zagreb (56,458) with Zagreb County in the second place, although already far behind Zagreb City with only 11,245 economic subjects. In all other counties the number of economic subjects ranged between 3,000 and 5,000, in total amounting to one third of Central Croatia.

Up to the year 2008 the number of economic subjects in all counties and in all activities significantly increased (see Figure 8). But this can be attributed also to a new methodology in statistical monitoring. The number of economic subjects in agriculture increased to 2,246, in processing industry to 14,402, in construction to 10,180. Also the number in real estate mediation increased to 21,019.

Thus, in comparison with the year 2001, all numbers significantly grew, which can be interpreted as the final stabilisation of the Croatian economy after war, and, to some extent, as being the result of better organized business conditions for economic entities.

The total number of economic subjects in Central Croatia in all activities amounted to 140,285 in 2008, of which 84,370 were located in the City of Zagreb, i.e. more than a half.

Figure 8: **Share of legal economic subjects (firms) in the counties of Central Croatia by branches in 2008**

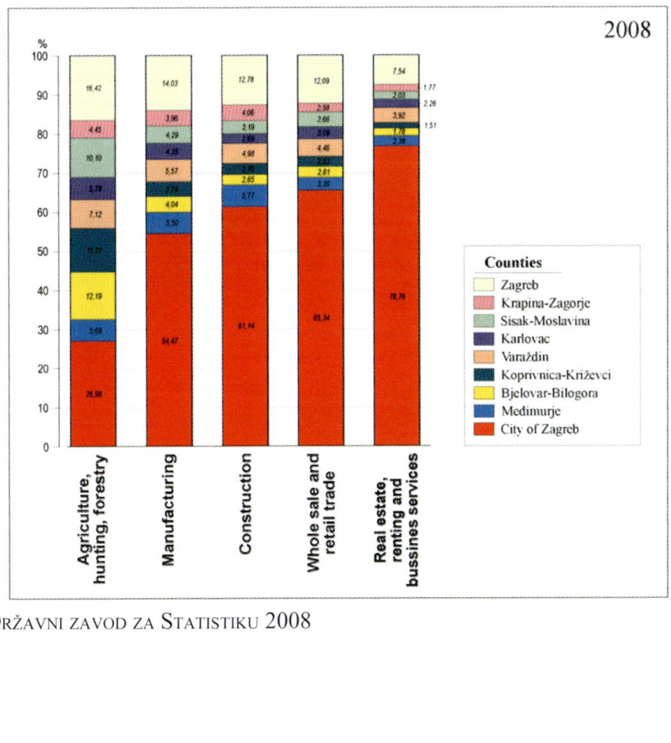

Source: Državni zavod za Statistiku 2008

7 Gross Domestic Product (GDP)

Data of the Gross Domestic Product (GDP) by counties were not collected before 2001 and are available only for the period 2001-2007. In general, GDP per capita data repeat the already well-known picture of the City of Zagreb as the peak of development followed by Zagreb County, which profits from its location in the city's surroundings and as well as from lower land prices and smaller communal utility fees (see Table 5). Many larger and smaller firms have relocated from the capital to its surroundings to mutual benefit, since this shift reduced also the pressure on the already overburdened city.

Next by GDP to Zagreb County is Varaždin County. Its prominent position is due to many exemptions and advantages offered by this county to domestic and foreign investors resulting in major investments. The lowest GDP has been documented for Bjelovar-Bilogora County and Međimurje.

It is worth to mention that GDP was constantly growing throughout these five years in all counties.

Table 5: **GDP per capita in the counties of Central Croatia 2001-2007 (in 1,000 USD)**

County	*2001*	*2002*	*2003*	*2004*	*2005*	*2006*	*2007*
Zagreb	3,038	4,000	4,949	5,998	6,775	6,813	10,062
Krapina-Zagorje	3,536	3,873	4,839	5,500	6,435	6,803	9,766
Sisak-Moslavina	3,882	4,213	5,135	5,975	6,874	7,993	9,844
Karlovac	3,801	4,435	5,183	5,929	6,638	7,507	10,697
Varaždin	4,256	5,093	6,279	6,872	7,375	8,303	11,242
Koprivnica-Križevci	4,629	5,287	6,389	7,272	8,028	9,348	12,498
Bjelovar-Bilogora	3,514	4,141	4,982	5,937	6,406	7,248	9,148
Međimurje	3,719	4,406	5,345	6,237	6,622	7,649	10,364
City of Zagreb	7,893	9,074	11,948	14,480	16,059	17,818	22,921

Source: Croatian Chamber of Commerce, Zagreb, 2008; GDP for the Republic of Croatia, spatial statistical units of the second degree and counties in 2007 (www.dzs.hr)

When the share of counties in Croatia's total GDP is calculated (see Table 6), it becomes apparent that although GDP of all examined counties has grown between 2001 and 2007, this growth oscillated in relation to the growth of the Croatian GDP. The share of Central Croatian counties in Croatia's total GDP varies between 2% (Međimurje) and 32.5% (City of Zagreb).

Table 6: **Share of Central Croatian counties in overall Croatian GDP (%)**

County	*2001*	*2002*	*2003*	*2004*	*2005*	*2006*	*2007*
Zagreb	*4.7*	*5.4*	*5.2*	*5.3*	*5.5*	*5.1*	*5.5*
Krapina-Zagorje	*2.5*	*2.3*	*2.2*	*2.1*	*2.3*	*2.1*	*2.2*
Sisak-Moslavina	*3.6*	*3.3*	*3.1*	*3.0*	*3.1*	*3.3*	*2.9*
Karlovac	*2.7*	*2.7*	*2.4*	*2,2*	*2.3*	*2.3*	*2.4*
Varaždin	*3.9*	*4.0*	*3.8*	*3.5*	*3.4*	*3.5*	*3.4*
Koprivnica-Križevci	*2.9*	*2.8*	*2.6*	*2.4*	*2.5*	*2.6*	*2.5*
Bjelovar-Bilogora	*2.3*	*2.3*	*2.2*	*2.1*	*2.1*	*2.1*	*1.9*
Međimurje	*2.2*	*2.2*	*2.1*	*2.0*	*2.0*	*2.1*	*2.0*
City of Zagreb	*30.9*	*30.6*	*31.4*	*31.7*	*32.3*	*32.5*	*30.7*

Source: HRVATSKA GOSPODARSKA KOMORA

8 Conclusion

Although Central Croatia is economically the strongest region in Croatia, it is composed of counties at different development levels. Based on various indicators of economic development (economic structure of the population, number of persons employed by economic subjects, number of economic subjects as such, GDP per capita) it can be concluded that the economic gradient declines primarily from the City of Zagreb towards the other eight counties of the Region, in the second line also from the counties in the Northwest towards the counties in the South and Southeast.

Transition affected this Region from the beginning of the 1990s prompting significant changes in economic structure of the entire area, especially in the industrial sector, but also as regards employment, levels of income, number of firms and size of firms.

9 Bibliography

BEJAKOVIĆ P. (2003), Nezaposlenost. In: Financijska teorija i praksa, 27,4, pp. 659–661.

BLAIR J.P., CARROLL M.C. (2009), Local Economic Development; Analysis, Practices and Globalization. Los Angeles – London – New Delhi – Singapore, Sage Publications Inc.

BOTRIĆ V. (2003), Regionalni aspekti nezaposlenosti u Hrvatskoj. In: Privredna kretanja i ekonomska politika, 95, pp. 27–46.

DRŽAVNI ZAVOD ZA STATISTIKU (ed.) (1994), Statistički ljetopis hrvatskih županija 1993. Zagreb.

DRŽAVNI ZAVOD ZA STATISTIKU (ed.) (several years), Statistički ljetopis Republike Hrvatske, several years. Zagreb.

DRŽAVNI ZAVOD ZA STATISTIKU, www.dzs.hr (9.7.2009)

DRŽAVNI ZAVOD ZA STATISTIKU (ed.) Statistički pokazatelji 2008, www.dzs.hr

DUJŠIN U. (1999), Nezaposlenost i politika zapošljavanja u zemljama u tranziciji: Hrvatska. In: Ekonomska istraživanja, 12, 1-2, pp. 1–19.

FRIGANOVIĆ M. (1992), Stanovništvo i naseljenost Republike Hrvatske. In: Geografski horizont, 2, pp. 49–61.

HRVATSKA GOSPODARSKA KOMORA, www.hgk.hr (9.7.2009)

HRVATSKI ZAVOD ZA ZAPOŠLJAVANJE, www.hzz.hr (9.7.2009)

LOKIN B., MLINAREVIĆ M., ŽIVKOVIĆ, M. (2007), Industrijska politika i EU. In: Ekonomska politika Hrvatske u 2008 (= Zbornik radova), pp. 120–138. Opatija, Inženjerski biro d.d.

LONČAR, J. (2011), Ekonomsko-geografsko restrukturiranje Središnje Hrvatske u uvjetima tranzicije. Doctoral dissertation, Geografski odsjek PMF-a, Sveučilište u Zagrebu, Zagreb.

LUKIĆ A. (2009), Tipologija ruralnih područja Hrvatske – geografski aspekt. Doctoral dissertation, Geografski odsjek PMF-a, Sveučilište u Zagrebu, Zagreb.

MAGAŠ D. (1998), Osnove geografije Hrvatske. Zadar, Filozofski fakultet Zadar, Odjel za geografiju.

MATKOVIĆ T. (2002), Restrukturiranje rada? Transformacija strukture zaposlenosti. In: Revija za socijalnu politiku, 10, 2, pp. 161–184.

MATKOVIĆ T. (2003), Zaposlenost u Hrvatskoj i izmjene radnog zakonodavstva. In: Revija za socijalnu politiku, 10, 2, pp. 255–262.

NEJAŠMIĆ I. (2008), Stanovništvo Hrvatske: demogeografske analize i studije. Zagreb, Hrvatsko geografsko društvo.

PEJNOVIĆ D. (2004), Depopulacija županija i disparitet u regionalnom razvoju Hrvatske. In: Društvena istraživanja, 13, 4-5, pp. 72–73.

ROGLIĆ J. (1974), Središnja Hrvatska. In: CRKVENČIĆ, I., DUGAČKI, Z., JELEN, I. et al. (eds.), Geografija SR Hrvatske, knjiga I., pp. 44–92. Zagreb, Institut za geografiju Sveučilišta u Zagrebu, Školska knjiga.

STIPERSKI Z. (1991), Industrijska područja Hrvatske s polazišta središnjosti odnosno rubnosti. In: Radovi, 26, 26, pp. 99–120.

STIPERSKI Z. (2007), Promjene u hrvatskoj industriji tijekom tranzicijskog razdoblja. In: BAJS, Lj. et al. (eds.), 4. hrvatski geografski kongres, zbornik radova, Poreč, 10-13. listopada 2007, pp. 285–302. Zagreb, Hrvatsko geografsko društvo.

TEODOROVIĆ I., BUTURAC G. (2006), Perspektive industrijske proizvodnje u Hrvatskoj i intra-industrijska razmjena. In: Ekonomski pregled, 57, 11, pp. 705–729.

VLADA REPUBLIKE HRVATSKE (ed.), Program poticanja zapošljavanja, http://hrcak.srce.hr (9.7.2009)

Changes in Polish Tourist Flows to the Eastern Adriatic

*Jan A. Wendt, Gdańsk**

with 1 figure and 6 tables in the text

Content

Summary 159
1 Methodological problems 160
2 Changes in Polish tourist flows 160
3 Polish tourists in Croatia and Slovenia 163
4 Conclusions 164
5 Bibliography 165

Summary

The paper aims at an analysis of changes in Polish tourist flows to the eastern coasts of the Adriatic after 1989, especially to Slovenia and Croatia. The analysis focuses on economic factors of tourism development as well as on factors of touristic attractiveness of these countries for Polish tourists such as cultural affinity, low prices and good accessibility.

* Jan Wendt, Prof. dr. hab., Department of Regional Development Geography, Gdańsk University, ul. Bażyńskiego 4, PL 80-952 Gdańsk, and Department of Tourism Economics, Academy of Physical Education and Sport, ul. Kazimierza Górskiego 1, PL 80-336 Gdańsk; e-mail: jan.wendt@ug.edu.pl

1 Methodological problems

The Adriatic region is besides Greece and Spain one of the most important tourist destinations in Europe. After 1989 this region has also become one of the most popular destinations for Polish tourists. It may therefore be interesting to identify the factors that cause the flow of Polish tourists to the Adriatic coast and to determine the changes since 1989.

As regards the concept of tourism we depart from the definition presented by the World Tourism Organization (WTO) saying that tourism includes all activities of people who travel for leisure, business or other purposes for no longer than a year without a break outside their everyday environment. So we define a tourist as a person, who resides in a place outside his/her home at least for one day or spends at least one night in a tourist accommodation. Persons staying less than a day are classified as excursionists.

A major problem in the context of this study is availability and reliability of data describing size and spatial spread of tourist traffic. Differences in statistical methods of national statistical agencies in Croatia and Slovenia let us prefer to use data published by the Central Statistical Office of Poland, since they are homogenous, collected and elaborated on the basis of a consistent methodological framework.

It has also to be mentioned that the owners of accommodation facilities are not so much interested in delivering reliable data, mainly for tax reasons. Furthermore, data on day trips and excursions are practically not available, although these forms of tourism play a major role with Polish tourists. Therefore, we use in addition to data provided by the Central Statistical Office of Poland a survey conducted by the Tourist Institute in Warsaw [Warszawa] (2010). For practical reasons, the study is confined to Croatia and Slovenia.

2 Changes in Polish tourist flows

After the political turn of 1989/90 economic transformation and economic reforms had strengthened the purchasing power of the Polish currency and the Złoty has become fully convertible. This made it possible for Poles to travel also under the conditions of commercial tourism, not only – as in Communist times – of Socialist welfare tourism. Thus, the years 1991-2000 saw an increase of Polish trips to abroad from about 20 to 56.7 millions. A weakening of the economy and a decrease of the real value of the Polish Złoty in 2003-2004 caused a decline up to 2004, when the number of Polish trips to abroad fell to the level of 37.2 millions (see Figure 1). Later, the Polish accession to the European Union (EU) and the Schengen Space resulted again in an increase of Polish trips to abroad.

Figure 1: **Polish trips to abroad including day trips 1991-2007 (in millions)**

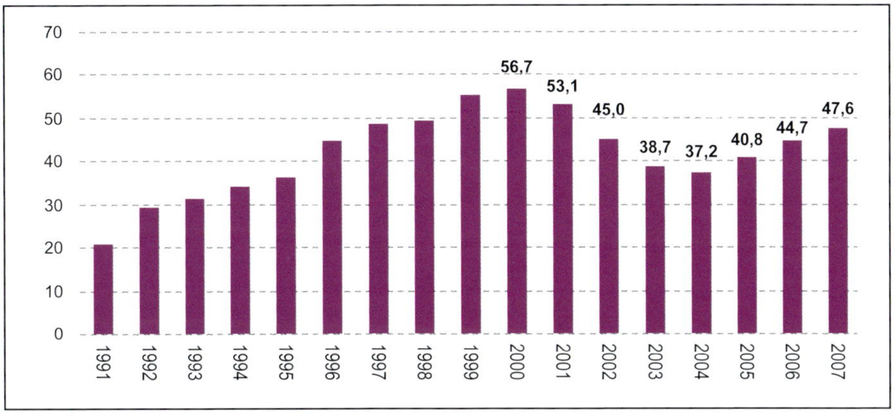

Source: Tourist Institute 2010, Warsaw

Also in terms of Polish tourists to abroad (in the sense of persons spending at least one night in a tourist accommodation abroad), the years 2000-2009 saw a significant decrease from 9.6 to 6.3 millions (see Table 1).

The most popular destination of Polish tourists is – not surprising, given the size of Polish religious and pilgrimage tourism – Italy with about 650,000 tourists in 2009. In the same year Croatia was visited by about 300,000 and Slovenia by only 30,000 Polish tourists. Besides Italy and Croatia also Egypt, Spain and France are popular tourist destinations of Poles in the Mediterranean. France, however, is not so much visited for its Mediterranean coast, but for urban attractions like Paris.

Compared to the overall decrease between 2000 and 2009, Egypt and Croatia stand out as winner destinations (see Table 1). From 2004 to 2009 the number of Polish tourists in Egypt has increased from 100,000 to 250,000 and in Croatia from 150,000 to 300,000. This is mainly due to economic factors like value for money, but also to the recreational values of the two countries. In contrast, Polish tourism to Spain and Greece declined or stagnated. During the same period the number of Polish tourists in Greece remained at the level of 150,000; in Spain it increased from 150,000 to 250,000, but did not return to the level of 2000, when Spain was visited by about 400,000 Polish tourists.

Table 1: **Polish tourists in selected Mediterranean countries (millions)**

Year/ Country	*2000*	*2001*	*2002*	*2003*	*2004*	*2005*	*2006*	*2007*	*2008*	*2009*
Croatia	0.40	0.50	0.30	0.20	0.15	0.25	0.25	0.25	0.30	0.30
Egypt	.	.	.	0.10	0.10	0.10	0.15	0.15	0.25	0.25
France	0.75	0.50	0.55	0.35	0.20	0.30	0.20	0.45	0.35	0.20
Greece	0.50	0.25	0.55	0.15	0.15	0.15	0.10	0.15	0.30	0.15
Italy	1.00	0.60	0.45	0.55	0.50	0.55	0.45	0.35	0.45	0.65
Slovenia	.	.	.	0.02	0.02	0.02	0.02	0.03	0.03	0.03
Spain	0.40	0.30	0.30	0.15	0.15	0.15	0.10	0.30	0.30	0.25
Turkey	.	.	0.10	.	.	0.10	0.10	0.10	0.15	0.15
Total	**9.60**	**7.70**	**8.40**	**7.20**	**6.30**	**6.20**	**7.30**	**6.90**	**7.60**	**6.30**

Source: Tourist Institute 2010, Warsaw

Poles prefer travelling individually. In the years 2004-2009 only about 15-20% of all trips were organized by travel agencies. About 10% were business trips, while 59-65% were organized individually. Among the trips undertaken individually, Croatia and Slovenia rank prominently as destinations. They can be reached by private car in about 18-20 hours from southern Poland. The distance between Gdańsk in northern Poland and Dubrovnik is about 1,900 km, between Wrocław in southwestern Poland and Split 1,200 km. This is feasible in two days with one overnight stay at the maximum.

Table 2: **Polish foreign tourism by purpose (%)**

Categories	*2002*	*2003*	*2004*	*2005*	*2006*	*2007*	*2008*	*2009*
Tourism	*44*	*48*	*38*	*47*	*44*	*42*	*52*	*52*
Family visit	*28*	*23*	*22*	*26*	*23*	*25*	*25*	*22*
Professional	*17*	*23*	*33*	*19*	*19*	*26*	*18*	*17*
Others	*11*	*6*	*7*	*8*	*14*	*7*	*5*	*9*

Source: Tourist Institute 2010, Warsaw

As regards travel purposes, classic tourism ranks first rising from 44% in 2002 to 52% in 2009 (see Table 2). The second place hold visits to family members and friends, the third business trips. Both have either declined or not grown since 2002 due to the weakening of the economy in Poland.

Table 3 shows expenditures of Polish tourists travelling abroad, perhaps the most important criterion from the destination's point of view.

Table 3: **Travel of Polish tourists to abroad (in Euro)**

	2002	*2003*	*2004*	*2005*	*2006*	*2007*	*2008*	*2009*
Travel expenses								
during travel	166	163	201	197	224	239	333	330
before travel	171	140	176	167	239	238	346	342
Daily cost of travel								
during travel	15	14	15	14	15	15	22	20
before travel	15	12	13	13	15	15	23	27

Source: Tourist Institute 2010, Warsaw

As Table 3 shows, expenditures almost doubled from 2002 to 2009. The increase was especially significant from 2005 to 2009, when the purchasing power of the Złoty and the Polish economy grew. The growth of daily expenses, however, was much smaller. This can be explained by two reasons. The first is the growth of purchasing power of the Polish Złoty from 2002 to 2009, which improved its exchange rate with the Euro from 5.5 to 3.9 to 1. In 2009 (February) for 1 Euro only 3.1 Złoty had to be paid. A second reason are longer holidays with more overnight stays.

3 Polish tourists in Croatia and Slovenia

Factors most relevant for Polish tourism to the Adriatic region are tourist attractions, economic factors and safety. In terms of tourist attractions, both Croatia and Slovenia dispose over a wealth of natural as well as cultural assets. This is reflected by the overall number of foreign tourists in these two countries, which is impressive and significantly growing especially in Croatia (see Table 4).

Table 4: **Foreign tourists in Croatia and Slovenia 2004-2008 (in 1,000)**

	2004	*2005*	*2006*	*2007*	*2008*
Croatia	9,412	9,995	10,385	11,162	11,261
Slovenia	1,499	1,555	1,617	1,751	1,771

Source: Tourist Institute 2010, Warsaw

Besides natural and cultural attractions as well as safety and security, major reasons for Poles to go for vacations to Croatia and Slovenia are cultural similarities with Poland such as a similar course of transformation, related languages or the common Roman Catholic denomination. Also similar features in history like having been occupied by neighbouring countries create an atmosphere of mutual understanding.

Table 5: **Polish tourists in Croatia and Slovenia 2003-2009 (in 1,000)**

	2003	*2004*	*2005*	*2006*	*2007*	*2008*	*2009*
Croatia	152,0	250,0	242,0	276,0	323,0	417,0	454,0
Slovenia	20,3	18,7	18,1	22,5	27,3	32,6	27,9

Source: Tourist Institute 2010, Warsaw

Table 6: **Polish tourists in Croatia and Slovenia 2003-2009, growth compared to the previous year in %**

	2003/2002	*2004/2003*	*2005/2004*	*2006/2005*	*2007/2006*	*2008/2007*	*2009/2008*
Croatia	*91*	*164*	*97*	*114*	*117*	*129*	*109*
Slovenia	*82*	*92*	*97*	*124*	*121*	*119*	*86*

Source: Tourist Institute 2010, Warsaw

Tables 5 and 6 show an increase in the number of Polish tourists in Croatia and Slovenia between 2003 and 2009. Especially the flow of Polish tourists to Croatia surpasses essentially the average growth of Croatian tourism. But also in Slovenia the increase in the number of Polish tourists exceeded the average growth of tourism more than twice. The accession of Slovenia to the Euro Zone, which may have resulted in a rise of prices for tourism services or was at least perceived so by Polish tourists, had a certain detrimental effect. This may also have been a reason for a shift towards Croatia. Growth rates for 2009 show for the first time an effect of the European economic crisis.

4 Conclusions

Based on statistical data it can be stated that Polish tourist flows to Croatia and Slovenia show a dynamic increase in the last two decades. Croatia became one of the main Polish tourist destinations. This is, apart from natural and cultural attractions, mainly due to economic factors, easy accessibility and cultural affinity. Especially

Croatia corresponds very well to specific demands of the Polish tourist market such as low costs – similar to Egypt, Tunisia or Turkey. This is confirmed by an analysis of changes in tourism volume compared to the economic development in Europe and economic changes in Poland.

The cost factor is certainly an advantage of both Croatia and Slovenia compared to alternative offers in the Adriatic region and its hinterland such as Italy and Austria. Bosnia and Herzegovina as well as Albania are relatively cheaper than Croatia and Slovenia and for their different cultures also attractive for Polish tourists, but lack the security level of Croatia and Slovenia. This makes it very likely that the two will remain major Polish tourist destinations for years to come.

5 Bibliography

GUS (ed.) (2000-2010), Rocznik Statystyczny Rzeczypospolitej Polskiej (years 2000-2010) Warszawa.

Tourist Institute, Warsaw (ed.), http://www.intur.com.pl/wyjazdy_polakow2009.pdf

ISR-Forschungsberichte

1 Zoltán CSÉFALVAY und Walter ROHN (1991): **Der Weg des ungarischen Arbeitsmarktes in die duale Ökonomie**

2 Elisabeth LICHTENBERGER (Hg., 1991): **Die Zukunft von Ostmitteleuropa. Vom Plan zum Markt**

3 Marlies SCHULZ (1991): **Der Tauschwohnungsmarkt in der zentralistischen Planwirtschaft – das Beispiel von Ostberlin**

4 Helga SCHMIDT (1991): **Die metropolitane Region Leipzig – Erbe der sozialistischen Planwirtschaft und Zukunftschancen**

5 Hugo PENZ (1992): **Entwicklungsstruktur und Zukunft von ländlicher Siedlung und Landwirtschaft in der ČSFR und in Ungarn**

6 Zoltán CSÉFALVAY und Walter ROHN (1992): **Die Transition des ungarischen und Budapester Wohnungsmarktes**

7 Alina MUZIOŁ-WĘCŁAWOWICZ (unter Mitarbeit v. Josef Kohlbacher, 1992): **Die Transformation des Wohnungswesens in Polen – eine Analyse des Warschauer Wohnungsmarktes**

8 Grzegorz WĘCŁAWOWICZ (unter Mitarbeit v. Josef Kohlbacher, 1993): **Die sozialräumliche Struktur Warschaus – Ausgangslage und postkommunistische Umgestaltung**

9 Markus SEIDL (1993): **Stadtverfall in Bratislava**

10 Heinz FASSMANN, Josef KOHLBACHER und Ursula REEGER (1993): **„Suche Arbeit" – Eine empirische Analyse über Stellensuchende aus dem Ausland**

11 Heinz FASSMANN, Zoltán CSÉFALVAY und Walter ROHN (1993): **Regionalstruktur im Wandel – Das Beispiel Ungarn**

12 Ursula BAUER (1994): **Europa der Regionen – Zwischen Anspruch und Wirklichkeit**

13 Heinz FASSMANN, Josef KOHLBACHER und Ursula REEGER (1995): **Die „neue Zuwanderung" aus Ostmitteleuropa – Eine empirische Analyse am Beispiel der Polen in Österreich**

14 Heinz FASSMANN (Hg., 1995): **Immobilien-, Wohnungs- und Kapitalmärkte in Ostmitteleuropa. Beiträge zur regionalen Transformationsforschung**

15 Heinz FASSMANN und Christiane HINTERMANN (1997): **Migrationspotential Ostmitteleuropa. Struktur und Motivation potentieller Migranten aus Polen, der Slowakei, Tschechien und Ungarn**

16 Heike JÖNS und Britta KLAGGE (1997): **Bankwesen und Regionalstruktur in Ungarn**

17 Konrad SCHERF (1998): **Die metropolitane Region Berlin. Genese und Niedergang, Revitalisierung und Innovation**

18 Heinz FASSMANN, Christiane HINTERMANN, Josef KOHLBACHER und Ursula REEGER (1999): **„Arbeitsmarkt Mitteleuropa". Die Rückkehr historischer Migrationsmuster**

19 Zoltán CSÉFALVAY (1999): **Die Wettbewerbsfähigkeit der österreichischen Großstädte. Theoretische Ansätze und empirische Befunde**

20 Axel BORSDORF und Michaela PAAL (Hg., 2000): **Die „alpine Stadt" zwischen lokaler Verankerung und globaler Vernetzung. Beiträge zur regionalen Stadtforschung im Alpenraum**

21 Walter ROHN (2000): **Forschungseinrichtungen in der Agglomeration Wien. Stellung im Innovationsprozeß und Einbindung in innovative Netzwerke**

22 Vera MAYER (2000): **Regionale Innovationspotentiale und innovative Netzwerke der Industrieunternehmen in der metropolitanen Region Wien. Ergebnisse einer Unternehmensbefragung**

23 Axel BORSDORF (Hg., 2000): **Perspectives of Geographical Research on Latin America for the 21st Century**

24 Wolfgang BERGER (2001): **Photovoltaics in Europe in the Year 2020. Utilities, Sustainable Development and Culture**

25 Heinz FASSMANN, Josef KOHLBACHER und Ursula REEGER (in Zusammenarbeit mit Katharina DEMEL und Irene STACHER, 2001): **Integration durch berufliche Mobilität? Eine empirische Analyse der beruflichen Mobilität ausländischer Arbeitskräfte in Wien**

26 Walter ROHN (2002): **Regelung versus Nichtregelung internationaler Kommunikationsbeziehungen. Das Beispiel der UNESCO-Kommunikationspolitik**

27 Vera MAYER (2002): **Wohnpräferenzen von Jugendlichen in Wien. Ein Beitrag zur Kultur- und Sozialgeographie des Wohnens**

28 Michael JANOSCHKA (2002): **Wohlstand hinter Mauern. Private Urbanisierungen in Buenos Aires**

29 Axel BORSDORF und Christof PARNREITER (Hg., 2003): **International Research on Metropolises – Milestones and Frontiers**

30 Heinz FASSMANN, Josef KOHLBACHER und Ursula REEGER (2004): **Polen in Wien. Entwicklung, Strukturmerkmale und Interaktionsmuster**

31 Josef KOHLBACHER und Ursula REEGER (2005): **Aus aller Herren Länder? Wien als Studienort und internationale Bildungsmetropole**

32 Josef KOHLBACHER und Ursula REEGER (2006): **„Gespanntes Nachbarschaftsverhältnis?“ Eine empirische Analyse des interethnischen Zusammenlebens in unterschiedlichen Wohnbaukategorien in Wien**

33 Josef KOHLBACHER und Ursula REEGER (2006): **Die Dynamik ethnischer Wohnviertel in Wien. Eine sozialräumliche Longitudinalanalyse 1981 und 2005**

34 Wolfgang BOSSWICK, Heinz FASSMANN, Josef KOHLBACHER and Doris LÜKEN-KLASSEN (2007): **Housing and Residential Segregation of Migrants. A state-of-the-art report**

35 Josef KOHLBACHER und Ursula REEGER (2008): **Staatsbürgerschaftsbonus beim Wohnen? Eine emprische Analyse der Unterschiede zwischen eingebürgerten und nichteingebürgerten Zuwanderern/-innen hinsichtlich ihrer Wohnsituation in Wien**

36 Heinz FASSMANN and Yvonne FRANZ (Hg., 2010): **Integration Policies on the Local Level: Housing Policies for Migrants. Examples from New York City, St. Paul, Antwerp, Vienna and Stuttgart**

37 Josef KOHLBACHER, Ursula REEGER and Philipp SCHNELL (2012): **Neighbourhood Embeddedness and Social Coexistence. Immigrants and Natives in Three Urban Settings in Vienna**